SHORT HISTORIES

Short Histories are authoritative and elegantly written introductory texts which offer fresh perspectives on the way history is taught and understood in the twenty-first century. Designed to have strong appeal to university students and their teachers, as well as to general readers and history enthusiasts, *Short Histories* comprise novel attempts to bring informed interpretation, as well as factual reportage, to historical debates. Addressing key subjects and topics in the fields of history, the history of ideas, religion, classical studies, politics, philosophy and Middle East studies, these texts move beyond the bland, neutral 'introductions' that so often serve as the primary undergraduate teaching tool. While always providing students and generalists with the core facts that they need to get to grips with, *Short Histories* go further. They offer new insights into how a topic has been understood in the past, and what different social and cultural factors might have been at work. They bring original perspectives to bear on current interpretations. They raise questions and – with extensive bibliographies – point the reader to further study, even as they suggest answers. Each text addresses a variety of subjects in a greater degree of depth than is often found in comparable series, yet at the same time in a concise and compact handbook form. *Short Histories* aim to be 'introductions with an edge'. In combining questioning and searching analysis with informed historical writing, they bring history up-to-date for an increasingly complex and globalized digital age.

For more information about titles and authors in the series, please visit: https://www.bloomsbury.com/series/short-histories/

A Short History of ...

the American Civil War	Paul Anderson (Clemson University)
the American Revolutionary War	Stephen Conway (University College London)
Ancient China	Edward L Shaughnessy (University of Chicago)
Ancient Greece	P J Rhodes, FBA (Durham University)
the Anglo-Saxons	Henrietta Leyser (University of Oxford)
Babylon	Karen Radner (University of Munich)
the Byzantine Empire	Dionysios Stathakopoulos (King's College London)
Christian Spirituality	Edward Howells (Heythrop College, University of London)
Communism	Kevin Morgan (University of Manchester)
the Crimean War	Trudi Tate (University of Cambridge)
English Renaissance Drama	Helen Hackett (University College London)
the English Revolution and the Civil Wars	David J Appleby (University of Nottingham)
the Etruscans	Corinna Riva (University College London)
Florence and the Florentine Republic	Brian Jeffrey Maxson (East Tennessee State University)
the Hundred Years War	Michael Prestwich (Durham University)
Irish Independence	J J Lee (New York University)
the Italian Renaissance	Virginia Cox (New York University)
the Korean War	Allan R Millett (University of New Orleans)
Medieval Christianity	G R Evans (University of Cambridge)

Medieval English Mysticism	Vincent Gillespie (University of Oxford)
the Minoans	John Bennet (University of Sheffield)
the Mongols	George Lane (SOAS, University of London)
the Mughal Empire	Michael H Fisher (Oberlin College)
Muslim Spain	Amira K Bennison (University of Cambridge)
New Kingdom Egypt	Robert Morkot (University of Exeter)
the New Testament	Halvor Moxnes (University of Oslo)
Nineteenth-Century Philosophy	Joel Rasmussen (University of Oxford)
the Normans	Leonie V Hicks (Canterbury Christ Church University)
the Ottoman Empire	Baki Tezcan (University of California, Davis)
the Phoenicians	Mark Woolmer (Durham University)
the Reformation	Helen L Parish (University of Reading)
the Renaissance in Northern Europe	Malcolm Vale (University of Oxford)
Revolutionary Cuba	Antoni Kapcia (University of Nottingham)
the Risorgimento	Nick Carter (Australian Catholic University, Sydney)
the Russian Revolution	Geoffrey Swain (University of Glasgow)
the Spanish Civil War	Julián Casanova (University of Zaragoza)
the Spanish Empire	Felipe Fernández-Armesto (University of Notre Dame) and José Juan López-Portillo (University of Oxford)
Transatlantic Slavery	Kenneth Morgan (Brunel University London)

the Tudors	Richard Rex (University of Cambridge)
Venice and the Venetian Empire	Maria Fusaro (University of Exeter)
the Wars of the Roses	David Grummitt (University of Kent)
the Weimar Republic	Colin Storer (University of Nottingham)

A SHORT HISTORY OF THE ETRUSCANS

Corinna Riva

BLOOMSBURY ACADEMIC
LONDON • NEW YORK • OXFORD • NEW DELHI • SYDNEY

BLOOMSBURY ACADEMIC
Bloomsbury Publishing Plc
50 Bedford Square, London, WC1B 3DP, UK
1385 Broadway, New York, NY 10018, USA

BLOOMSBURY, BLOOMSBURY ACADEMIC and the Diana logo are trademarks of Bloomsbury Publishing Plc

First published in Great Britain 2021
Reprinted 2022

Cover design: Terry Woodley
Cover image © Leonardo Bochicchio, courtesy of SABAP-RM-MET

A catalogue record for this book is available from the British Library.

Library of Congress Cataloging-in-Publication Data
Names: Riva, Corinna, author.
Title: A short history of the Etruscans / Corinna Riva.
Description: London; New York: Bloomsbury Academic, 2020. |
Series: Short histories | Includes bibliographical references and index.
Identifiers: LCCN 2020032477 (print) | LCCN 2020032478 (ebook) |
ISBN 9781780766164 (hardback) | ISBN 9781780766157 (paperback) |
ISBN 9781350182066 (epub) | ISBN 9781350182059 (ebook)
Subjects: LCSH: Etruscans. | Etruria–History.
Classification: LCC DG223 .R58 2020 (print) | LCC DG223 (ebook) |
DDC 937/.501–dc23
LC record available at https://lccn.loc.gov/2020032477
LC ebook record available at https://lccn.loc.gov/2020032478

ISBN: HB: 978-1-7807-6616-4
PB: 978-1-7807-6615-7
ePDF: 978-1-3501-8205-9
eBook: 978-1-3501-8206-6

Series: Short Histories

Typeset by Deanta Global Publishing Services, Chennai, India
Printed and bound in Great Britain

To find out more about our authors and books visit www.bloomsbury.com and sign up for our newsletters.

To the memory of Luciano and our impossible dreams.

Contents

List of figures		x
Preface		xiii
Acknowledgements		xvii
Chapter 1	The Etruscans from the Middle Ages to the Late Twentieth Century	1
Chapter 2	Beginnings: Moving Settlements and Emerging Hierarchies	37
Chapter 3	Etruscan Urbanization: Towns and New Networks	61
Chapter 4	The Etruscan Non-*polis:* Urban Growth in the Archaic Period	91
Chapter 5	Beyond Tyrrhenian Etruria: Human Mobility in a Changing Society	123
Chapter 6	Etruria and Rome	155
Epilogue: From Globalization to New Questions		187
Glossary		197
Notes		201
Select bibliography		205
References		208
Index		245

Figures

0.1	Map of Italy in the central Mediterranean with sites mentioned in the text	xix
0.2	Map of southern Etruria with sites mentioned in the text	xx
1.1	The church of Sant'Andrea, Mantova	6
1.2	The Medici villa at Poggio a Caiano	8
1.3	Salone dei Cinquecento, Palazzo Vecchio, Florence	10
1.4	Ceiling and tondo, Salone dei Cinquecento, Palazzo Vecchio, Florence	11
1.5	Frontispiece, Johann Joachim Winckelmann 1764 *Geschichte der Kunst des Alterthums*, Dresden	18
1.6	Orvieto, George Dennis 1878 *The cities and cemeteries of Etruria*, London	28
1.7	The Piacenza Liver	29
1.8	The Walking Apollo, Portonaccio sanctuary, *Veii* (Villa Giulia Museum)	32
2.1	Luni sul Mignone	38
2.2	The plateau of Tarquinia, Digital Terrain Model without vegetation	42
2.3	Sorgenti della Nova, elevation and plan of Sector III by E. Negroni; artist's impression of the houses and other buildings (below)	45
2.4	Sheet-bronze helmet, Arcatelle *necropolis*, Tarquinia	53
2.5	House-shaped bronze laminated urn	55
2.6	Tomb AA1, Quattro Fontanili, *Veii*, grave goods	57
3.1	The Monterozzi hill, Tarquinia	62
3.2	*Tumulo del Re*, *Tumulo della Regina*, Doganaccia, Tarquinia	63
3.3	*Bucchero oinochoe*, *Caere* (Villa Giulia Museum)	67
3.4	*Tumulo della Regina* under excavation, Doganaccia, Tarquinia	69

3.5 *Tumulo della Regina* under excavation, tomb entrance, Doganaccia, Tarquinia 70
3.6 *Tumulo della Regina* under excavation, monumental staircase leading to tomb entrance, Doganaccia, Tarquinia 70
3.7 *Tumulo della Regina* and nearby tombs, plan, Doganaccia, Tarquinia 71
3.8 Couple of hands in laminated silver and gold leaf, Tomb of the Silver Hands, Osteria *necropolis*, Vulci 74
3.9 Tomb 5, Monte Michele, *Veii*, the grave goods 75
3.10 Silver-laminated urn, *Tomba del Duce*, Poggio Bello *necropolis*, Vetulonia 77
3.11 Banditaccia *necropolis*, *Caere* 78
3.12 Tomb of the Five Chairs, *Caere*, reconstruction of side-chamber interior 79
3.13 San Paolo Olpe, San Paolo Tumulus, *Caere* (Villa Giulia Museum) 83
3.14 Earliest structure (EPOC 4 from south-west), Poggio Civitate (Murlo) 88
3.15 Orientalizing complex, reconstruction, Poggio Civitate (Murlo) 89
3.16 Archaic complex, reconstruction, Poggio Civitate (Murlo) 90
4.1 Piazza d'Armi, *Veii* 92
4.2 So-called *oikos*, reconstruction, Piazza d'Armi, *Veii* 93
4.3 Gravisca, aerial view of the sanctuary 100
4.4 Inscribed stone anchor with *Sostratos* dedication, Gravisca 102
4.5 House of Amphorae, the site under excavation, Marsiliana d'Albegna 107
4.6 House of Amphorae, plan, Marsiliana d'Albegna 108
4.7 House of Amphorae, virtual reconstruction, Marsiliana d'Albegna 108
4.8 Pech Maho lead tablet, Greek text (above), Etruscan text (below) 110
4.9 *Pyrgi*, the plan of the site 111
4.10 Golden plaques with *Thefarie Velianas*' dedication, *Pyrgi* (Villa Giulia Museum) 113
4.11 Pediment illustrating the myth Seven against Thebes, Temple A, *Pyrgi* (Villa Giulia Museum) 115
4.12 Dedication of bronze artefacts, Civita sacred complex, La Civita di Tarquinia, Tarquinia 116
4.13 Portonaccio sanctuary, *Veii* 118
4.14 Large-scale terracotta *acroteria*, Portonaccio sanctuary, *Veii* (Villa Giulia Museum) 120
5.1 Marzabotto 125

5.2 Marzabotto, town plan 127
5.3 The temples of *Uni and Tinia*, virtual reconstruction, Marzabotto 128
5.4 Spina, town plan 132
5.5 House unit, Spina 133
5.6 Prato Gonfienti 135
5.7 Porticoed house unit (lotto 14), hypothetical reconstruction, Prato Gonfienti 136
5.8 Vicchio Stele 136
5.9 Mars of Todi (Musei Vaticani) 139
5.10 The *tufa* outcrop of Orvieto (ancient *Volsinii*) emerging from the clouds 140
5.11 Crocifisso del Tufo *necropolis*, *Volsinii* 141
5.12 Crocifisso del Tufo *necropolis*, aerial view, *Volsinii* 142
5.13 Ara della Regina, Tarquinia 144
5.14 *Dado* tombs, Banditaccia *necropolis*, *Caere* 147
5.15 Tomb of the Lionesses, Monterozzi *necropolis*, Tarquinia 149
5.16 Monumental staircase, Sodo Tumulus II, Cortona 151
6.1 Tomb of the Infernal Chariot, Pianacce *necropolis*, Sarteano 157
6.2 Tomb of the Ships, Monterozzi *necropolis*, Tarquinia 159
6.3 Tomb of Hunting and Fishing, Monterozzi *necropolis*, Tarquinia 160
6.4 Right-hand wall of back chamber, Tomb of the Shields, Monterozzi *necropolis*, Tarquinia 162
6.5 François Tomb, reconstruction of the painting of the *tablinum*, Ponte Rotto *necropolis*, Vulci 167
6.6 The temple pediment, Talamone 179
6.7 Fortification, Rofalco, Selva del Lamone nature reserve (VT) 180
6.8 View from the site, Rofalco, Selva del Lamone nature reserve (VT) 180
6.9 The *Arx* or sacred hilltop, *Cosa* 182
6.10 Circuit wall, *Cosa* 182
6.11 The Roman theatre, Volterra 184
7.1 Aerial view of the site, Campo della Fiera, Orvieto (ancient *Volsinii*) 188
7.2 The excavation, Campo della Fiera, Orvieto (ancient *Volsinii*) 188
7.3 Trachyte stone base with inscription of *Kanuta*, Campo della Fiera, Orvieto (ancient *Volsinii*) 190
7.4 Site plan, Campo della Fiera, Orvieto (ancient *Volsinii*) 191

Preface

The Etruscans have agency and have been given their due: I borrow these phrases from the introductions to two of the latest specialist companions to the Etruscans, namely *A Companion to the Etruscans*, edited by S. Bell and A. Carpino (Wiley-Blackwell, 2016), and *The Etruscan World*, edited by J. MacIntosh Turfa (Routledge, 2013). Other such companions, all written in English, and including *Etruscology*, edited by A. Naso (De Gruyter 2017), have appeared recently, showcasing the enormous steps that the modern scientific academic discipline of Etruscan archaeology or Etruscology, as it is known primarily in Italy, has taken since its beginnings in the middle or so of the twentieth century. The publication of all these companions in less than ten years, along with their contributing authors, also speaks highly of the international scholarly environment in which these steps have been taken.

With this has thus come the recognition that to study classics or classical antiquity today one can no longer limit oneself to ancient Greece and Rome: the Mediterranean basin in which these civilizations flourished was culturally diverse, matching the equally lively social and cultural interaction between different regions and other civilizations, among which were the Etruscans, one of Rome's closest neighbours. It is symptomatic of this that, amidst all these companions, a short introduction to the subject has been written by an ancient historian (C. Smith *The Etruscans. A Very Short Introduction*. 2014, Oxford). And herein lies the core issue, from which we cannot escape: since the early modern period when an antiquarian interest in the Etruscans first emerged, we have always been told, by ancient Greek and Roman writers, what and how to think of the Etruscans, of their beliefs and traditions. If this has long shaped our knowledge of them, it has been so not solely because of our reliance on written sources for our studies; after all, these writers have dealt with other non-Greek and non-Roman civilizations. When it comes to the Etruscans, however, our own interpretations have also been strongly influenced by a constant succession of ideas about them deriving from those writers, forming and transforming throughout the centuries under the ideological stakes and claims made by those who needed them most, whether in Renaissance Italy or in the European Enlightenment; I shall explore why in the first chapter of this book. At the same time, archaeological discoveries, though often made to suit those claims, also raised new questions, some of which are still with us today, as the scientific study of the past took shape across European academic establishments and museums.

We cannot discount all of this when we try to write a history of the Etruscans. In this book, I wish to start here and from these ideas, and then gradually move the reader through changing scholarly perspectives and debates by providing a context to them in the excavation history, old and recent, of Etruscan Italy. In doing so, I hope that the reader will appreciate that the primarily archaeological study of this subject and the questions it poses, from urbanism to religion and the economy, requires a critical consideration of the relationship between the ancient written and archaeological sources, and of how this relationship has been treated by scholars of different generations.

In Chapter 2, I trace the emergence of what we know as Etruscan civilization and begin from the Bronze Age in order to show that this emergence was a long-term process which gained momentum between the end of the Bronze Age and the earliest phases of the Iron Age, when we see significant shifts in the location of settlements and material culture, inaugurating the beginnings of urbanism. Chapter 3 is devoted to the urbanizing phase of the seventh century BCE when we see not only the sociopolitical and economic transformations that urbanization brought to Etruscan Italy but also a phase of heightened interaction with the outside world. This is, in fact, the century in which the growth of newly settled Phoenician and Greek communities in the central Mediterranean is documented; these latter, together with indigenous towns, led to the formation of an urban network whose links expanded and nodes thickened in the course of the late seventh and into the sixth century BCE. The sixth century, the heart of the so-called archaic period, and subject of Chapter 4, is a period of growing trade links between Etruscan cities and other cities across the Italic peninsula and the central Mediterranean. This is shown by the export of Etruscan goods throughout this broader region, the increasing importation of goods into Etruria, and the establishment of trading posts. While scholars have traditionally viewed this century as a phase in which the Etruscans became 'Hellenized' as they acquired Greek goods and seemingly adopted Greek customs, we recognize today that the acquisition of those goods is evidence of a buoyant Etruscan economy that went hand in hand with the demands and needs of a changing society, in which new traditions, materials and ideas were incorporated into pre-existing social practices. One sphere of society where these changes are most visible is religion. If the sixth century BCE was a period of growth, the following century was a phase of major shifts and transformation; Chapter 5 thus examines the fifth century as a dynamic period rather than one of crisis, which was a view held for a long time but now in need of more nuance. This dynamism came from the opening up and expansion of the economic and trade networks beyond Tyrrhenian Etruria, from the Adriatic and further afield; the settlement and burial evidence offers a picture of further mobility across the peninsula and a changing social and urban landscape. Chapter 6 will focus upon the period from the fourth century BCE onwards, which saw the gradual absorption of Etruscan city states into Rome's political orbit. For this phase, too, we are fortunate to have an increasing amount of archaeological evidence that reveals a much more nuanced picture of this absorption and its consequences than what was previously assumed. As we shall see, this was not a one-way process whereby Roman culture and policies were imposed on Etruscan states, but rather a two-way process of interaction where some Etruscan cities and elite groups within them had much to gain from the Roman conquest. As always in human history, there were winners and losers, but the archaeological evidence at our disposal shows that not everyone in Etruria was losing out in 'becoming Roman'. The book ends with an epilogue that returns to the history of ideas by considering the place of Etruscan Italy in the context of current debates within the broader discipline of archaeology vis-à-vis a research agenda for the future; the intention is to give the reader a taste of the vibrancy of Etruscan archaeology as a contemporary discipline that can be best appreciated by placing it in a critical dialogue with its past.

The last but not at all least aspect of note that I bring to the attention of the reader is the fragility of the archaeological heritage that anyone studying Etruscan Italy has to confront and deal with: much of this fragility is a result of the illicit market in antiquities, which encourages and feeds illegal excavations and hence the destruction of this heritage.

Highly eloquent of this deplorable state of affairs is the fragment of a painted terracotta architectural slab that is on the book cover: the fragment is currently (at the time of writing) on show at the Centrale Montemartini in Rome as part of a remarkable exhibition 'Colori degli etruschi. Tesori di terracotta alla Centrale Montemartini'[1] It belongs to a large group of other such fragments coming from the territory of Cerveteri (Etruscan *Caere*) that were looted and illegally exported: the group was identified in Geneva in 2016 by the Carabinieri of the Nucleo Tutela Patrimonio Culturale, a branch of the Italian police devoted to the protection of cultural heritage, and returned to Italy. Through the painstaking study and process of restoration by the Soprintendenza we are able to know more about the production of this material, but its archaeological context is irretrievable. Without knowledge of such a context we lose a huge amount of information that would help us answer key research questions about Etruscan society. Ultimately, the cultural value of this material for the reconstruction of Italy's ancient past is also lost: herein lies the violence of the illicit market in antiquities.

London, 5 May 2020

Acknowledgements

This book took a long time to write: its beginnings took place amidst life-changing circumstances and plenty of thinking and re-thinking of what a *Short History of the Etruscans* could be like, and why any non-specialist reader, student or bookshop visitor should want to read such a book. In the meantime, I have accumulated plenty of debts to friends and colleagues who have come to the rescue either as honest advisers or as generous readers of parts of the manuscript or of its entirety.

Mike Rowlands has been an attentive listener to the earliest ideas on how to develop this project and the spin-off coming out of it, that has appeared elsewhere[1]: his encouragement towards reflecting on how ideas about the Etruscans shaped our understanding of them has been highly influential. Jas Elsner, too, has driven me further into this direction: I thank them both for helping me turn this project into what has been for me an all-consuming journey into antiquarian scholarship and intellectual history.

Caroline Morcom has been my champion non-specialist reader: her precious advice, and her contagious enthusiasm, has been a blessing for a novice of non-academic English prose. Christopher Smith has been there for advice on all sorts of themes and topics that have fed into this book (and elsewhere), and for reading the early stages of the text. Gabriele Cifani has also been a most generous reader of the entire semi-final draft. The specialist reviewers of the submitted manuscript have provided encouraging feedback and incisive comments that have improved the text although, I hasten to add, neither of them nor anyone else is responsible for it. Mark Pearce has diligently corrected my readings of early prehistory; Cristiano Iaia has answered final, last-minute doubts. Lindsay Allen has helped polish the epilogue, and has forced me to clarify my Italian-style long sentences; more polishing has come from Lena Isayev. Andrea Zifferero, who has kindly lent me the images of *Casa delle Anfore* at Marsiliana, has also been generous with his time: to him I am indebted for our past fruitful discussions on wine consumption in Etruria. Lorenzo Zamboni has not only lent me the illustrations on Spina, but he has also discussed with me the trickiest questions about Verucchio. Carlo Casi has lent me plenty of photographs and made contacts to this end for me, but he has also been a constant presence as a friend and colleague over the years and through our field collaboration at Vulci. In Athens, Denitsa Nenova has been, as always, the most efficient colleague in drawing the maps.

Several other colleagues have generously intervened to provide me with their own images and illustrations during a time when I should have been travelling from site to site to take my own photographs, but I could not due to the Covid-19 emergency. I thank them all: Giovanna Bagnasco, Cristina Biella, Antonio Baragliu, Mariagrazia Celuzza, Eric Gailledrat, Elisabetta Govi, Massimo Legni, Alessandro Mandolesi, Matilde Marzullo, Laura Michetti, Nuccia Negroni Catacchio, Andrea Pessina and Gabriella Poggesi, Lisa Pieraccini, Simona Rafanelli, Simonetta Stopponi, Tony Tuck, Nancy Winter. Sincere thanks also go to Alessia Argento at the Villa Giulia Museum and Daniele Maras, Rossella Zaccagnini and Enrico Ciavoni at the Soprintendenza archeologia, belle arti e paesaggio per l'area metropolitana di Roma, la provincia di Viterbo e l'Etruria meridionale.

Abigail Lane and Emily Drewe at Bloomsbury also deserve my warmest thanks for their patience and professionalism. Likewise, I would like to cordially thank Alex Wright (once at I.B. Tauris, now at Cambridge University Press) who first invited me to this project and commissioned the book.

This book could not have been written without the library at the Institute of Classical Studies of Senate House and the Warburg Library in London: I thank the staff at both libraries for all their patience and help. I also wish to thank UCL for continuing to offer us full-year-long research leave, which is essential to complete book-length, single-authored projects.

Last, but by no means least, extremely special thanks go to Stephen and Silvia for, well, everything. This book is dedicated to the memory of Luciano and to the memory of our dreams of a life together.

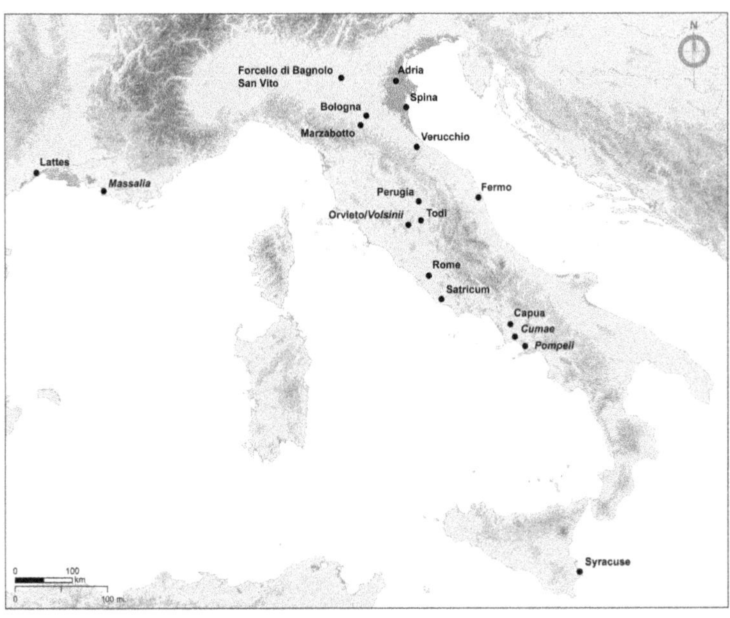

Figure 0.1 Map of Italy in the central Mediterranean with sites mentioned in the text (drawing D. Nenova).

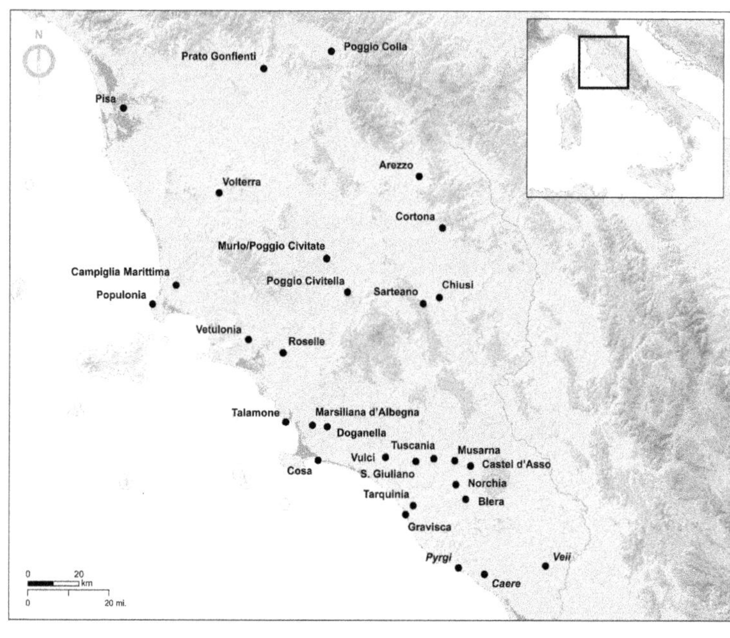

Figure 0.2 Map of southern Etruria with sites mentioned in the text (drawing D. Nenova).

1

THE ETRUSCANS FROM THE MIDDLE AGES TO THE LATE TWENTIETH CENTURY

INTRODUCTION

> Historians of antiquity who believe in weighing the claims of archaeology against the claims of literary tradition can be dismissed as too naive members of their profession. The real task of the historian is to analyze all the data he has and to try to account for all of them. But the process of analyzing data is never an individual performance. It is invariably, though in varying degrees, a collective enterprise of scholars of different countries, different academic traditions, different generations – indeed, different centuries. Especially in the study of Classical antiquity, we cannot lightly ignore the fact that the texts we study, the inscriptions we read, the monuments we see, have for the most part been known to previous generations of scholars and in some cases have been studied uninterruptedly since antiquity. The editions we use, the meanings we attribute to the texts, the identification and the description of ancient monuments, are the result of the work of centuries. Any new interpreter must be aware of past interpreters: he [or she] who is not aware of past interpreters will still be influenced by them, but uncritically, because, after all, awareness is the foundation of criticism. The historian must therefore be able to account not only for all the data he possesses but also for all the interpretations he is aware of.
>
> (Momigliano, 1975, pp. 196–7)

Thus, Arnaldo Momigliano, the late Italian ancient historian, acutely reflected on the relationship between archaeology and the ancient literary tradition. Although Momigliano was writing about the origins of the

Roman Republic, this observation seems to be particularly pertinent for Etruscan archaeology, a discipline that sometimes sits awkwardly within studies of classical antiquity because of the lack of a direct literary tradition which characterizes Greek and Roman antiquity and, at the same time, the wealth of a material record that is comparable to that of its neighbouring Greek and Roman archaeology. In reality, archaeology more broadly has made enormous advances since Momigliano wrote; thanks to these, Etruscan archaeology nowadays is couched within Mediterranean archaeology, where Etruria can be examined through a whole suit of archaeological methods that encourage the scholar to focus on material culture in all its facets, the challenges of how to interpret it and the opportunities for overcoming these challenges. This is, in fact, the field of enquiry within which this short history of the Etruscans will be approached. Yet, Momigliano has still much food for thought to offer, largely for two reasons. First, like its Greek and Roman counterparts, Etruscan antiquity has been written about, interpreted and studied for several centuries. Some scholars argue that interest in Etruscan history began, in fact, in antiquity, most notably with the Greek historian Dionysius of Halicarnassus, active in Rome in the first century BCE and author of a book on the history of Rome, *Roman Antiquities*, and his near-contemporary Livy whose monumental history of Rome, *Ab Urbe Condita*, stretched to the author's own times (Bonfante, 1986, pp. 18–46). Both books dealt with the origins of the city and its neighbours, and therefore with Etruscan cities and their relationship with Rome. Other scholars, as I wish to do here, prefer to distinguish an ancient literary and historical tradition from later documents, beginning in the early modern period when we see evidence of an awareness, by humanist historians, poets and writers, of a rupture with the ancient past (Hankins, 1991) and the growth of what has been called 'a spirit of historical criticism' (Quint, 1985).

Over the centuries, the Etruscans have been subjected to a myriad of theories in relation to their origins, their place within both historical narratives of Italy as a nation and beyond, and localized narratives of those regions in which they flourished. Above all, it is the relationship of the Etruscans with Rome that has always proven critical in the construction of those very narratives. Several of these theories, born within the antiquarian tradition of early modern Europe, were discredited by subsequent scientific scholarship for being erroneous antiquarian findings or, in the most sensational cases, discredited by their contemporaries for being fantasies deriving from skilled forgeries. Indeed, the lack of a direct literary tradition coupled with the survival of ancient monuments is arguably accountable for making Etruscology particularly susceptible to fantasies and forgeries since antiquity (Rowland, 2005). But as I shall show, a succinct glance at these theories, interpretations, even fantasies, on the Etruscans through the centuries encourages us to look closely at the use or, in worst cases, manipulation of a people's history for political advantage and ideological ends. This is particularly so when that history is constructed primarily through material traces and only indirectly through near-contemporary or much later literary and historical traditions.

The second aspect of note in Momigliano's words is the very relationship between archaeology and the literary tradition. For centuries, Greek and Roman ancient written sources have directed our appreciation of the Etruscans and our own interpretations of the material remains they have left behind. Only recently have we come to acknowledge that a deeper understanding of their civilization comes from scrutinizing closely the tension between what Greek and Roman authors had to say about the Etruscans and our own interpretations of those authors on the one hand, and of the archaeological record on the other; to capture this tension is no easy feat and, as we shall see throughout this book, it often leads to a somewhat more speculative, but what I hope can be a more intellectually honest history. Ultimately, such a history is primarily, though not exclusively, archaeological if we recognize that our only direct source for reconstructing that history is material remains. However, this was not so in fourteenth- and fifteenth-century Florence where, early modern historians contend, the so-called Etruscan myth was born (Cipriani, 1980),[1] that is to say, the cultural construction of an Etruscan past, which served ideological ends of those in power and hence able to construct that past. It is here and a couple of centuries earlier that I would like to commence. The aim for beginning here is twofold: to highlight the role that antiquity, and within it the Etruscans, played in the cultural politics and the political thought of those centuries, on the one hand, and, on the other, to ask how and to what extent that role was transformed and shaped by the cultural politics of later centuries down to the twentieth century.

THE ETRUSCAN MYTH: FLORENTINE HUMANISM AND THE MEDICI'S DYNASTY RISE TO POWER

In the fourteenth century, the Etruscans first caught the attention of contemporary historians who wrote of Etruscan historical figures known from Roman sources. Livy's *Ab Urbe Condita*, for example, was the main source for our first early modern account, by Giovanni Villani, of the deeds of the Tuscan king Porsenna. His universal history, *Nuova Cronica*, however, linked the Tuscan past with Rome's past, and does not contain the terms 'Etruria' and 'Etruscans' (Salvestrini, 2002; Schoonhoven, 2010). This is perhaps surprising if we consider Livy's extensive reference to both. What one can infer from this is that, to Villani and his contemporaries, the ancient Roman past was critical to the shaping of Florence's power, while Etruria had not yet entered their imagination as a historically and politically relevant entity. In particular, that power and Florence's civic identity were enhanced by highlighting Rome's republican legacy, with which Florence sought to legitimize its growing hegemony in Tuscany. The use of antiquity for shaping a Roman republican heritage must be viewed in relation to the novel interest in ancient literature, which forms the essence of humanism, and in relation to the development of political thought and literature from the end of the thirteenth century (Rubinstein, 2004). In fifteenth-century Florence, some of that political literature and the values it promoted such as virtue and liberty served as political propaganda and its values as a 'civic myth', created to legitimize the status quo of the Florentine political system of the time (Najemy, 2000).

Rome's republican heritage, in fact, was a more strongly driving force in the definition of Florence's ancient past in the late fourteenth century as attested by contemporary historical documents such as the official and private letters of Coluccio Salutati (1331–1406), then chancellor of the Florentine republic (Baldassarri, 2009). In these letters, Salutati also talked of the pre-Roman past of Italy alongside Florence's Roman republican values in order to emphasize the freedom of Italic city states in pre-Roman times (Witt, 2000, p. 313). Leonardo Bruni of Arezzo (1370–1444), Salutati's successor to the chancellorship, pursued this ideal of political freedom and republican values further: in his *Historiae Florentini Populi Libri XII* (1416–42), a history of Florence renowned among his contemporaries, he saw the origins of these ideals in the independent Etruscan city states and their government run by *Lucumones*, the cities' magistrates (Bruni, 2001, Volume 1, Introduction). As the Etruscans entered Florence's republican ideology and were conveniently moulded to its 'civic myth', so did they attract the attention of those humanists responsible for forging the myth, and stimulated their curiosity in their literary activities. Interestingly, the championing of republicanism left the Etruscans largely indistinct and on equal footing with their other fellow ancients. Only with Cosimo I, as we shall see, were they explicitly singled out and turned into a local heritage.

What fuelled the growing interest in Etruscan civilization was also its archaeological discovery that gained momentum in the fifteenth century, inspiring artists and architects. Prominent figures of Florence's artistic and cultural world became familiar with the Etruscan legacy, largely known from Vitruvius and Pliny the Elder, in ancient sculpture, painting and architecture, and sought to inject it into their work (Chastel, 1961, pp. 32–69; Cipriani, 1980, pp. 19–21). Less was known about Etruscan artefacts and architectural structures, which began to be investigated. A renowned example is the discovery, made at the turn of the century, in 1507, of the Castellina Tumulus in the Chianti hills, a tomb talked about in letters and documents of the time (Bocci Pacini and Bartoloni, 2003). The growing central role that antiquarian discoveries played into the Etruscan revival of the fifteenth century mirrors the equally growing antiquarian interest elsewhere in Italy, which led to the creation of private collections of ancient artefacts.

If, however, ancient art was familiar because of its presence in the urban landscape, especially in Rome, although as yet unrecognizable to the untrained fifteenth-century eye, Etruscan remains were all the more difficult to understand because of the lack of a local ancient literary tradition (Chastel, 1961, pp. 32–7). However, those remains provided a new heritage to study and from which to extract suitable pride. Indeed, because of the lack of an Etruscan literary tradition, Florentine humanists' understanding of Etruscan civilization was driven more by ancient writers than by material culture. A prime example of this are the writings of Leon Battista Alberti, the famous Florentine architect and theorist. Alberti's sensitivity to ancient architecture, shaped by Vitruvius, led him to use the concept of the temple *Etruscorum more* (in the Etruscan manner) – as he described in his own treatise – in his design of the church of Sant'Andrea, begun in the mid-1470s in Mantova, the city that was known to have Etruscan origins. Vitruvius' influence did not drive Alberti's choice in architectural form or design, but in spatial proportions: as the ratio between the length and width of the Vitruvian Etruscan temple had to be six to five, the plan of Sant'Andrea's main nave followed these prescribed proportions. This, along with the lack of remains of Etruscan temples known at the time, may explain Alberti's misreading of the original Vitruvian plan, a single set of *cellae* (inner temple chambers) facing a portico. In fact, the overall design of Sant'Andrea was inspired by the biblical temple of Solomon and the Basilica of Maxentius in Rome, which, he thought, displayed the features of Etruscan temples (Tavernor, 1998, pp. 176–8). Yet, while Roman ancient architecture is behind much of the church's design, it remains rather suggestive of the value that this most famous architect placed on an autochthonous expression of antiquity that he chose the Etruscan manner as he saw it for what was a most important architectural project towards the end of his professional career. And it was architecture which, to Alberti and his contemporaries, the Etruscans excelled at. Most emblematic of these ancient skills was the labyrinth and tomb of Porsenna, described by Pliny in great detail, and illustrated by the famous Sangallo architects (Borsi, 1985) (Figure 1.1).

At the same time, one has to wonder what exactly the quality of being autochthonous meant to Alberti. At that time, after all, artists and architects adopted the classical form and the antique not because of their desire to study it, understand it and apply it philologically,

Figure 1.1 The church of Sant'Andrea, Mantova, photograph by Bjoern Eisbaer (CC BY-SA 3.0), from Wikimedia Commons.

but rather because the ancients and the antique helped them nurture their own imagination and fulfil their own objectives, of which the achievement of naturalism was paramount. The antique and the ancients, in other words, acted as a passive element in fifteenth-century art, architecture and poetry (Holberton, 1985). This use of the antique belongs to a broader High Renaissance approach to the ancients, which must have affected how people made sense of the material past surrounding them: historian James Hankins has noted that critical study and method of analysis of the ancients' oeuvres were not part of that approach. In the fifteenth and early sixteenth centuries, historical truth was not achieved via a process of critical enquiry, but rather via a hermeneutics which did not distinguish fact from value, and which was therefore perfectly adapted in maintaining or even strengthening contemporary values and needs (Hankins, 1990, pp. 362–3). In Florence, such values and needs were inextricably entangled with, even coincided with, those of noblemen who protected and supported artists and poets.

Of these, Lorenzo Medici (1449–92) encapsulates par excellence the ideal of the Florentine patron of the arts, and was, by far, the most avid collector of antiquities (Fusco and Corti, 2006). Aside from his own art collection, Lorenzo's thinking around antiquity is most visible in the project for the villa he had built on one of his country estates at Poggio a Caiano. The villa was to be decorated with sculpture and a temple façade *all'antica*, both realized in Lorenzo's time. The temple façade, the first in the Renaissance to adorn a domestic residence, was a bold move and followed architectural theory of the time, after Alberti. As a true expression of the revival of antiquity, the villa also embodied the interest, by Lorenzo and his circle, in bucolic and pastoral culture and life, intended as the ancients did (Kent, 2004, pp. 75–125). Whether that revival explicitly harked back to the Etruscan past in the form of the temple façade, with its broad pediment and widely positioned columns, as Etruscologists have argued (Bonfante, 1986, p. 26), or in the maiolica frieze decorating the pediment (Cox-Rearick, 1982), as others have suggested, seems to be contentious: it is perhaps correct to see the villa as a combination of different sources of inspiration that came together in that humanist taste for the antique. Any attempt to extract, from that combination, what was Etruscan is not only impossible but also misleading exactly because that taste was informed by an eclectic use of the sources. No one knew or, rather, no one cared to understand, philologically, what an Etruscan temple looked like (Figure 1.2).

Figure 1.2 The Medici villa at Poggio a Caiano, photograph by Sailko (CC BY-SA 3.0), from Wikimedia Commons.

The temple façade together with the later decorative programmes of the villa under later Medici suggests a continuity, noted by scholars, in the Medici's political ideology from Lorenzo up to the family's restoration in Florence in the early sixteenth century. Whether, however, we can speak of continuity in respect of the ways in which the Etruscans served that ideology is debatable: only in the later sixteenth century, not earlier, was the emphasis on Etruscan kingship becoming explicit and closely tied with Etruscan autochthony, which had by then become politically relevant. In the sixteenth century, the Tuscan architectural order was codified as an architectural canon by Sebastiano Serlio, who, in his treatise on architecture, not only saw the Tuscan order as the strongest and most rustic, but also associated it with architectural rustication. This association reveals a significant intention to establish rustication not as an architectural language inspired by Roman antiquity, but rather as an autochthonous Tuscan language that stood vis-à-vis the classical Greek orders just as vernacular Italian, increasingly more frequently used in learned circles, stood vis-à-vis Latin (Ackerman, 1983). And this is where Serlio and his contemporaries departed from the earlier generations of architects like Alberti: for Serlio that autochthony had become significant. Furthermore, like the other orders, such an autochthonous language was defined by both architectural proportions and allegorical characteristics: rustic, solid, warrior-like and virile, all qualities that would well serve the cultural–political ideology of another Medici, Cosimo I.

FROM COSIMO MEDICI TO THE SEVENTEENTH CENTURY

The convergence of Etruscan kingship and autochthony thus emerged slowly and was only exploited for the first time and forcefully by Cosimo I in order to shape his political–cultural ideology. The efforts of Cosimo to build on a local heritage – linguistic, archaeological, artistic and historical – went hand in hand with his successful attempts at gaining sovereign rights beyond Florence and the ultimate kingly title of Grand Duke of Tuscany, which Pope Pius V bestowed upon him in 1569 followed by his coronation as Grand Duke in 1570 (Schoonhoven, 2010, pp. 464–6). Scholars agree that the 1540s and 1550s were a crucial phase for Cosimo's reign as he attempted to resolve political strife at home, while intervening in strengthening the economy of the region and extending his rule to other neighbouring states. His cultural agenda also generated a 'cultural miracle', as Cosimo promoted culture at all levels from supporting artists and poets, and reopening the University of Pisa, to founding and becoming patron of learned academies like the *Accademia Fiorentina*, and championing the Tuscan language and its writers (Eisenbichler, 2001).

For the first time, a Medici ruler explicitly used culture and the arts as tools for political propaganda, not only to legitimize his own rule but also to impose such a rule as dynastic and monarchic: this propaganda had inevitably a strong impact upon changing views of Etruscan antiquity, and particularly so in relation to Cosimo's intention to emphasize his absolute regal authority (Eisenbichler, 2001). Even so, Cosimo shrewdly exploited Florence's republican past and its historical civic values to his own political ends, succeeding in demonstrating that his power was simply the culmination of Florence's great civic (republican) traditions (van Veen, 1992). The *Palazzo della Signoria* (or *Palazzo Vecchio*), the seat of the Florentine Republic, where he took up residence, was redecorated to suit his political propaganda (Allegri and Cecchi, 1980, pp. 235–73). The *Salone dei Cinquecento*, the Republic's Hall of the Great Council, was redesigned by Giorgio Vasari and turned into the main reception

Figure 1.3 Salone dei Cinquecento, Palazzo Vecchio, Florence, photograph by Benjamín Núñez González (CC BY-SA 4.0), from Wikimedia Commons.

hall for Cosimo's principate (Blake Macham, 2006, pp. 125–ff). Its painted walls and ceilings spoke to his power linked to the history of Florence and to the dynastic line of his family: here, Etruria appears as a unifying theme strengthening Cosimo's duchy, and later Grand Duchy as a regional power (Figure 1.3).

In 1563, the depiction of Cosimo's apotheosis in the tondo at the centre of the ceiling of this hall shows the city of Fiorenza, personified, crowning him with oak leaves (Figure 1.4); Cosimo, named *optimus princeps* in the inscription, is seated on a *sedes curulis*, a symbol of ancient Roman consular, and hence republican, authority. That the scene conveys a message of historical continuity is seen in the rest of the inscribed words of the tondo, CONSTITUTA CIVITATE/AUCTO IMPERIO/PACATA ETRURIA; Van Veen (van Veen, 1992, pp. 203–4) has suggested that *constituta civitate* be read as 'organized the state after its foundation by Augustus/Octavian', while *aucto imperio* as a reference to Florence's expansion and the conquest of Siena. Interestingly, in this tondo, the ancient political pedigree of Florence is Roman, both imperial and republican at once, but the present (*pacata Etruria*) harked

Figure 1.4 Ceiling and tondo, Salone dei Cinquecento, Palazzo Vecchio, Florence, photograph by Benjamín Núñez González (CC BY-SA 4.0), from Wikimedia Commons.

back to an Etruscan past. Etruria, in other words, was stripped of any connotation of political authority but acted as a gelling agent for the regional state of Tuscany under the figure of the Duke. In fact, the idea of Etruria was inseparable from the Duke as a figure of imperial power and ruler of the state at once. Hence, at Cosimo's death, Piero Vettori and Giovan Battista Adriani who composed the funeral orations addressed Cosimo as *Etruriae Dux* (Cipriani, 1980, pp. 109–12). At the Uffizi, the seat of the bureaucratic administration of the duchy, designed by Giorgio Vasari, the sculptural decoration of the recessed façade facing the *Piazza della Signoria* also spoke of Cosimo's rule and his imperial aspirations: towering a sculpture gallery was a statue of Cosimo, represented as Augustus/Hercules (Allegri and Cecchi, 1980, pp. 97–101; Cipriani, 1980, pp. 75–7; Crum, 1989).

Etruscan antiquity took centre stage, not only for antiquarian matters, which were stimulated by new important discoveries, but also in respect of interest in language. The latter must be seen in the context of Cosimo's promotion of vernacular Florentine. The activities of the *Accademia*

Fiorentina, founded by him in 1542 and born as *Accademia degli Umidi* a year earlier with the goal to learn and study Florentine, were absolutely vital channels for this promotion (Watt, 2001, pp. 127–31). In reality, interest in the Etruscan language was not new: a century earlier, a Dominican friar, Giovanni Nanni, who went by what he saw as an Etruscan name, Annius of Viterbo, reached fame through his *Commentaria super opera diversorum auctorum de antiquitatibus loquentium*, a long commentary intertwining biblical and classical texts, artefacts and inscriptions, published in 1502, and already widely condemned as being a crafty forgery by the later generation of humanists. In it, Annius claimed to have published a series of ancient texts, which he forged. What transpired from these texts was the deep antiquity of the Etruscans who descended from Comerus, the grandson of Noah or Janus, and were the first to settle after the Flood. Annius saw them as the most religious of people, while Viterbo, the first city built after the Flood, was their capital; just as ancient, he claimed, was their language, older than Hebrew and coming from Aramaic, the most ancient of all languages (Ligota, 1987, p. 50; Stephens, 2004). Under Cosimo, on the other hand, interest in the Etruscan language is highly indicative of the value of Etruscan for stressing the regional integration and identity of the duchy, no longer focused on Florence alone (Bertelli, 1981, pp. 203–5). Indeed, it has been argued that it is the central decade of the sixteenth century that saw interest in Etruria or *etruscheria* reach its highest point (Cristofani, 1981, p. 197; Galdy, 2009, p. 48; Schoonhoven, 2010, p. 465).

In the mid-sixteenth century, newly discovered artefacts which added to the lustre of Cosimo's collection included famous Etruscan artefacts, namely the bronze Minerva of Arezzo, found in 1542 and purchased ten years later, and the Chimera, found in 1553–4 along with a series of small bronze statuettes at Arezzo. Despite being a fortuitous discovery, the Chimera and its Etruscan inscription aroused the interest and curiosity of antiquarians and artists alike, including Vasari and Titian, both in Tuscany and elsewhere, who all attempted to trace the fabulous animal iconographically (Cristofani, 1979); by the second half of the century, the Chimera was considered a typical example of Etruscan art. In the middle of the century, beside Arezzo, other cities in Tuscany saw a surge in antiquarian interests for the search for new artefacts outside Florence: Chiusi, for example, was a favoured destination for antiquarians (Cristofani, 1981).

Ancient Etruria continued to be a constant presence during the reign of Cosimo's successors who continued the Medici dynasty and the political ideology that claimed both Etruscan ancestry and a Roman imperial past at once. Francesco, Cosimo's son, supported the newly born *Accademia della Crusca* (Cipriani 1980, p. 150), and patronized other learned societies. He also oversaw important transformations of the Uffizi that involved the creation of a gallery in the higher level of the loggia, an early concept of museum (Berti, 1967, pp. 131–8). His brother Ferdinando, who succeeded upon his premature death in 1587, also created several new galleries, each devoted to a science and a particular set of objects (Acidini, 2009, p. 26).

The following reigns of the seventeenth century, however, saw a general intellectual decline: historiographical writing and the sharp critical political theory on authority and the state that had so much characterized the previous centuries lost impetus. The cultural life of the duchy and the activities of intellectuals and learned societies wilted into provincial erudition and lack of innovative thinking save for a few exceptions such as the *Accademia della Crusca* and the publication of its vocabularies, Galileo's followers at the University of Pisa and the *Accademia del Cimento*, founded in 1657, and devoted to an experimental approach to the natural sciences (Diaz, 1976, pp. 452–5; Beretta, 2000). To this atmosphere belong the seven books of *De Hetruria Regali*, a work written between 1616 and 1619 by Thomas Dempster, a Catholic Scotsman who left Britain and France to go to Rome, and then, under papal auspices and with the support of Cosimo II, taught civil law at Pisa where he was commissioned by the Duke's secretary of state to write an Etruscan regal history (Leighton and Castelino, 1990). The manuscript was never published, but was purchased and later published posthumously by the English Thomas Coke (Bruschetti, 2014). It was a compilation of classical, medieval and humanist sources, some of which turned out to be forgeries, with the addition of Latin inscriptions. *De Hetruria Regali* was undoubtedly the most complete compilation of sources on Etruscan antiquity up until then by an erudite scholar who genuinely intended to write the history of the Etruscan ancient origins of the Medici family as accurately as possible. In it, the Etruscans were viewed as the only autochthonous people of Italy as attested by their language, which, according to Dempster, did not derive from Aramaic or Hebrew, and could not be deciphered. The era of the ancient Etruscan kings was seen as the most flourishing, a view that, once again, validated the authority of the Medici regal dynasty (Cristofani, 1983, pp. 20–3; Leighton and Castelino, 1990, pp. 347–9).

Dempster's attempts at collating all the sources in an encyclopaedic way must be placed in the broader context of seventeenth-century antiquarian studies that anticipated the development of these studies a century later. The trend towards the systematization of sources for reconstructing different aspects of an ancient culture and the interest towards specific genres of ancient monuments such as sculpture, glyptic art or coins is discernible in antiquarian studies of the sixteenth century. This slowly led to the conception of ancient cultures as peculiarly different from contemporary culture and the realization of the growing separation between the two and the superiority of the latter (Wrede, 2000). Furthermore, interest in the natural world, which must have come from the novel theories proposed by Galileo, pushed seventeenth-century antiquarians and artists both in Tuscany and in Rome to integrate the natural landscape with the antiquities in their work; this is seen, for example, from the paintings of antiquarian scenes of Salvator Rosa and the encyclopaedic work of Rome-based Jesuit Athanasius Kircher. This attitude towards linking antiquity to its landscape foreshadows the approach to the archaeological landscape by travelling antiquarians of the eighteenth century and Grand Tourists, namely northern European social elites whose visits to Italy completed their education into Greek and Roman classical culture (Fiore, 2012).

THE LONG EIGHTEENTH CENTURY: FROM *DE ETRURIA REGALI* TO LANZI'S OEUVRE AND THE *MUSEO ETRUSCO* AT THE UFFIZI

Thomas Coke, himself a young Grand Tourist who visited Cosimo III's court, bought *De Hetruria Regali* during his tour in the first half of the eighteenth century (Dezzi Bardeschi, 1976, p. 245). Coke published the manuscript in Florence between 1720 and 1726: Dempster's text was revised and illustrated as *De Etruria Regali* with the help of Florentine Filippo Buonarroti (Cristofani, 1983, pp. 23–8). The illustrations were accompanied by captions, which were arranged in such a way as to provide a synthesis in regard to Etruscan customs and traditions from religion, public and private life to art, coinage and sciences; remarkable, in these captions, is the small number of references to literary sources, and conversely the addition of information from archaeological sites and findspots almost in the guise of an excavation report (Cristofani, 1983, pp. 34–5). Buonarroti was not the only Florentine antiquarian with an interest in sites. His friend Anton Francesco Gori was another. Author of several works on ancient inscriptions and antiquities, Gori also published accounts of antiquarian discoveries outside Tuscany, sometimes accompanied by illustrations, and most notably an account of the discovery of *Herculaneum* in 1749. With indefatigable spirit, he travelled and visited sites throughout Tuscany and further afield, developing an innovative way of exploring antiquities, namely in the field (Dezzi Bardeschi, 1976, pp. 249–51). Gori's publications included the *Museum Florentinum*, one of the earliest illustrated museum catalogues in eight volumes (1731–62). His major work, however, was the *Museum Etruscum*, in which, starting in 1737, Gori assembled and published all the antiquities he saw and sites he visited in his travels across the Grand Duchy and further afield in Perugia (Cruciani Fabrozzi, 1976, pp. 282–6; Cristofani, 1983, pp. 53–9).

The decision to accompany these published texts with appropriate illustrations is part of a broader European 'visual turn' from the seventeenth century, of which the *museo cartaceo* or paper museum represents a forerunner; this was an unpublished, but widely known assembly of over 7,000 watercolours by Roman collector Cassiano del Pozzo (Burke, 2003). Indeed, it has been suggested that Buonarroti's illustrations in *De Etruria Regali* were inspired by the publication of the first volumes of *L'Antiquité expliquée et répresentée en figures*, which French scholar Bernard de Montfaucon published in France between 1719 and 1724 in fifteen volumes containing over 1,000 tables of illustrations (Cristofani, 1983, p. 28; Schnapp, 2009). Both the illustrated *De Etruria Regali* and Montfaucon's publication reflect a critical shift that had occurred, beginning from the latter part of the seventeenth century, both in Italy and across Europe, in regard to the consideration of ancient material remains vis-à-vis ancient literary sources, which now came to be seen as a support to those remains and not vice versa, as had been the case with earlier text-focused antiquarians (Momigliano, 1950). Such a shift corresponded to a key recognition, from the late seventeenth century onwards, of the importance and greater authenticity of original sources, namely the material remains that were illustrated through printed images, vis-à-vis the secondary ones, that is, the literary sources (Momigliano, 1950, pp. 293–4, 301–3). These developments, in fact, represent the beginnings of the modern historical method as we know it, which is grounded on the fundamental difference between evidence and interpretation; it ultimately derived from the experimental method involving observation used in the sciences, from the natural to the medical sciences (Momigliano, 1950, p. 300; Burke, 2003, pp. 275–7, 294–5). Consideration of the authenticity of antiquities bore a further consequence: antiquarians of the classical world and antiquarians of the non-classical world, particularly in northern Europe, began to converge (Momigliano, 1950, p. 293; Schnapp, 2009). For antiquarians interested in Etruria such as Buonarroti and Gori, this convergence meant that the Etruscans could be written about much more extensively than before thanks to the increase of finds and excavations.

The enormous growth of antiquarian collections among the nobility and rich families in Florence, as elsewhere in Italy, especially Rome and beyond, was a result of this intensification of excavations. This also led to the concept of the museum which developed thanks to the activities of learned academies that were devoted to antiquarianism. Prominent among these was the *Accademia Etrusca* at Cortona, born in 1727 under the initiative of a clutch of *cortonesi*, which swiftly became respected beyond Cortona: the president of the *Accademia*, known as *lucumone*, the first of whom was Buonarroti himself, was appointed among influential figures such as foreign affairs ministers at the duchy and cardinals (Cristofani, 1983, pp. 49–51). As the museum at Cortona was established through the *Accademia*, the stimulus to creating museum collections was also growing in other cities such as Siena and Volterra. At Volterra, frenetic excavations in search of Etruscan urns even led to the imposition, by the Ducal Regency, of a local commission that included the local antiquarian Mario Guarnacci to administer excavation permits (Cristofani, 1983, pp. 61–74).

In reality, the concept of museum had already been born in Florence under Francesco Medici with the Uffizi Gallery, although no designated space had ever been given to Tuscan antiquities. The intellectual exchange among erudites and antiquarian activities remained restricted largely to private occasions and learned circles. Some of these learned circles, however, were remarkably cosmopolitan thanks to the travelling of Tuscans abroad, particularly to Rome, the most cosmopolitan city in Italy (Gallo, 1999; Pieraccini, 2009), and of foreign visitors to sites and cities in Italy on their Grand Tour or for other reasons. In the eighteenth century, Rome, in fact, hosted the most cosmopolitan community of antiquarians drawn from all over Italy and beyond, from the Veronese Francesco Bianchini who established an antiquarian academy in Rome, to the Venetian artist–antiquarian Giambattista Piranesi who used to socialize with English Grand Tourists (Cristofani, 1983, pp. 103–ff). To this community and the larger Republic of Letters that characterized the late seventeenth century and the century of the Enlightenment belonged two towering figures for the history of modern Etruscology, namely Joan Joachim Winckelmann and Luigi Lanzi, for whom special treatment must be reserved (Riva, 2018);[2] their work explains why we should consider the eighteenth century the long century for the advancement in ideas about Etruscan civilization.

German-born art historian Winckelmann is the founding figure of modern classical archaeology and art history. His interest in classical antiquities, which had begun in Dresden while in post as a librarian at the castle of the *Reichsgraf* Heinrich von Bünau, developed after his arrival in Rome in 1755. First employed by Cardinal Archinto and papal secretary of state as his librarian, Winckelmann later worked under the patronage of Cardinal Alessandro Albani until he was appointed as papal antiquarian, perhaps the most powerful office for an antiquarian in Rome. Trips to ancient sites and access to the antiquities' collections of Rome's nobility provided him with an unmatched in-depth knowledge of classical antiquities. Among his writings, his *Geschichte der Kunst des Alterthums* (*A History of the Art of Antiquity*), first published in Dresden in 1764, and then republished in a revised version soon after his premature death, remains the backbone of all subsequent studies of classical art. Imbued with ideas from Enlightenment writers, from Montesquieu to Rousseau, Winckelmann's famous thesis was that the excellence of art depended upon the degree of freedom and a benign climate that could foster art and benefit the ancients. He also established an evolutionary framework for the understanding of ancient art in order to identify its development, pinnacle and decline. In this framework, classical Greek art encapsulated that pinnacle. The impact of this framework upon modern classical art and archaeology cannot be overstated (Décultot, 2000; Potts, 2000; Winckelmann and Potts, 2006; Harloe, 2013). Less well known is Winckelmann's treatment of Etruscan art, which he deemed to be particularly ancient and therefore unable to reach the sublime beauty of Greek art. The character of Etruscan art according to Winckelmann, in fact, appeared in an earlier work of his, *Description des pierres gravées du feu baron de Stosch*, published in Florence in 1760: this was a catalogue of the gem collection of Prussian baron Philipp von Stosch, who held one of the most impressive private museums and libraries in Florence at the time. In the catalogue, Winckelmann considered one of these gems, the Stosch gem (or *gemma Ansidei*), as being equivalent to what Homer had achieved among the poets (Cristofani, 1983, p. 147). This gem would go on to illustrate the frontispiece of the first edition of the *Geschichte*. Conversely, the Tydeus gem, also part of the catalogue, was, in his eyes, the pinnacle of the achievements of Etruscan art (Winckelmann, 1760, pp. 347–8). In fact, in this publication, one can already see Winckelmann's thoughts on artistic changing styles, from the rise of an art to its decline, which he systematically applied in his *Geschichte* (Harloe, 2013, pp. 79–86) (Figure 1.5).

The third chapter of the *Geschichte*, devoted to the 'art of the Etruscans and their neighbours', was based upon Winckelmann's analysis of the Etruscan antiquities that he knew first hand and from published illustrations, from Gori's *Museum Etruscum* to Buonarroti's images in

Johann Winckelmanns,
Präſidentens der Alterthümer zu Rom, und Scrittore der Vaticaniſchen Bibliothek,
Mitglieds der Königl. Engliſchen Societät der Alterthümer zu London, der Maleracademie
von St. Luca zu Rom, und der Hetruriſchen zu Cortona,

Geſchichte der Kunſt
des Alterthums.

Erſter Theil.

Mit Königl. Pohlniſch. und Churfürſtl. Sächſ. allergnädigſten Privilegio.

Dreſden, 1764.
In der Waltheriſchen Hof-Buchhandlung.

Figure 1.5 Frontispiece, Johann Joachim Winckelmann 1764 *Geschichte der Kunst des Alterthums*, Dresden.

De Etruria Regali (Cristofani, 1983, pp. 144–7). It represents the earliest systematic attempt at classifying Etruscan antiquities and producing a synthesis of ancient art. Here, Winckelmann's classification followed the evolutionary paradigm and stylistic criteria that closely followed those applied to Greek art (Harloe, 2013, pp. 107–10). Thus, he considered Etruscan art as divided into three styles: an initial first style, a second 'mannered' style, and a third style, in which he saw the decline of Etruscan art together with the process by which Etruscan art imitated Greek art following the establishment of Greek colonies in Italy (Winckelmann and Potts, 2006, pp. 170–4). The most salient aspect of this Etruscan chapter is his juxtaposition between a style and the 'temperament' of the Etruscans, melancholic, violent and full of passion, and his emphasis upon the freedom of the Etruscan republics in determining the style of their art, echoing the link between Greek art and Greek freedom developed in the second part of the *Geschichte* (Winckelmann and Potts, 2006, pp. 159–60). Political freedom, in particular, was key, in his eyes, to the flourishing of Etruscan art as much as it was for Greek art. The revised Etruscan chapter in the posthumous 1776 Viennese edition of the *Geschichte* dealt primarily with the introduction to the chapter (Cristofani, 1993a, pp. 135–6; Winckelmann and Borbein, 2002, pp. 132–7). The themes of free, industrious Etruscans and of freedom stimulating the arts remained, but it is implicit in Winckelmann's revised explanation of the Etruscan democratic elective governments, bearers of peace and tranquillity (Winckelmann and Borbein, 2002, pp. 137–9).

Winckelmann's emphasis on the causes for these styles and the character of Etruscan art is inherent in his conceptualization of a 'system' for explaining artistic development through universal causes (Potts, 2000, pp. 33–46). This concern for universal history derives from Winckelmann's reading and adaptation of the works of philosophic historians of the French and English Enlightenment; however, Winckelmann's eclecticism derived from his ability to draw from a range of sources, including contemporary works on the connoisseurship of antiquities, including Comte Caylus's *Recueil d'antiquités égyptiennes, étrusques, grecques, romaines* (Harloe, 2013, pp. 110–16). For Winckelmann, the political was inextricably linked to art; indeed, art provided the means through which one could throw light upon political forms and conditions (Potts, 2000, pp. 36–7). While the Etruscan chapter remained on the fringes of the core of the *Geschichte*, it nevertheless sought to provide a specific political setting for the evolution of Etruscan art that did not place the latter in an entirely subordinate position vis-à-vis Greek art. On the contrary, the affirmation, in the first edition, that Etruscan desire to emulate derived from Etruscan freedom and, in the second edition, that Etruscan elective democratic governments provided the context for art's beginnings explicitly endorsed Etruscan art's prominence at the beginning of the history of art and the political. Winckelmann, however, was well aware of the scarcity of sources on Etruscan art, which led to much uncertainty. His inference on the Etruscans' temperament for explaining the reasons why the development of their art stalled exemplifies the role of conjectural reasoning that is nevertheless central to the entire *Geschichte*, but was even more necessary in the case of poorly known Etruria (Harloe, 2013, pp. 119–27).

After the second Viennese edition, subsequent translations were made of Winckelmann's *Geschichte* into other languages. Two Italian translations were made by Carlo Amoretti in Milano in 1779, and Carlo Fea in Rome in 1783–4, which provided much criticism to Winckelmann's ideas (Ferrari, 2003, pp. 4–14). Fea's translation, however, failed to convey some key concepts used by Winckelmann, such as the sublime, deriving from a platonic or neoplatonic aesthetic and philosophical approach to art (Potts, 2000, pp. 113–17) because of the well-established roots of the Enlightenment and of empiricism in Italy (Ferrari, 2003; Tortarolo, 2003, pp. 140–7). That both translations included, at the beginning, the panegyric that Göttingen philologist Heyne wrote for Winckelmann is indicative of the negative reception that the *Geschichte* received in Italy (Gauna, 2003, p. 66): Heyne's panegyric was a strong attack on Winckelmann's abstract and systematic method, and on the possibility of explaining artistic development according to external phenomena (Sassi, 1984; Ferrari, 2003, pp. 17–18; Harloe, 2013, pp. 171–88).

Another critic of the *Geschichte* was Winckelmann's contemporary Luigi Lanzi, a Jesuit antiquarian who also lived in Rome in the 1760s and belonged to the cosmopolitan community of antiquarians there. In 1775, he was called upon by the Grand Duke of Tuscany, Peter Leopold, to collaborate with the director of the *Real Galleria* of the Uffizi for the reorganization of the museum. Author of a study of Etruscan and Italic languages and arts, the *Saggio di lingua etrusca e di altre antiche d'Italia: per servire alla storia de' popoli, delle lingue e delle belle arti*, in three volumes (first published in 1789), Lanzi has been rightly acknowledged as the founder of modern Etruscology for introducing an analytical method that successfully built a historical narrative for Etruscan art that diverged from antiquarianism and approached a perspective akin to that developed by Winckelmann. His *Saggio*, furthermore, represents a major watershed for the decipherment of the Etruscan alphabet: rejecting previous comparisons with Oriental languages and Hebrew and the etymological method of earlier antiquarians, Lanzi applied a strictly philological and epigraphic method to Etruscan inscriptions and compared them closely to Greek and Latin inscriptions, noting the similarity between the Greek and Etruscan alphabets. He also considered other Italic pre-Roman languages, and proposed that all these languages, including Etruscan, derived from a common Greek root (Cristofani, 1983, pp. 179–80).

Lanzi's entire oeuvre, however, went much further than this: it included *Storia pittorica della Italia* (1809), a vast history of Italian painting from the Middle Ages up to Lanzi's times. In his work, Lanzi emphasized experiment and comparison as key to his analytical method both for the study of ancient Italic languages, and the study of Etruscan art (Perini, 1982; Rossi, 2006). He furthermore conceived of history as a cyclical process, so that different eras in time and space could be compared (Rossi, 2006, pp. 21–4). In fact, the coexistence of cycle and permanence in Lanzi's view of history, which brought him to consider Etruscan art vis-à-vis the arts of early modern Tuscany, owes much to Winckelmann (Rossi, 2006, pp. 106, 114–16); similarly, Winckelmann's debt is clear in Lanzi's adoption of the tripartite classification of different epochs of artistic development, which, however, led Lanzi to strikingly different conclusions (Cristofani, 1983, p. 170).

Lanzi's interpretive approach to explaining change in Etruscan art was, in fact, highly innovative thanks to three aspects, which I shall now turn to: first, an attention to chronology through the painstaking study of inscriptions; second, the use of the concept of 'school' to explain a style; third, the employment of wide comparisons and parallels for building eventually a universal history. First, Lanzi approached Etruscan art from the point of view of linguistic development through a close study of Etruscan and other Italic inscriptions. In fact, inscriptions were to him the means through which to date the art (Lanzi, 1824–5, p. 14). In this way, and having a much more in-depth knowledge of artefacts than Winckelmann, Lanzi established a much more sound relative chronology of Etruscan art than Winckelmann ever could, and one which stayed valid well into the nineteenth century (Cristofani, 1976b, pp. 19–20). Like Winckelmann, he discerned the impact of Greek art upon the second Etruscan style, but he affirmed convincingly that the Etruscans never imitated the Greeks slavishly (Lanzi, 1824–5, pp. 145–7), and developed their own *scuola* or 'school', the second key aspect of

Lanzi's novel approach to art (Rossi, 2006, pp. 42–3). The comparison with other pieces of evidence and, above all, with similar objects, in the manner of a rudimentary typology, was of utmost importance to Lanzi's understanding of these objects. Hence, according to Lanzi, the object was not simply to be understood in relation to the story of a people and in relation to its style and its time but was also to be placed according to a 'school' identified through such a comparison (Lanzi, 1824–5, pp. iii–xi). The concept of *scuola* allowed for synthesis and for an accurate grasp of temporality, which Lanzi matured thanks to his work at the *Real Galleria* of the Uffizi (Gauna, 2003, pp. 84–6; Rossi, 2006, pp. 223–43; Spalletti, 2010, p. 98).

The reorganization of the museum at the Uffizi was realized in 1782. The objective was to eliminate the encyclopaedic format of the display and create a new display for a wider public that would single out the best art and antiquities. This display would be composed of new objects and paintings acquired for the purpose of filling the gaps of the collection (Gauna, 2003, pp. 70–5; Spalletti, 2010). The Grand Duke's ultimate aim was to provide a didactic experience for the public, and as such, the project was a political–ideological one, much in line with other late eighteenth-century and nineteenth-century museums (Pommier, 2001, pp. 280–1; Rossi, 2006, pp. 243–4; Findlen, 2012, pp. 96–106; 2013). An Etruscan section, the *Museo Etrusco* as Lanzi called it, was created. Other antiquities were arranged throughout the museum: the *Galleria delle Statue* was altered due to the increasing number of Greek and Roman sculptures that came into the collection; other objects and paintings were placed in twenty smaller rooms or *gabinetti* (Barocchi, 1983, pp. 97–115; Gregori, 1983; Spalletti, 2010). Art historians have already underlined the variety of interpretive frameworks underpinning the new displays, illustrated in Lanzi's museum guide published in 1782 (Lanzi, 1982): for example, the busts of the Medici family are introduced in the guide through a distinctly historical interpretation (Spalletti, 2010, p. 98); the *gabinetti*, on the other hand, were organized according to their own genre, and a geographical arrangement was used for the *Museo Etrusco* (Barocchi, 1983, pp. 111–15). What is most remarkable, however, is the unique placement of Etruscan antiquities throughout the *gabinetti* and corridors. The *Museo Etrusco*, located in a small room, contained funerary objects arranged by provenance and accompanied by captions. All the other Etruscan antiquities were arranged in other rooms together with other ancient and modern material that encouraged the visitor to compare it with this other material in order to see the 'schools' and artistic change through time: hence, for example, the Arringatore, Minerva and Chimera, Etruscan pieces held in the Medici collection since the sixteenth century, were placed near one another in the Gallery of the Statues (*corridoio/Galleria delle Statue*) together with other ancient and modern, namely Renaissance, sculpture (Spalletti, 2010, pp. 34–64). In his museum guide, Lanzi invited the visitor, upon entering the museum, to amble through the long corridors displaying busts and paintings, all the way to the *Museo Etrusco* and to begin from there: the very beginnings of art were therefore placed in Etruria, where the geographical differentiation of sepulchral art distinguished the alabaster urns from Volterra from the terracotta ones from Chiusi (Lanzi, 1982, pp. 46–50).

Lanzi's interpretive framework, however, has no resemblance to the eighteenth-century published collections and histories of art and antiquities, which, as shown exemplarily in Caylus's *Recueil d'Antiquité*, functioned as a published gallery or a paper museum corresponding to the development of museum displays (Gauna, 2003, pp. 183–7; Rossi, 2006, pp. 214–15; Décultot, 2010). In contrast to these, Lanzi's publications were not illustrated or they were poorly so. In fact, his museum guide reveals his quite profound distance from the contemporary illustrated collections and histories of antiquities: the image, which, to Caylus, Winckelmann and others, constituted the history of art, was, to Lanzi, auxiliary to the autoptic examination of the objects displayed in the museum, which was the indispensable accompaniment to the text. The third key aspect of Lanzi's intellectual innovation may partly provide an explanation of his idiosyncratic approach to image reproduction. For him, changes in language were analogous to changes in art and, as he showed in the *Storia Pittorica*, in literature, too; his approach allowed him to employ analogy and comparison as structuring principles of analysis to the extent that his entire oeuvre could explain language, art and literature and links between them through a series of parallels, and thus provide the possibility for a universal history (Perini, 1982, p. 240; Rossi, 2006, pp. 7–8, 33–4, 74). While such a potential is fully realized in the *Storia Pittorica*, the *Saggio* is inevitably constrained by the poverty of the sources. Lanzi nevertheless emphasized here the almost 500 inscriptions collected.

Lanzi's approach and aims were of a very different calibre from those of antiquarians in Tuscany whose interests and activities were largely localized and provincial. It is worth reminding the reader, in fact, that antiquarians' provincial and regional interests were characteristic of a politically fragmented Italy (Firpo, 2008). In Tuscany, this is exemplified by the publication of two major works in the latter part of the eighteenth century: the first is Giambattista Passeri's three volumes on vase painting, *Picturae Etruscorum in vasculis*, and the second is the three volumes of *Origini Italiche* (*Italic Origins*) by the Volterran antiquarian Mario Guarnacci, both first published in 1767. Passeri, who had collaborated on Gori's *Museum Etruscum*, maintained the widely held view that painted vases excavated from Tuscany to Campania were Etruscan. Devoted to excavations at Volterra and to his own collection and library, Guarnacci was highly esteemed in Gori's time by those interested in Etruscan antiquities or *etruscherie*, but he remained very traditional, almost *à la* Dempster, in his treatment of these antiquities; the reaction to his *Origini Italiche* was, as a result, rather unenthusiastic (Cristofani, 1983, pp. 96–102).

THE SHORT NINETEENTH CENTURY: EXCAVATIONS, CATALOGUING, ORIGINS AND THE NEW NATION STATE

For the history of ideas and the development of Etruscology, the nineteenth century appears at first sight as momentous: the explosion of excavations throughout Italy and across the Mediterranean, fostered by the myriad colonialist projects and military interventions of emerging European nation states in the east of the basin, provided archaeologists with masses of new finds and tantalizing discoveries; concurrently, ideas about classical antiquity evolved. That evolution also occurred through the intellectual and institutional changes that transformed classical archaeology into a scientific discipline, shedding its antiquarian past. German scholarship was at the forefront of such changes with the institutionalization of the 'sciences of antiquity' or *Altertumswissenschaft*, which was based on the combined study of ancient texts and archaeological evidence that was, in turn, aimed at a complete historical understanding of classical antiquity; textual sources, however, took precedence over the archaeological ones (Marchand, 1996, pp. 41–6; Rebenich, 2011). By classical antiquity the initiators of *Altertumswissenschaft*, such as Friedrich August Wolf, and subsequent German scholars meant ancient Greece, a bias that turned philhellenism into a veritable scholarly science. And yet, the origins of these ideas and therefore the basis of the *Altertumswissenschaft* are already in Winckelmann, whose writings on Greek beauty and artistic genius had a fundamental impact upon German thinkers and intellectuals; in fact, Winckelmann became a legendary founding father of the *Altertumswissenschaft*. His evolutionary framework formed the basis for subsequent chronological sequences of art, for the formulation of 'national' styles as well as for shaping the thoughts of romantic scholars on the Greek spirit embodied in classical Greek sculpture (Marchand, 1996, pp. 7–16; Harloe, 2013, Ch. 1).

This is relevant for the state of Etruscan studies in the nineteenth century because the *Altertumswissenschaft* and the philhellenism underlying it went on to shape classical archaeology in Italy, especially in the aftermath of Italy's unification (Barbanera, 1998, pp. 3–90; 2015). The consequence of this is that no critical intellectual advances as those that Lanzi brought were made. This is not to undermine or diminish the evolution of Etruscology as such, but rather to suggest that the nineteenth century was largely a period of major discoveries and findings, which was followed by the need to catalogue and systematically publish these findings. Ultimately and because of that philhellenism, the scholarly understanding of Etruscan antiquity had to suit a philhellenic straitjacket, from which Etruscology took some time to distance itself and certainly not before the following century. Not by accident the most influential nineteenth-century handbook of Etruscology, *Die Etrusker*, was written by one of the founders of *Altertumswissenschaft*, German archaeologist K. O. Müller.

First published in 1828, *Die Etrusker* was to have wide success in subsequent revised publications, most notably that of 1877 by Wilhelm Deecke. The book was a compendium of the latest knowledge to date, combining all the sources available for the Etruscans. It was a total Etruscan history, but one in which the ancient texts were the primary evidence: in it, Müller sought to establish the relationships between the different components of Etruscan culture, from religion and political systems to art and language, framing them into an organic whole. But his views on art were limited by his philhellenism: in fact, *Die Etrusker*'s chapter on art shows Müller's difficulty in characterizing Etruscan art beyond asserting its emulative stance towards Greek art, which he explained by portraying Etruscan art as an offshoot of Greek artistic roots on foreign soil (Müller and Deecke, 1877, p. 273). In addition, because of the essential role that he attributed to religion and mythology in the study of art, Müller was unable to read the Etruscan character of the art through its mythology (Müller, 1847, p. 383; Blok, 1984, pp. 26–52; Settis, 1984, p. 1089; Isler-Kerényi, 1998, pp. 259–61); in his view, not only did Etruscan art borrow from Greek mythology, but

Etruscan religion was also dominated by superstition, and was therefore ill-suited to figurative representations (Müller, 1847, p. 160; Müller and Deecke, 1877, pp. 1–195).

The development of these ideas was contemporary with the progressive periodization of art and archaeology that was fuelled by the new excavations, not just in Italy, but across the Mediterranean, from Egypt and Anatolia to the Aegean, from the middle to the late nineteenth century. The Etruscan Regolini Galassi Tomb was excavated at Cerveteri, ancient *Caere*, in 1836 by Archbishop Alessandro Regolini and General Vincenzo Galassi. Nine excavation reports were made by Regolini, which were then edited by Giovanni Pinza in 1907, but news of its discovery was already given in 1836 (Pareti, 1947). Ten years later, in 1847, the first Assyrian museum in the world was inaugurated at the Louvre to house newly excavated finds from Khorsabad; in 1853, Henry Layard published the engravings of a selection of bronze bowls he excavated at the North-West Palace at Nimrud. Examination of these finds and their style gave rise to the conceptualization of the ancient Orient in artistic and cultural terms, and the eventual recognition of an Orientalizing period in ancient art. It was Alexander Conze who first applied the term 'Orientalizing' to distinguish the Geometric style of Greek vase painting, and then to Etruscan art in 1870 (Riva and Vella, 2006; Nowlin, 2016, pp. 29–33). These categorizations were inherently shaped by the philhellenic *Altertumswissenschaft*; indeed, the idea of an Orient was part and parcel of philellenism (Marchand, 1996, pp. 188–227), and was to colour scholarly views on antiquity as much as cultural and political constructions of the east Mediterranean, leading to Orientalism (Said, 1995). I will return to this topic in Chapter 3.

Closer to home, in Italy, the rhythm of excavations at sites known from the ancient sources, from *Caere* and Tarquinia to Chiusi and Perugia, was frenetic. Among them were those of newly discovered sites in the Po Valley, notably Marzabotto and Villanova (see Chapter 2), which prompted questions in the latter part of the nineteenth century on the Etruscanness of these sites and the relationships of these new findings with other prehistoric ones, and hence of the origins of prehistoric people (Pearce and Gabba, 1995). The new finds filled private and public museum collections. In fact, most Etruscan collections in the major national and international museums nowadays from London to Paris and Berlin largely derive from this golden age of excavations in Italy, which fuelled the antiquities market both at home and abroad. Preference was given to cemeteries and tombs that could provide riches of precious objects and Greek painted vases, which up until then were thought to be Etruscan. Renowned are the excavations of banker and antiquity collector Giovanni Pietro Campana at *Caere* and the sale of much of his collection to Napoleon III, which went on display at the Louvre in 1863 (Gaultier, Haumesser, and Santoro, 2013, pp. 45–7). More often than not the potential for gains from the selling of antiquities led to the plundering of tombs, but in other cases, especially towards the end of the century, the excavations led to important documentation of sites such as the fundamental publication of *Fouilles dans la Nécropole de Vulci* by Stéphane Gsell in 1891 following his work at Vulci upon the invitation of local landowner Prince Giulio Torlonia. Before Gsell, Vulci came to represent the most extraordinary case of extensive excavations of Etruscan cemeteries, which led to a disconcerting dispersion of finds all over Europe. There were several owners of the lands (known as *tenute*) where the cemeteries were located. Among them was Lucien Bonaparte, brother of Napoleon, who came to own some of these lands upon becoming Prince of Canino in 1824; soon after this his excavations began, leading to the flooding of the art market with thousands of painted vases. Prominent in this market were Vincenzo Campanari and his sons, based at Tuscania, who also and concurrently excavated at Vulci in the 1830s in collaboration with the Vatican (Buranelli, 1991; Della Fina, 2004). The *Museo Gregoriano Etrusco* at the Vatican Museum was founded after these activities and the discovery of the Regolini Galassi Tomb, which was put on display in 1838.

The pillaging of Vulci was noted (Dennis, 1907, pp. 430–3) by a preoccupied English diplomat George Dennis in his *The Cities and Cemeteris of Etruria* (1848), an account of trips he took to Etruria with his artist friend Samuel James Ainsley, which was to have a lasting fortune in its later reprints and brought Etruria to the attention of the larger Anglophone public (Potter, 1998). What also particularly intrigued the public was the first ever exhibition of Etruscan material, which the Campanari organized in 1837 in London, one of the major hubs of the international art market, thirty or so years after the Elgin marbles had been put on display. The exhibition at Pall Mall recreated to scale eleven Etruscan tombs decorated with copies of tomb paintings, with *sarcophagi* and grave goods placed within them (Barbanera, 2008). The exhibition was extremely successful: much of this material was, in fact, bought by the British Museum. Among the visitors was Lady Hamilton Gray who subsequently visited Etruria, published her travel diary as *Tour to the Sepulchres of Etruria in 1839* in 1840, which further promoted interest in the Etruscans to the English public (Orestano, 2016) (Figure 1.6).

Figure 1.6 Orvieto, George Dennis 1878 *The cities and cemeteries of Etruria*, London from Wikimedia Common.

For scholars, on the other hand, the main channel of communication for reporting new finds and excavations was ensured by the founding of a research institute in Rome, the *Instituto di Corrispondenza Archeologica* (the future German Archaeological Institute), which was not simply at the centre of classical archaeology in Italy but also the centre of international scholarship of the classical world: with the publication of its bulletin (*Bullettino dell'Instituto*), it was conceived as a point of exchange for archaeologists and for gathering news from across the Mediterranean (Blanck, 2008). The *Instituto* grew thanks to the Prussian government's financial support that included post-doctoral scholarships allowing young scholars to travel and learn about classical monuments; one of the first of such scholars was Conze himself. In fact, Conze was a pupil of Edward Gerhard who was the first director of the *Instituto* and a friend of Müller (Marchand, 1996, pp. 96–101). This may partly explain Conze's proximity to and impact upon new perspectives on Etruscan art and its Orientalizing period. Gerhard furthermore was responsible for the systematic publication of finds catalogues: his initiatives included the corpus of Etruscan mirrors (*Etruskische Spiegel*) completed at the end of the nineteenth century in several volumes, and the *Rapporto intorno i vasi volcenti* (1831) in which he settled once and for all the debate about the Greek identity of the painted vessels dug at Vulci, already identified as Greek by Lanzi.

Beside the questions on Greek painted vessels, a significant advance was made in the field of epigraphy and Etruscan language as more and more inscriptions were discovered, among which were the now renowned so-called Zagreb mummy, a fragmented text painted on linen (1862), and the bronze liver of Piacenza (1877): Wilhelm Deecke introduced a new method for studying the linguistic evidence that became standard, and large epigraphic corpora were assembled. The first publication of *CIE* (*Corpus Inscriptionum Etruscarum*), nowadays still in publication and a standard reference point for any epigraphist or linguist of Etruscan, appeared under the vision of German linguist Carl Pauli (Benelli, 2017) (Figure 1.7).

Beside these scholarly developments, Italian studies on antiquity more generally, from Etruria to the Roman empire, were enmeshed with the political ideas and debates underpinning the turmoil of the *Risorgimento*, which led to revolutionary uprisings, the wars of independence and eventually the unification of Italy as a nation state. Some of these debates had to do with the future of Italy and the different visions for a united country on the eve of the 1848 uprisings, which included anti-Rome positions and visions of a federal state (De Francesco,

Figure 1.7 The Piacenza Liver, © This image is from Getty.

2013, pp. 30–132). As happened in all other European nation states, antiquity played a key role in defining the new nation and its identity: national ancestral origins were a particular European-wide concern. In fact, debates on origins in German scholarship also touched on the Etruscans, whose northern origins were upheld by some primarily by a linguistic argument based on epigraphic evidence. In Italy, on the other hand, the autochthony of ancient Italic people became crucial. In these debates, Giuseppe Micali's monumental *L'Italia Avanti il Dominio de' Romani* (*Italy before the dominion of Rome*), first published in 1810 in four volumes and republished, was highly influential: in asserting the autochthony of different Italic peoples in the pre-Roman era as a common trait among them, with pre-eminence given to the Etruscans, *L'Italia* served all sorts of political visions for a united Italy. Furthermore, the variety that characterized pre-Roman antiquity and the possibility this gave for exalting an era of Italic people, united under autochthony, without the need to deal with Rome's role in the assimilation of Italy, gave Micali's work much ideological flexibility and therefore made it attractive to the politically radical and moderate alike, according to modern historian De Francesco (De Francesco, 2013, pp. 70–1).[3] Micali, however, was a traditional scholar writing in the eighteenth-century tradition of local Etruscan studies (Momigliano, 1966, p. 804). His ideas about autochthony, furthermore, were categorically scorned by Italian and German scholars. Combined with this was the Germanism that came to dominate scholarship in antiquity in Italy and that brought Rome into the centre, shifting focus from the study of classicism to a distinctly historical analysis of the Greek and Roman world (De Francesco, 2013, pp. 121–3).

THE TWENTIETH CENTURY: ETRUSCOLOGY, AN INDEPENDENT FIELD

Among the main priorities after Italy's unification was the creation of institutions needed for the new nation state in all spheres of life; in the case of archaeology, the administrative bodies for the protection of the country's artistic and archaeological heritage included the *Deputazione per la conservazione e l'ordinamento dei musei e delle antichità etrusche* established in 1871 for the specific protection of the Etruscan heritage. Important changes, too, were brought to the teaching of archaeology at university and in the field, all of which ultimately led to the professionalization of the discipline. State museums were established: the

Etruscan Museum in Florence was opened in 1870, the *Museo Civico* in Bologna in 1881, and the National Museum at the Villa Giulia in Rome in 1889, conceived as a museum of pre-Roman Italic civilizations (Barbanera, 1998, pp. 3–90; Moretti Sgubini, 2000).

In this context, the years from 1919 to the early 1940s were momentous in the history of studies of Etruscan art; 1919 is the year of publication of the sixth-century BCE terracotta sculpture excavated by Giulio Quirino Giglioli in 1916 at the Portonaccio temple at the Etruscan city of *Veii* (Figure 1.8): among it was the 'walking Apollo' (*l'Apollo che cammina*), so named by Carlo Anti in 1920 in the scientific journal *Bollettino d'Arte* (Anti, 1920). The discovery of this archaic sculpture led to the recognition of the originality of Etruscan art, up until then considered to be less accomplished than Greek art, a bias still present in *L'art Etrusque* by Jules Martha published in 1889 as the earliest handbook on Etruscan art, still very much antiquarian in spirit and content. That recognition was boosted by the crisis affecting classicism, not only in scholarly debates on ancient figurative art, but more generally in contemporary European culture where a taste for non-classical art was fostered by the artistic experiences turned towards cubism and expressionism and a widely spread interest in 'primitive' and African art (Harari, 1993; Barbanera, 2009; Bagnasco Gianni, 2016). The protagonists in those debates were art historians Aloïs Riegl and Franz Wickhoff at the University of Vienna, whose studies on medieval art led them to re-evaluate Roman imperial art, which, in the world view of philhellenism, belonged to a phase of artistic decline. Riegl's concept of *kunstwollen*, according to which artistic expression was the result of the taste and cultural inclinations of a specific historical era and thus impossible to judge *a priori*, debunked Winckelmann's evolutionistic view of classical art as the pinnacle of artistic accomplishment in antiquity. The art historian most influenced by these ideas was Ranuccio Bianchi Bandinelli, a young Etruscologist at the time, whose first thinking on Etruscan art along these lines was formulated in his contribution at the First National Congress of Etruscology held in Florence in 1926 (Barbanera, 1998, pp. 119–26; 2009, pp. 22–3). The ideas and debates about the Etruscan character of art were furthermore entangled in, and influenced by, the needs to articulate a national identity based on the conception that art and material culture were the expression of a people's ethnicity. Bianchi Bandinelli problematized this ethnic view, using a linguistic metaphor to explain the originality of Etruscan art, comparing this art to a dialect of Greek art. These discussions, however, did not go any further partly because of the still unresolved question of

Figure 1.8 The Walking Apollo, Portonaccio sanctuary, *Veii* (Villa Giulia Museum), photograph by Sailko (CC BY-SA 4.0), from Wikimedia Commons.

origins, and partly as the fascist regime turned towards imperial Rome as a key feature of its propaganda (Harari, 2012). Research in the post-war years, in fact, would turn towards art production and craftsmanship, iconography and iconology.[4]

Etruscan origins had been perhaps the object of greatest contention among scholars in the nineteenth century, partly as a result of differing ideological positions on nation-building as we saw earlier, partly as a result of a general interest in migration and attempts at explaining ancient people's movement through the archaeology. This question, however, was to take a decisive turn towards a solution. That the question was still a matter of hot debate can be gauged by the discussions at the First International Congress of Etruscology held in 1928 in Bologna: while Italian Etruscologists maintained Etruscan autochthony, German scholars sustained Oriental origins, a view that accompanied debates on the Etruscan language and the Orientalizing phase of Etruscan art among others (Miller, 2015). These discussions extended to prehistorians who, following the discovery of a 'Villanovan civilization' after the site of Villanova and excavations at several other Iron Age cemeteries from Bologna to Tarquinia, debated the origins of such a civilization (Dore and Morigi Govi, 2014). I will return to all these issues in the following chapter; here it is sufficient to say that the matter was once and for all settled in the post-war period with the refinement of chronological sequences and the concurrent research of Renato Peroni, professor of European proto-history in Rome since 1974, and Massimo Pallottino, the most prominent figure in Etruscology of the second half of the twentieth century. To Pallottino, in fact, we owe the key shift of focus from one of origins to one of formation and transformation: the Villanovan civilization was none other than the Etruscan civilization of the Iron Age, and its development could be traced all the way back to the Bronze Age (Pallottino, 1942, 1947; Bagnasco Gianni, 2012).

There is little doubt that, while the flourishing of Etruscology in the post-war period came following one of the many devastating consequences of the war, namely the ideological abuse of Roman imperial antiquity by the fascist regime that left an intellectual vacuum, equally decisive were Pallottino's efforts, and that of his colleagues and students, to turn Etruscology into an independent scientific field within classical archaeology, in which all types of documentary sources had to be examined and given equal weight in advancing our knowledge. The post-war era was also a period of discoveries of sites that were not cemeteries, facilitated by the introduction of the Agrarian Reform in 1948 and national development policies that saw a boom in the construction industry. Sanctuary sites took centre stage: the coastal harbours and sanctuaries of *Pyrgi* and Gravisca were among these momentous discoveries leading to a series of excavation campaigns between the early 1960s and 1970s that are continuing today, still enriching our archaeological record and providing a training ground of several generations of Etruscologists. At *Pyrgi*, the recovery, in 1963, of a set of golden plaques engraved with an almost bilingual Phoenician and Etruscan inscription recording a religious dedication by a ruler of *Caere* is particularly notable: its contribution to our knowledge of this Etruscan city and of archaic religion more generally cannot be overstated, as we shall see in Chapter 4.

These and other sites ushered in new possibilities for constructing a social, economic and political history of the Etruscans, which were accomplished by the generation of scholars after Pallottino, some of whom were influenced in their interpretations by currents of thought from the social and historical sciences, from structuralism and semiotics to Marxism.[5] The concurrent excavations of sites in *Latium* such as *Lavinium*, where fieldwork of another noteworthy sanctuary site, the Sanctuary of the Thirteen Altars, began in the middle of the 1950s, Castel Di Decima and Osteria dell'Osa augmented the evidence from that region and fed into these new possibilities, fuelling exciting debates around key themes concerning the early phases, not just of Etruria but also of *Latium* and Rome, such as urbanization. Indeed, in those years we can trace the beginning of the convergence in archaeological research on early Rome and *Latium* on the one hand, and Etruria on the other: the exhibition *Civiltà del Lazio Primitivo* on the archaeology of *Latium* from the Late Bronze Age to the seventh century BCE was organized in Rome in 1976 by Pallottino himself as president of the *Istituto di Studi Etruschi e Italici*, and marks that beginning (Acanfora, 1976). The culmination of that convergence is marked by another major exhibition, *La Grande Roma dei Tarquini*, held in Rome in 1990; its organization was conceived as part of a series of initiatives and other exhibitions devoted to the Etruscans held in 1985, a year which was proclaimed as 'the Year of the Etruscans' (Pallottino, 1990). All of the above ultimately led to the prospect of historical syntheses that were realized from the 1980s onwards with the growth of field research, conferences, publications and other exhibitions. The 1990s was a particularly lively decade for grand exhibitions, from the travelling European exhibition *Gli Etruschi e l'Europa* (1992), again under the direction of Pallottino, to *The Etruscans* (2000) at Palazzo Grassi in Venice under the direction of Mario Torelli.

Further promotion of new debates and questions, and adding to our evidence, was also new attention focused on the Etruscan landscape, the topography of urban centres, and smaller sites. Much of this attention came from foreign teams of archaeologists based at the foreign academies in Rome who benefitted from the rich legacy of topographical and field research, which, in the aftermath of Italy's unification, led to the planning and implementation of a national archaeological map, still in progress today under the name of *Forma Italiae*. British archaeologists, who introduced landscape archaeology and its best-tested field method, the field-walking survey (or field survey), to Italy, particularly benefitted from this legacy: the earliest systematic survey, the South Etruria Survey, could not have been done without it. Begun in the mid-1950s by John Ward-Perkins, the then director of the British School at Rome, it produced masses of data, only recently re-studied and published (Potter, 1979; Smith, 2018). In 1966, a North American team from Bryn Mawr College (United States) began excavations, continuing till today, of a site near Murlo (Poggio Civitate), not far from Siena, uncovering an archaic residential complex that has helped shape our views on Etruscan architecture and building technology. In the same year, excavations began at another residential complex at the settlement of Acquarossa near Viterbo by the Swedish Institute of Classical Studies in Rome, which, a few years earlier, had become involved in the investigation of a prehistoric site at Luni sul Mignone (Pallottino and Wikander, 1986). This is where I shall begin.

2

BEGINNINGS

MOVING SETTLEMENTS AND EMERGING HIERARCHIES

A BRONZE AGE SETTLEMENT: LUNI SUL MIGNONE

Luni sul Mignone is a large (5 hectares) plateau of *tufa*, the local name for volcanic rock, not far from the Mignone river and lying north-west of Bracciano Lake in today's province of Viterbo, north of Rome, in what is one of the largest ancient volcanic areas of southern Europe: here, high, steep-sided volcanic rock formations like Luni dot the landscape cut by river courses, offering the determined visitor with good orientation skills and a willingness to scale the challenging terrain breathtaking views. The area was known to the local archaeological association and to archaeologists from the Swedish Institute who had begun excavating a nearby site, San Giovenale, in 1956; in 1960, they proceeded to investigate the plateau, then known locally as Pian di Luni and called 'acropolis' by the Swedes, after realizing its archaeology potential. Historical sources reported by Östenberg, who published the excavation, confirm that *Lunum* was the name given to the place in the Middle Ages: it was cited as *civitas* in the ninth century and *castrum* or *castellum* in the thirteenth century; by the seventeenth century it was abandoned (Östenberg, 1961, pp. 128–70) (Figure 2.1).

Between 1961 and 1963, the Swedish team, comprising king of Sweden Gustav VI Adolph, who had a keen interest in archaeology, and Princess Margrethe, heiress to the Danish crown and archaeology student, began work. They discovered, among other finds that included Etruscan-period fortifications and prehistoric tombs, a Bronze Age settlement on the

Figure 2.1 Luni sul Mignone, photograph by Alessandro Mandolesi.

plateau. This settlement was composed of a village of huts, in which five fragments of Mycenaean pottery imported from Greece were found, and a monumental Iron Age house; the village, Östenberg concluded, was established in the fourteenth century BCE and existed for 300 to 350 years before its abandonment. A small plain below and to the east of the plateau known as Tre Erici was also excavated: the remains there of five huts dated from the Neolithic and into the Iron Age attested to a long-term habitation of the site. Osteological and palaeobotanical analyses were carried out as was radiocarbon dating on selected samples of material. The innovative approach to fieldwork comprising such ground-breaking investigative techniques and the momentous discoveries cannot be overstated enough at a time when hardly anything was known of prehistoric settlements in Etruria and these techniques were hardly ever applied. Indeed, the swift publication of the excavation in Italian, focused on the prehistoric phases of the site, from the Neolithic, through to the 'Chalcolitic' or Copper Age and Bronze Age, was motivated by the need to disseminate the finds which were to radically alter our view of the Bronze Age in Etruria, the period that, it will become clear later, is key to understanding what this part of Italy became in Etruscan times (Östenberg, 1967).

Up until then, Bronze Age sites across Italy were studied and dated largely on the basis of tomb finds and metal hoards, as we shall see further on Iron Age tombs, and the decorated pottery that was ordered according to stylistic and typological criteria, an approach that was to become particularly strong under the influence of Peroni's school of proto-history (Peroni, 1971, 2004; Cocchi Genick, 2014). Interpreting these sites, given the lack of detailed knowledge on settlements, cannot have been easy. What archaeologists could see was that these sites, especially at high altitude, increased in number in the Bronze Age; hence, the phrase 'Appennine culture' used to characterize this period (Peroni, 1959; Puglisi, 1959). In 1959, on the basis of this knowledge and of other materials such as a specific type of pottery vessel with holes for straining liquids known as milk-boilers, prehistorian Salvatore Puglisi put forward the so-called pastoralist hypothesis which characterized Copper and Bronze Age society as one of nomadic transhumant pastoralists before the re-establishment of settled agricultural communities in the Recent Bronze Age (known as 'Sub-Appennine' phase). This hypothesis put seasonal transhumance – the movement of shepherds between the Appenninic highlands and the coastal lowlands – on the map of our interpretations of these prehistoric periods (Puglisi, 1959; Barker, 1981, pp. 90–5). Puglisi's hypothesis derived from late nineteenth- and early twentieth-century diffusionist ideas, based on the presence of copper and stone weapons in Copper Age burials, of invading warlike populations of so-called warrior–shepherds (*pastori–guerrieri*) who defeated local farmers at the end of the Neolithic and occupied upland sites like Luni (Cella, Gori, and Pintucci, 2016, p. 76). His suggestions, however, inspired by ethnographic parallels drawn from traditional lifestyles of Italian nomadic shepherds, were far more sophisticated than that. They provided an explanation of the economies of these proto-Etruscan societies and also of their symbolic and ideological world (Lugli, 2014).

Following the publication of the excavation of Luni, along with Palidoro in modern northern Lazio, Luni was one of only two settlements known with a stratified sequence dating from Neolithic, Copper Age to Bronze Age. It therefore not only provided a sound basis for investigating the development of the Bronze Age in Etruria but also crucially demonstrated a continuity in pottery types at a single site, and furthermore that communities from the Copper Age were settled and had a fairly sophisticated economy in contrast with Puglisi's hypothesis. This could not have been possible without scientific analyses of palaeobotanical and faunal remains which provided information on what was cultivated, gathered and consumed at Luni, from wheat and barley to pulses and acorns. The faunal sample, aside from recording wild animal species, also comprised pig, cattle and sheep bones, all together comprising 94 per cent of the entire sample and with a ratio of 1:2:1

between these three different species: this ratio, which indicates the use of cattle as workforce for agriculture, lasted from the Copper Age down to the Iron Age, Östenberg contended, showing the continuity of a mixed subsistence economy (hunting, animal rearing and agriculture) over the long term. The great quantity of millstones inside the 'Appennine houses' and terracotta storage containers added to the view of well-organized agricultural production by prehistoric communities living in stable settlements.

Luni was one of only two sites at the time that delivered a reliable faunal sample; the other was Narce, a settlement in the Treia valley, north-east of Bracciano Lake, that also had a long stratified sequence from prehistory to Roman times (Potter, 1979, pp. 37–46). Unlike Narce, however, Luni was a sizeable settlement comprising several huts located at the centre of the plateau. The excavated huts themselves were considered to be of a very strange type: their perimeter was cut into the volcanic rocks at a depth of over 2 metres at most, and their size varied from 7 metres to 42 metres in length; beaten floors, refuse material and hearths were found inside the perimeters, as were the remains of collapsed stones which would have formed low drystone walls for the huts. They were interpreted as long houses and dwellings for family groups, at the head of which a leader with supreme authority, it was thought, ruled the community. This interpretation proved problematic as we shall see, but this was the first time archaeologists could begin to see details of the internal social organization of a proto-Etruscan community. Invasion or migration theories were thus dismissed and Anglophone prehistorians who were closest to Puglisi's anthropological perspective provided further stimulus to the debate on the nature of Bronze Age society and economy, which, by the late 1970s and early 1980s, were seen as developing locally along with cultural contacts with the outside eastern Mediterranean world (Barker, 1972, 1981; Potter, 1979, pp. 36–51). Such contacts were no doubt stimulated by the richness of metal ore deposits of the Tyrrhenian Etruscan region (see From the Bronze to the Iron Age: Continuity and change).

Beside the continuity of occupation, another notable finding at Luni was evidence of those very contacts, namely fragments of Mycenaean imported pottery which put Luni on the map of Mediterranean prehistory for two main reasons: first, the fragments provided a firm basis for dating the site's pottery sequence and, hence, a framework for dating the material from other contemporary sites; second, important questions were raised on the nature of those contacts that brought this pottery to an inland location and to what was, and currently still is, considered to be the most ancient northernmost reach of this material. Östenberg saw these contacts as sporadic and Luni as a 'conservative world of the Apennine farmers and stockbreeders' (Östenberg, 1967, p. 260). Sixty or so years later, our knowledge and the presence of these imports at many more sites throughout the Italian peninsula have completely altered this interpretation: scientific analysis, in particular, has shown that several examples of this pottery are, in fact, imitations of Mycenaean pottery – hence, the adjective Italo-Mycenaean – and were probably made at southern Italian workshops located in coastal areas near the Adriatic and Ionian Sea. At Luni itself the earliest fragment was, we now know, imported from the Aegean, while the later ones come from such Italo-Mycenaean vessels (Jones, Levi, Bettelli, and Vagnetti, 2014). The scenario that this evidence offers today therefore is one of a dynamic Bronze Age society involved in regional and long-distance contacts across the Italic peninsula and beyond (Vagnetti, 1999; Vianello, 2005).

Other earlier interpretations of Luni have since been discounted: we now know that Luni was inhabited from the second millennium to the tenth century BCE, that the settlement grew largest in the Final Bronze Age, the so-called proto-Villanovan phase (between the twelfth and tenth centuries), and that no more trace is known of habitation until the Etruscan period proper. The so-called Iron Age monumental building is now known to be coeval with the Final Bronze Age growth of the settlement; alternative interpretations have been offered for it – a cult place or storage area for meat given the faunal remains – that differ from Östenberg's original one. Despite all this, the momentous discoveries and excavation at Luni uncovered prehistoric developments that fundamentally affected our perspectives on prehistoric Etruria (Barbaro, 2010, pp. 169–72).

FROM THE BRONZE TO THE IRON AGE: CONTINUITY AND CHANGE

The plateau of Luni and its neighbouring areas, the terraces of Tre Erici and a ridge above these, known as Fornicchio, are an 8-hectare settlement unit that exemplifies the high altitude, naturally defended settlements that, we now know, characterize the Final Bronze Age landscape of southern Etruria. There are currently over 200 Final Bronze Age settlement and cemetery sites known in the region today; of these, over a 100 are settlements only, fewer than ten are only cemeteries and several more are cemeteries associated with a settlement (Barbaro, 2010, p. 350); some are high-altitude sites like Luni, others are not as naturally defended or are open-space sites. A few of them, including Luni, acted as central places, that is to say, larger settlements commanding a territory from which natural resources could be drawn, and where smaller settlements were conceivably dependent on the larger ones: in other words, we see a well-organized territorial system of human occupation across the landscape. Towards the last phases of the Final Bronze Age open-space locations were abandoned and naturally defended sites increased in number and grew in size as is the case at Luni; at this same time, the future Etruscan cities also show evidence of occupation (Pacciarelli, 2000, 2010; Peroni, 2004, pp. 302–407). Much of this evidence consists of archaeological material collected from the plough soil during field-walking surveys and spread across the enormous *tufa* tablelands of southern Etruria that would host some of the largest cities in the first millennium BCE such as *Caere* (Cerveteri), Tarquinia, Vulci and *Veii* (Figure 2.2).

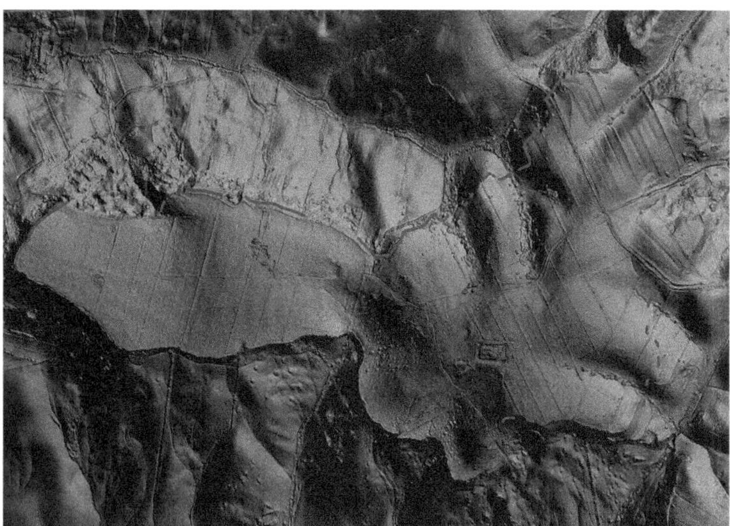

Figure 2.2 The plateau of Tarquinia, Digital Terrain Model without vegetation, from Garzulino, A. 2019 LiDAR, territory and archaeological areas: new results and perspectives for the knowledge, analysis and preservation of complex context, in ISPRS International Archives of Photogrammetry, Remote Sensing and Spatial Information Sciences, Vol. XLII-2/W11, 549–555, ISSN: 2194-9034, https://doi.org/10.5194/isprs-archives-XLII-2-W11-549-2019.

In some cases, as at Vulci and Tarquinia, other evidence includes burials (Barbaro, 2010, p. 351), but it is Tarquinia that shows some remarkable evidence for long-term habitation: here, Final Bronze burials coexisted with a settlement located at La Castellina, a rocky spur jutting out just north of the large plateau, which would become the future city; on this large plateau at Pian della Regina, the site of a much later monumental temple, have been found traces of a settlement, also dated to the Final Bronze Age (Mandolesi, 1999). Adjacent to Pian della Regina, at so-called Pian di Civita, traces of religious activities dated to the second half of the tenth century BCE have also been found: they include offerings placed into a natural rock cavity, and ritual terracotta vessels found in a small hut near the cavity; both the cavity and the hut lie under a monumental sacred complex that grew in the course of the eighth century BCE, as we shall see (Bonghi Jovino, 1997, pp. 146–9; Bonghi Jovino, 2001). What precise form this early settlement took is difficult to assess given that those traces mostly consist of pottery fragments collected from the ground surface or plough soil: in all likelihood, it comprised several households spread out over open spaces on this vast *tufa* plateau (Pacciarelli, 2000, pp. 128–69). This is what is also hypothesized for other future southern Etruscan cities, albeit with some differences between them: in the case of *Caere*, for example, the occupation of the final phases of the Bronze Age is not as widespread, and only at the beginning of the Iron Age do we see traces of an expanding settlement, coeval with a fairly sizeable high-altitude settlement at Monte Santo, north of the future city, that began in the final phases of the Bronze Age (Barbaro, 2010, p. 352). At *Veii*, the closest Etruscan city to Rome, traces of Final Bronze Age human occupation are known from Isola Farnese only, another high-altitude site south-east of the plateau of the future city, but no other significant traces are known so far except for a single pottery fragment found on the plateau (Barbaro, 2010, pp. 138–9). Other sites that would become cities beyond southern coastal Etruria were also inhabited at this early stage: they include Bisenzio, overlooking Lake Bolsena, inland sites such as Chiusi in the Valdichiana, Vetulonia and a little later Populonia, both of which are located in northern Etruria, Tuscany today.

It should be clear by now why the final phases of the Bronze Age, which we know much better in southern Etruria than anywhere else, is where a history of the Etruscans must begin (Carancini, 2018): as Luni's excavation first showed, the transition between the Final Bronze Age and Early Iron Age is a key period of continuity as well as change. Continuity is seen in the earliest occupation of those sites that would become cities to the extent that some archaeologists now agree that this moment of transition can be considered as a proto-urban phase, that is to say, a phase when communities began living in settlements that were to become urban and, in some cases, would stay urban to the present day (Vanzetti, 2002; Riva, 2010b, pp. 13–22); Rome is also part of this picture (Fulminante, 2014, pp. 66–104). It is also, however, a phase of profound change: when these future cities came to be inhabited, several other settlements were abandoned soon after. Some of them were later reoccupied in the eighth and seventh centuries BCE as Luni itself or later as Sovana near Lake Bolsena; others were never settled again until several centuries later. Sorgenti della Nova, a Final Bronze Age high-altitude and naturally defended settlement discovered in the early 1970s and located on a *tufa* plateau inside the nature reserve of Selva del Lamone on the border between modern Tuscany and Lazio, was established in the eleventh century BCE; it was abandoned a century later in the early Iron Age, only to be inhabited again in the Middle Ages. Just like Luni, Sorgenti consisted of a series of oval huts, 10 to 20 metres long, which were first built on the hilltop; further dwellings were subsequently built on the terraced slopes and these included rooms cut into the rock face of the slope, some of which were used for storage and/or food processing. Through this terracing system, the settlement, in fact, grew to become a 15-hectare village that, according to its excavators, may have reached a population of 1,500 (Negroni Catacchio, 1995; Dolfini, 2013). The presence of other structures such as drainage channels and basins for water storage provides further evidence of a sophisticated spatial organization for the community here and its social activities, whether food processing, storage of animals and other resources, household tasks such as spinning and weaving and sacrificial activities. Its excavators have suggested that such an organization is appropriate for a proto-urban settlement, and yet, unlike other such settlements that grew into cities, Sorgenti was abandoned; it is thus highly likely that its inhabitants moved and re-settled at the much larger plateau of Vulci, just south of Sorgenti in the Fiora river valley (Dolfini, 2013, pp. 35–6) (Figure 2.3).

Much like the other large south Etruscan proto-urban and future urban settlements that occupied vast tablelands extending over 100 hectares, Vulci is not comparable in size to Final Bronze Age sites like Sorgenti, and herein lies the key to understanding the early Iron Age as a radically new phase for the history of the Etruscans: in Tyrrhenian southern Etruria, these vast plateaux where the cities grew were, like their earlier and much smaller counterparts, naturally defended but, unlike

Figure 2.3 Sorgenti della Nova, elevation and plan of Sector III by E. Negroni (Negroni Catacchio, N. 1995 *Sorgenti della Nova: L'Abitato del Bronzo Finale*. Florence: Istituto Italiano di Preistoria e Protostoria); artist's impression of the houses and other buildings (below) (Negroni Catacchio, N. and Domanico L. 2001 L'abitato protourbano di Sorgenti della Nova: dagli spazi dell'abitare all'organizzazione sociale. In J.R. Brandt and L. Karlsson (eds.), *From Huts to Houses: Transformations of Ancient Societies*, 337–359. Stockholm: Paul Åström's Förlag.).

them, they were nearer the coast, accessible from the sea and placed within a vast agriculturally fertile plain. In other words, their position for urban growth was optimal. That access to the coast was an important resource for early Iron Age communities is also seen in the continuous habitation of some coastal Final Bronze Age sites into the Iron Age, such as Castellina del Marangone, a high-ground site overlooking the coast between Tarquinia and *Caere* (Prayon, 2016). Accessibility to natural resources, whether agricultural, mineral or other, was also critical to the early urban growth of other settlements, both inland and further north where the landscape and geomorphology are notably different from those of southern Etruria: Bisenzio located on a hill overlooking Lake Bolsena; Orvieto (ancient *Volsinii*) perched on an imposing *tufa* outcrop, best seen as one approaches the city from Bolsena; Chiusi developing on adjacent hills along the Valdichiana in central Tuscany; Vetulonia overlooking the plain of Grosseto; Volterra also on high ground between Florence and Siena; Populonia, the only coastal site facing the island of Elba, one of the richest areas for mineral sources in the Mediterranean. All of these settlements were ideally placed to access enough resources to sustain a large urban population in the first millennium BCE (Riva, 2010b, pp. 23–9). Some of these sites such as Volterra or *Volsinii* are less well known than others because the Etruscan-period town was obliterated by the later city, but, as we shall see, much knowledge can be gained from other areas of these towns such as their cemeteries and sanctuaries.

The urbanization of all these settlements went hand in hand with the establishment of the earliest Greek and Phoenician settlements in the central Mediterranean, a phenomenon not limited to this region. In fact, the contemporary settling of new permanent non-indigenous communities across the Mediterranean engendered new forms of cross-cultural interaction and social relations, and represents one of the earliest instances of ancient colonialism (van Dommelen, 2012); the consequences of this phenomenon cannot be overstated not only for the broader region in which Etruscan cities grew, but also for the entire Mediterranean basin. Indeed, Greek, Phoenician and indigenous settlements such as Etruscan and Latin ones including Rome were part of the same phenomenon in the central Mediterranean, namely the urbanization of this broader region, which was accelerated by embryonic trading networks that were to expand in later centuries (Cunliffe and Osborne, 2005). Interestingly, Populonia's earliest occupation of Poggio del Telegrafo, the main hilltop of the future city opposite Elba, detected by pottery fragments and the presence of four chamber tombs on the slopes of Poggio al Castello nearby, dates to the ninth–eighth centuries BCE (Cambi and Acconcia, 2011). This is a century or so earlier than the date of the establishment of Pithekoussai, the earliest Greek settlement west of the Aegean, located on the island of Ischia in the Bay of Naples. The presence of a metalworking quarter at Pithekoussai points to the role of natural resources like mineral ore deposits, in which Elba and the Tuscan metal-bearing hills were rich, in the interaction between indigenous and these new non-indigenous settlements as well as their respective growth (Giardino, 2013). Hence, while we may surmise from this and other evidence that knowledge of these resources and opportunities was gained prior to the birth of these new settlements, once these latter were established and began interacting with local indigenous societies we see the beginnings of a new phase in Mediterranean antiquity.

IRON AGE CEMETERIES AND GROWING COMMUNITIES

As the earliest urban phase, the early Iron Age therefore represents a momentous period for Etruria, engendering all the transformations that urbanization brought, social and political, not just economic. The best vantage point from which to view these transformations are the cemeteries that developed on the hilltops surrounding the proto-urban settlements, and featured cremation burials placed in pits dug into the ground. The incineration of the dead was a common funerary ritual throughout Etruria from the twelfth century BCE and a much broader ritual custom spreading throughout Italy and Continental Europe. This is known as Urnfield Culture or phenomenon: in Etruria and other areas across Italy, the cremated bones were deposited in a so-called biconical ceramic urn that was covered by a ceramic bowl (Iaia and Pacciarelli, 2012). If the earliest Final Bronze Age cremation pits only contained the urn, later urns were accompanied by a set of objects which distinguished the dead by reflecting the status he or she held in life and portraying an image of him or her in death: at the very beginning of the Iron Age, that image largely related to the gender of the deceased; in later burials, larger sets of grave goods projected a more complex image (Iaia, 1999; Riva, 2010b, pp. 72–84). The latter, however, is anything but a mirror image of life: the selection of grave goods made by the burying group was driven by the social and ideological concerns of the living, acting as a filter which archaeologists only recently have come to recognize, and through which it is possible, with caution, to read and interpret those intentions. Indeed, in the Final Bronze Age, formal burials were likely to be reserved for a few distinguished members of the community, ushering in the funerary realm as the place in which to express social differentiation, as we shall see.

But these are current interpretations which we have arrived at after more than a century of discoveries and heated debates on how to extrapolate information of Etruscan society from cemeteries. The discoveries and excavations of Iron Age cemeteries belong to much earlier times than those of Luni; I briefly turn to the history of these now in order to trace the development of ideas with regard to the Etruscan Iron Age. These excavations date mostly after the unification of the Italian state and later, when central governmental authorities were established in order to manage the enormous and, up until then, divided historical and archaeological heritage of the new nation state. Thus, for example, at *Veii*, while the earliest excavations took place in the 1830s by Luigi Canina at Quattro Fontanili, a cemetery subsequently extensively excavated from the early 1960s, the other Iron Age cemeteries were excavated from 1889. This was the year when Rodolfo Lanciani, best known for his work on the topography and monuments of Rome, dug the Vaccareccia *necropolis* south of Quattro Fontanili on behalf of the Empress of Brasil, Teresa Cristina di Borbone; the other Veientan cemeteries at Casal del Fosso and Grotta Gramiccia north-west of the city were excavated in the early twentieth century (Delpino, 1999). Similarly, at *Caere*, the Iron Age Sorbo cemetery, now under the modern town and near the monumental Regolini Galassi Tomb, was excavated by Raniero Mengarelli, then director of the excavation agency of Civitavecchia and Tolfa, between 1911 and 1916 (Pohl, 1972). In the 1880s and 1890s, the cemeteries of Vetulonia and Populonia were also the subject of discovery and excavation by Isidoro Falchi, a doctor and local archaeologist, who located Vetulonia in the hamlet of Colonna di Buriano (Falchi, 1965). And so it happened at Volterra where archaeologists Gherardo Ghirardini and Antonio Minto, founder of the Institute for Italic and Etruscan Studies, dedicated their time to the excavation of the cemeteries there towards the end of the nineteenth century (Minto, 1930). Indeed, one might say that the Iron Age was discovered in those decades: in 1871, the Fifth Congress of Prehistoric Archaeology that took place in Bologna brought to wider audiences the momentous excavations of prehistoric cemeteries across Italy, especially in Emilia Romagna; subsequently, from the late 1880s, under the rigid and centralized control of archaeological fieldwork by the Italian government and by Luigi Pigorini, the most influential prehistorian in Rome, scholarly attention was drawn towards the study of the Iron Age (Peroni, 1992, pp. 18–38; Pacciarelli, Cupitò, Grifoni Cremonesi, Cremaschi, and Tagliaferri, 2014).

Ghirardini, who studied at Bologna under Edoardo Brizio, a key figure of the intense archaeological fieldwork of this season in Emilia Romagna, went on to direct several excavations at sites all over central Italy. One such excavation was that of one of the richest Iron Age cemeteries at Tarquinia or Corneto-Tarquinia as the modern town was known then from 1881 to 1885, a period of equally frenzied archaeological fieldwork there, supported by the town mayor Luigi Dasti. The cemetery was in an area known as 'Le Arcatelle' on a hill known as Monterozzi that stretches for about 6 kilometres in front of the plateau of the ancient city and became the largest urban cemetery starting from the seventh century BCE. In 1876, Brizio himself had written a first official written report on Tarquinia with fellow archaeologist Felice Barnabei that appeared in the very first edition of *Notizie degli Scavi*, the journal that has ever since reported excavations on Italian soil. Ghirardini, who had been sent to Tarquinia by Giuseppe Fiorelli, then at the Directorship of Antiquities, distinguished himself for publishing systematically on his excavations at Le Arcatelle in the *Notizie degli Scavi*; he was soon followed by Angelo Pasqui and Wolfgang Helbig who continued to report on the excavations until the end of the nineteenth century (Delpino, 1991). The result is a precious series of detailed and competent excavation reports that has allowed archaeologists after them to study closely one of the best records of Iron Age burials in Etruria.

In 1882, Ghirardini reported on the newly dug *tombe a pozzo*, or pit cremation tombs; he immediately recognized the tombs, their objects and the burial ritual from similar burials, familiar to him, that had been excavated near and around Bologna (Ghirardini, 1882). Some of the first to be found there had been brought to light in the early 1850s at Villanova di Forlì by Count Giovanni Gozzadini on his estate. Gozzadini, however, an amateur archaeologist who carried out his own private excavation, had no expertise in recording details of the almost 200 tombs and their contents that went to form his own private collection. Archaeologists like Brizio himself and others went on later to excavate other cemeteries in Emilia Romagna and noticed the similarity of burial ritual and style of objects deposited in the graves with those found at Villanova. Hence, the adjective 'Villanovan' was coined and has been used ever since to denote the Iron Age in Etruria and the specific aspects of the cremation ritual that are also found outside Etruria; similarly, 'proto-Villanovan', coined in 1937 by Giovanni Patroni but first identified by palaeontologist Giuseppe Colini in his study of the excavated finds from Tolfa and Allumiere in the Tolfa Hills between *Caere* and Tarquinia, has been used to describe the final phases of the Bronze Age when the biconical urns were first adopted (Colini, 1909; Fugazzola Delpino, 1979; Cavani, 2009).

In those years, however, at the end of the nineteenth century, when archaeologists were debating the date of these newly dug 'primitive' artefacts and therefore the historical development and relationships between different graves, 'Villanovan' also came to characterize a people: much debate ensued upon the origins of these primitive people, and migration theories, widely popular among scholars, provided a means for interpreting those origins. While some, including Brizio and Patroni, objected to these theories, by the 1880s the idea that new incoming populations migrated through Italy bringing with them the cremation rite gained momentum, particularly under the influence of Pigorini. According to him and others, early prehistoric Indo-European populations migrated to Italy from across the Alps, settling in Emilia Romagna and bringing with them the incineration rite; the Villanovan civilization resulted from these populations moving further south towards the end of the Bronze Age. In reality, migration theories were common across Europe between the end of the nineteenth and the early twentieth century, and were used to explain the presence of artefacts that were stylistically or typologically different from uniform archaeological assemblages (Fugazzola Delpino, 1979, pp. 32–4; Peroni, 1992, pp. 30–3; Nizzo, 2014). While Pigorini's theory incidentally served the purpose of constructing a national identity for the young nation state by sustaining a narrative of amalgamation of ancient peoples, migration theories were also deployed to explain the presence of eastern-looking artefacts and stylistic traits in later tombs, particularly at southern Etruscan sites, that were thought to have been brought by peoples from the east Mediterranean. This will be a topic for the next chapter, but it is sufficient here to say that questions on origins with regard to these later tombs were also influenced by the views of ancient authors such as Herodotus and Dionysius of Halicarnassus who wrote about Etruscan origins.

As briefly discussed in the previous chapter, it was only in the post-war period that ideas on the Villanovan question on the one hand, and eastern origins of the Etruscans on the other, matured along parallel lines and merged together in the early 1960s. Importantly, these developments led to a consensus on the terms proto-Villanovan, Villanovan, Appennine and Sub-Appennine and their chronological relationships, and an agreement that ultimately they all referred to stylistic and cultural traits only. While many scholars contributed to these developments, two among them stand out, Renato Peroni and Massimo Pallottino, who both built on the work of influential scholars such as Hermann Müller-Karpe on the chronology of Late European prehistory. In his studies on the relationship between proto-Villanovan and Sub-Appennine, Peroni saw proto-Villanovan as the transitional phase between the Bronze and Iron Age in the eleventh and tenth centuries BCE, and stressed the continuity between proto-Villanovan and Villanovan (Peroni, 1959, 1960).

In a much earlier article (Pallottino, 1939), Pallottino tried to elucidate the relationship between the Bronze and Iron Age in Etruria, emphasizing regional variations in material culture across Italy in these periods; he thus established a chronological framework for the first half of the first millennium BCE, which he divided into four different cultural *facies*, namely groups of stylistic and cultural traits belonging to a specific chronological phase. In doing so, however, he importantly recognized that traits belonging to different phases, proto-Villanovan and Villanovan for instance, could be contemporaneous at different sites as a result of interaction between these sites or lack thereof; he thus differentiated between a typological and a chronological or historical phase. In his subsequent work it became clear to him that the beginnings of Villanovan material culture marked the beginning of the Iron Age that coincided with the earliest Greek colonization in the central Mediterranean (Fugazzola Delpino, 1979, pp. 34–40). The finding of Mycenaean fragments at Luni sul Mignone and the excavations of other prehistoric settlements in the 1960s ultimately confirmed the cultural continuity between the Bronze and Iron Ages and the chronological frameworks that scholars went on to refine.[1]

WARRIORS IN TOMBS

Among the rich incinerations with bronze objects that Ghirardini excavated at the Arcatelle cemetery at Tarquinia was what he described as a 'typical' terracotta urn covered with a bronze helmet, which he reported as 'without a crest' and decorated by a series of repoussé small studs and points and small holes along the lower part of the helmet (Ghirardini, 1882, p. 188). This is a sheet-bronze bell helmet, held at the National Museum of Tarquinia, belonging to a small group of similar helmets all coming from the Arcatelle cemetery, which Pallottino in 1939 assigned to the first cultural *facies*, and saw as characteristic of the Villanovan phase of southern coastal Etruria. In those years, the 1930s, decorated sheet-bronze objects such as shields, vessels and other types of helmets were studied mainly by Scandinavian and German archaeologists who, like previous scholars, were interested in the relationship between these and other sheet-bronze objects with similar decoration found north of the Alps, and therefore the relations between Italy and Continental Europe: the key issue among scholars was identifying the origins of these objects, their decoration and craftsmanship, either south or north of the Alps, and the direction of diffusion. A decade later, German archaeologist Gero von Merhart wrote a seminal work on European sheet-bronze helmets and later settled the debate by recognizing the Danubian–Carpathian basin as the area where these objects were first made (Iaia, 2005, pp. 15–16). Indeed, our helmet, in form and decoration, is particularly close to other helmets and cups coming, respectively, from the Carpathian and Danubian region; that similarity, we now know thanks to recent studies (Iaia, 2005), suggests the hand of a group of itinerant metalworkers who were active in the Carpathian–Danube basin and moved from there to north-eastern Italy and further south to Tyrrhenian central Italy. The largest cluster of sheet-bronze helmets is, in fact, found at the proto-urban settlements of southern Etruria, although isolated ones are known elsewhere in northern Etruria, northern and central Adriatic Italy (Iaia, 2005, p. 224). The helmet's simple decoration furthermore allows us to date it to the transition between the Bronze Age and the earliest phases of the Iron Age: this makes it the earliest group of helmets from Arcatelle, which were all found in cremation burials (Iaia, 2005, p. 49) (Figure 2.4).

In fact, this group of graves from Arcatelle comprises the earliest examples of graves with helmets, an Iron Age phenomenon detected in Etruria and elsewhere in Italy that inaugurated the equally distinctive phenomenon of the warrior grave, that is, a burial, often a cremation, in which the grave goods alluded to warriorhood and pertained to deceased individuals of high social status (Iaia, 2009–12; Riva, 2010b, pp. 74–95). The burial containing the bell helmet that Ghirardini excavated also contained two horse bits and an iron rod, which archaeologists have interpreted as a 'sceptre', an object symbolizing not simply high social status, but also the political authority of the deceased individual over the community; the horse bits, on the other hand, heralded another feature of later burials emphasizing the military status of the deceased, namely the presence of a chariot inside the grave. The chariot was to become a distinctive feature of elite tombs both in Etruria and further afield across the Italic peninsula (Emiliozzi, 1999; Riva, 2010b, pp. 95–107); first appearing in the last decades of the eighth century BCE particularly at the cemeteries of *Veii* and Bologna, the funerary deposition of chariots characterized very wealthy monumental burials in the following century, as we shall see in the next chapter. The cremation burial that held the

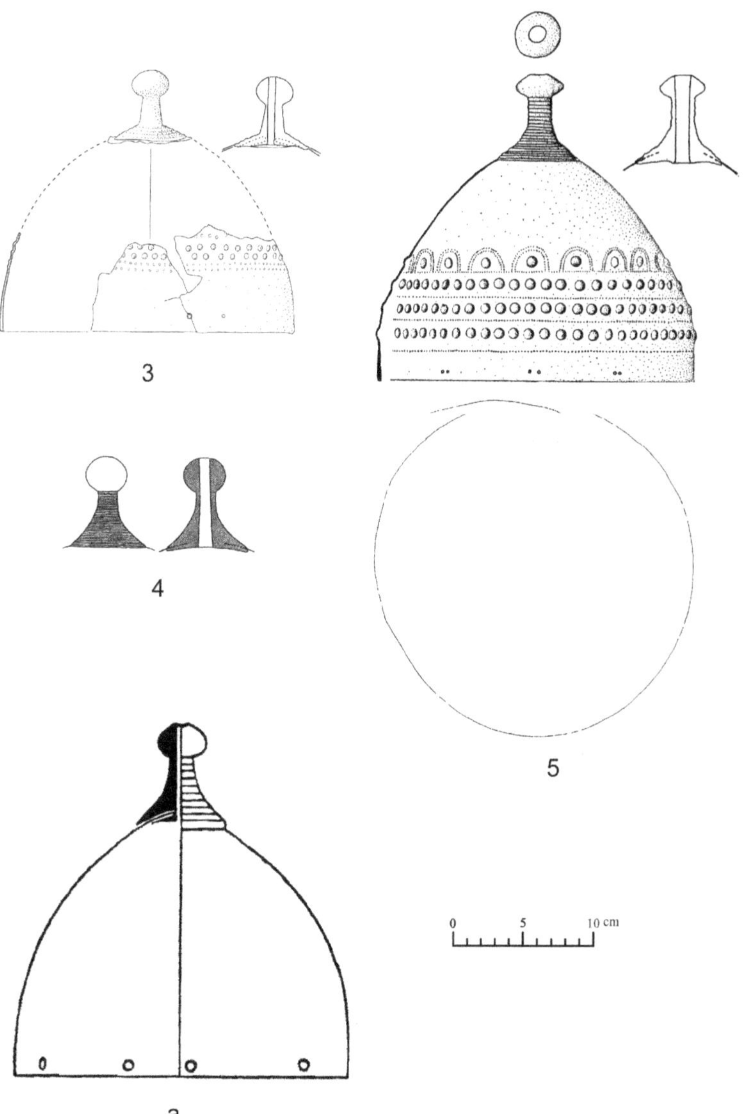

Figure 2.4 Sheet-bronze helmet, Arcatelle *necropolis*, Tarquinia, from Iaia, C. 2005. *Produzioni toreutiche della prima età del ferro in Italia centro-settentrionale. Stili decorativi, circolazione, significato*, Pisa-Roma, fig. 5.5.

bell helmet, however, was different from the later warrior graves: the grave was not rich with grave goods as seen, for example, in a near-contemporary chamber tomb at Populonia (Tomb 1, Poggio del Molino/del Telegrafo) where more than one deceased individual were buried together with personal ornaments, bronze *fibulae* (brooches) and two bronze-sheet bell helmets that were most probably manufactured at Tarquinia. Yet, it was at Tarquinia, at the very beginning of the Iron Age, in the tenth century BCE, that high-status individuals such as those buried at Arcatelle were able to attract particularly sophisticated workmanship in the form of bronze-sheet decorated objects (Iaia, 2010, 2013). These objects, first the helmets and later other items of military equipment and banqueting vessels, were not simply displayed at burial rituals as rare and precious, but were crucially exploited as symbolic devices for expressing political and social power at the cemetery (Iaia, 2005, p. 133). This points to two critical developments for the history of the future cities of Etruria: first, much sooner than might have been expected we find the materialization of symbols of political authority. This is first seen at Tarquinia in the funerary display of warriorhood, which reveals a community characterized by an emerging social hierarchy where local elites or aristocratic groups jostled for political power. Second, the use of these symbols to enhance social status and express political authority, and the exploitation of funerary rituals to this end, were to have a remarkable longevity in Etruria, as we shall see in the following chapter.

Another feature that was exploited as a symbol to these ends is the image of the house that appeared in the form of cinerary urns shaped like a miniature hut and of miniature hut roofs reproduced on the peak of terracotta bell helmets covering urns: these hut-shaped urns, used since the Bronze Age in *Latium* and southern Etruria and largely found at Tyrrhenian coastal early Iron Age cemeteries in very limited numbers, highlighted the status of the male deceased as confirmed by their association with specific sets of grave goods. At the same time, the merging of helmet and hut into the urn cover emphasized an intriguing symbolic association between the warrior and the house, intended in its inherent aspects, namely the family group, land ownership and the household as economic unit (Riva, 2006). As we shall see in the following chapter, the symbolism of the house endured in a monumentalized form (Figure 2.5).

Although this varied from one settlement to another and indeed at *Caere* we see a notable lack of this phenomenon, the exploitation of military symbolism in death reached other centres in a process of elite

Figure 2.5 House-shaped bronze laminated urn © This image is from Getty.

emulation that went hand in hand with this urbanizing phase and culminated in the warrior burials of the eighth century BCE. Nowhere else is this better seen than at *Veii*, for which we have a particularly good documentation of the cemeteries excavated in the 1960s and 1970s (Berardinetti, De Santis, and Drago, 1997). Here, the presence of military insignia and weapons such as the sword and spear signalled the high status of the deceased, while the symbolism of warriorhood also appeared in the form of terracotta helmets imitating metal ones covering the urns of individuals of lower social status (Iaia, 2005, pp. 132–4). In the eighth century BCE, some cremation burials held an exceptional set of grave goods that make them unique in the panorama of elite emulation of this period: it is the case of burial AA1 at Quattro Fontanili that displayed a pair of horse bits, a full panoply of offensive and defensive weapons, including a bronze-sheet crested helmet and shield, an axe, a spearhead and a sword with an ivory and bone pommel, as well as items of personal ornaments, *fibulae* and an imported scarab from the east Mediterranean (Boitani, 2004). Although one may see this tomb as the warrior grave par excellence along with other warrior graves at *Veii* and elsewhere, at

Poggio alle Croci, a cemetery of Volterra, and the aptly named Tomb of the Warrior at the Ripagretta cemetery on Tarquinia's Monterozzi hill, it also represents the joining link between the Iron Age cremation burial and the overwhelmingly wealthy elite burials of the following century. With these later burials it shared new forms of expression of power in the deposition of non-functional, ceremonial objects that were fit for display rather than use, such as a shield and a richly decorated pectoral (Iaia, 1999, pp. 126–35). In fact, Tarquinia's Tomb of the Warrior, brought to light in 1869 and only recently thoroughly studied (Babbi, Peltz, and Benelli, 2013), may be considered as the first example of such elite burials that belong to the so-called Orientalizing period beginning from the closing decades of the eighth century BCE (Figure 2.6).

Outside coastal southern Etruria, this period or horizon of warrior graves that ushered in a heroic ethos for expressing social status occurred with regional variations: at Bologna, for example, the absence of ceremonial warrior accoutrements used for display such as helmets and shields indicates a different attitude towards funerary symbolism in eighth-century BCE warrior graves, as is the absence of spears, found in south Etruscan graves and interpreted as belonging to individuals of lesser status (Iaia, 2005, p. 137). Interestingly, however, these differences are not due to geographical distance, but rather ideological choices by the burying groups on what was deemed worthy of display and best suited to symbolize the deceased's status. At Verucchio, a settlement inland from Rimini on the Adriatic side of central Italy, the combinations of weapons deposited in warrior graves are not unlike those seen in coastal Tyrrhenian burials, particularly those from central-northern Tuscany as seen at Vetulonia (Iaia, 2005, p. 138; Negrini, Mazzoli, and Di Lorenzo, 2018). At Verucchio, an example parallel to what we see at Tarquinia with the Tomb of the Warrior may be found in Tomb 89 of the Lippi cemetery: an exceptionally wealthy warrior grave containing, among other objects, remains of chariots and two helmets, one crested and for display, the other a fully functional one with a conical shape (Eles, 2002).

Tomb 89 also contained a wooden chair, the so-called Verucchio throne, with a rounded back of a type also found in southern Etruria in sheet bronze, an example of which is on display at the British Museum. The back of the chair of the Verucchio throne was carved with a rich figurative decoration depicting warriors, female figures and chariot processions, as well as various activities pertaining to the household of the deceased and the life of the aristocratic group (Eles, 2002, pp. 235–72; Mazzoli and Pozzi, 2015). Among the activities depicted is textile

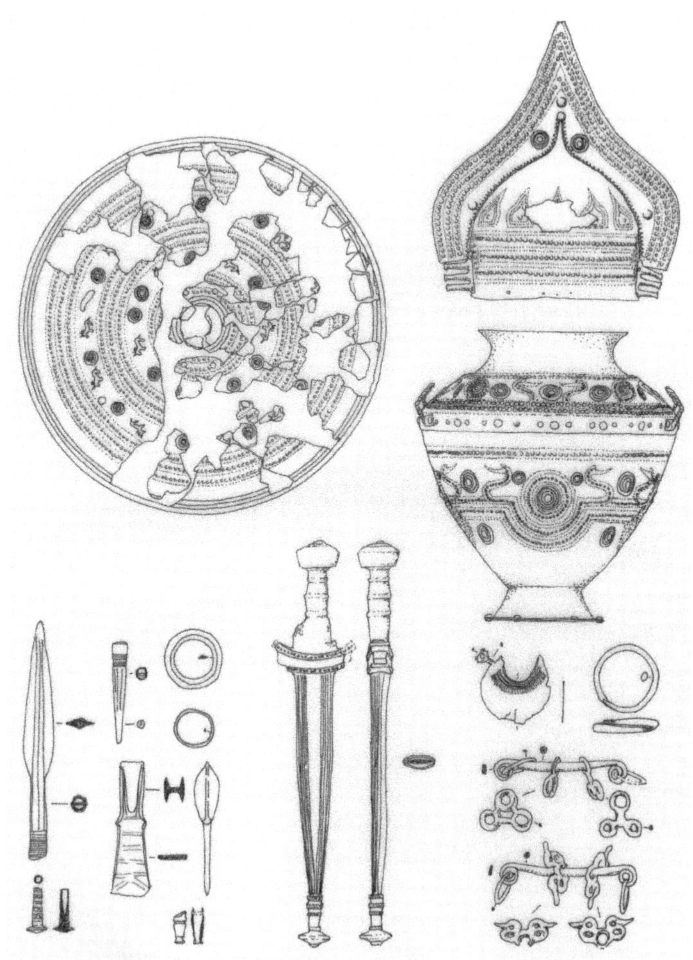

Figure 2.6 Tomb AA1, Quattro Fontanili, *Veii*, grave goods, adapted by L. de Camillis from Pacciarelli, M. 2006 *Dal Villaggio alla Città. La Svolta Protourbana del 1000 a.C. nell'Italia Tirrenica*. Firenze: All'Insegna del Giglio.

production, a craft that is visible in the burial record of Iron Age Etruria in the form of spinning and weaving implements such as spindle whorls, spools and distaffs that were deposited mostly in female burials; this is confirmed by the limited osteological analyses carried out at some cemeteries in central Italy, and by figurative evidence such as the very carved images of the Verucchio throne (Gleba, 2008). Although these implements were excavated along with other goods from the nineteenth century, it is only relatively recently that archaeologists have begun to explore their significance in greater depth than had been done previously when they were simply used to sex a burial with no osteological or other supporting evidence.

Two aspects in particular may be drawn out from this evidence, which recent studies have noted: first, the funerary deposition of these textile-making implements point to their symbolic meaning, which is confirmed by the manufacture of some of these in precious materials such as bronze, glass or ivory, that rendered them unfit for use; they are, in other words, analogous to the sheet-bronze weaponry discussed above that were created for display purposes and symbolized the deceased's status. As different combinations of weapons and other military accoutrements differentiated the social status of the deceased according to his military role, emphasizing social hierarchy in death, so did different combinations of textile-making tools. These tools indicated different levels of specialization and skills in textile production among women: those made in precious material and distaffs, used in the spinning of the fibre, for example, were deposited in wealthier burials (Gleba, 2009). Second, and related to this, textile production was a highly valued economic activity in Iron Age Etruscan households to the extent that its visibility in burials provided the symbolic means through which social status and hierarchy were expressed. Importantly, as textile production continued to play a significant role in the economy of Etruscan cities and settlements as it moved outside the household and into specialized workshops, these implements ceased to be buried with the dead beyond the seventh century BCE (Gleba, 2016). What this shows is that emphasis on gender-specific activities in death turned gender into a symbolic medium for expressing social differentiation that was no longer deployed after the seventh century BCE. In fact, it is a little bit more complicated than that. From the late eighth century and more so in the seventh century BCE some deceased individuals were distinguished by traits pertaining to warrior burials, of which the chariot was most glaring, but this time there was no clear-cut gender distinction as the tomb came to flaunt the aristocratic family group (Riva, 2010b, pp. 96–106).

This shift is symptomatic of profound social and political transformations across Etruria which we turn to in the next chapter. In the present chapter, however, we have seen that such transformations did not occur in a vacuum; on the contrary, they were the outcome of a series of complex developments over a considerable amount of time. It is for this reason that only by beginning a history of the Etruscans in the Bronze Age can we truly appreciate how and why the early Iron Age became such a pivotal turning point in Etruria; by then, we can already speak of an urbanizing society with all the advantages, opportunities and problems that urbanism brought, as we shall see in due course. As examined here, however, communities slowly began gelling together before the end of the Bronze Age, as best seen at Tarquinia. And it is at Tarquinia that our gaze shall linger.

3

ETRUSCAN URBANIZATION

TOWNS AND NEW NETWORKS

OPENING UP TO THE OUTSIDE WORLD

The Monterozzi hill, the location of the largest cemetery of ancient Tarquinia, is named after the numerous mounds, *monterozzi*, dotting it, which, already in the seventeenth century, were believed to host ancient burials. Only in the first half of the nineteenth century, however, were these burials excavated and found to be chamber tombs, and their funerary architecture and painted decoration explored by archaeologists, architects and foreign travellers. Famous are the drawings of Italian architect Luigi Canina who, like other visitors, copied the tomb paintings, and proposed fanciful reconstructions of these *tumulus* burials. That these mounds captured travellers' imagination is clear from their writings and illustrations: equally famous are those of Hamilton Gray, in her *Tour to the Sepulchres of Etruria in 1839* and of George Dennis. The excavations of these chamber tombs, known then as 'tombe egizie', continued in the latter part of the nineteenth century under Ghirardini himself, and then in the 1920s when Giovanni Cultrera continued the work of his predecessors (Figure 3.1).

The deterioration of these *monterozzi* either through natural erosion or human activity had been noticed since the nineteenth century as was the damage done by the looting of the burials. Thanks to the financial help of British navy captain A. Hardcastle, Cultrera was able to intervene and decided to excavate one of two enormous *tumuli* overlooking the sea in the area known as Doganaccia on the western side of Monterozzi.

Figure 3.1 The Monterozzi hill, Tarquinia, adapted from Canina, L. 1846 *L'antica Etruria marittima*, Roma.

The excavated *tumulus*, 35 metres in diameter and known as *Tumulo del Re* (Tumulus of the King), standing next to a similar *tumulus* known as *Tumulo della Regina* (Tumulus of the Queen), was found to have a small court preceding an entrance to the tomb chamber and facing the sea. Although plundered, Cultrera could see that the drum of the mound, the court and chamber were carved from limestone and that the upper parts of the structures were completed with carefully cut blocks of stone. Cultrera noted the similarity of the drum with those of *tumuli* excavated at *Caere* and that the architectural elevation of the chamber, ending in an ogival vault, was not unlike that of other chamber tombs already excavated on Monterozzi (Cultrera, 1932). What was different from these was the monumentality of the chamber and the use of several stone blocks to complete its construction (Figure 3.2).

What had remained of the plundered tomb was enough for Cultrera to date it to the seventh century BCE; the date we can attribute to this burial today is more precise, the second half of the seventh century or the late Orientalizing period (Mandolesi, Lucidi, and Altilia, 2015). Among the goods left in the tomb were large vessels made of *impasto*, an Etruscan ceramic ware used since the Iron Age, including large *ollae*, containers

Figure 3.2 *Tumulo del Re*, *Tumulo della Regina*, Doganaccia, Tarquinia, photograph by Università degli Studi di Torino.

for mixing liquids at the banquet, as well as plenty of fineware including Italo-Geometric *oinochoai* or jugs and *skyphoi* or drinking cups, so-called because their painted decoration imitated Greek Geometric pottery that the Etruscans imported; only a few vessels of *bucchero*, an Etruscan ceramic ware produced from the seventh century BCE and deriving from *impasto*, were left inside the burial. As Cultrera noticed, this *bucchero* ware was particularly fine; some fragments bore incised figures of lions, deer and palmettes, while others were small supports of bowls in the shape of palmettes and Egyptianizing heads, all stylistic motifs that were in line with the eastern-looking decoration of other objects and that gave the period the name 'Orientalizing'. Other notable finds included golden fragments, meagre remains of what would have been precious jewellery, iron fragments of a chariot and a fragment of a fineware *oinochoe*, nowadays lost, painted with a personal name *rutile hipucrates*, which Cultrera recognized as a combination of an Italic name and, the second, an Etruscanized Greek name. He was right: *Rutile* is the Etruscan for Latin *praenomen* or personal name *Rutilus*, and *Hipucrates* the Etruscan for the Greek *Hippokrates*, attesting to the range of contacts that the local aristocratic family owner of this enormous *tumulus* would have entertained with the outside world both in Italy and beyond (Ampolo, 2009; Bagnasco Gianni, 2010).

Cultrera's excavation revealed what we consider to be the most characteristic aspects of Orientalizing Etruria, from the use of writing and the eastern-looking decorative motifs of artefacts, to the monumentality of the burial and the lavishness of its grave goods; this is, in other words, very dissimilar from the earlier burials we encountered in the previous chapter, and representative instead of the social, cultural and political changes which Etruria, particularly the settlements closer to the Tyrrhenian coast, underwent within the space of a century. In Cultrera's time, however, scholarly views on those changes were not that different from those which, from the end of the nineteenth century, contributed to invasion hypotheses in order to explain the Villanovan period, discussed in the previous chapter. For the seventh century BCE and its eastern-looking culture, matters were complicated by the claims by ancient sources on the origins of the Etruscans: if Dionysius of Halicarnassus (*Antiquitates Romanae* I.26–30) alleged autochthony, he was alone in doing so; the Greek historian Herodotus, like other sources, claimed eastern origins (*Histories*, 1.94).

Pallottino's article of 1939 mentioned in the last chapter was fundamental for tackling these issues in relation to these changes: he not only established a more precise chronology of this Orientalizing period as he did with the Villanovan period, dividing it in two distinct phases but also provided a convincing explanation for changes towards a new, eastern-looking material culture by suggesting that these changes revealed a process of social and cultural transformations. He further saw Etruscan elites as active contributors to those transformations as they embraced an Orientalizing way of life thanks to the wide-ranging commercial contacts with the east Mediterranean (Pallottino, 1965). Prior to Pallottino's article, the term 'Orientalizing' was largely used as an art historical term to explain new styles in material culture and imported objects from the east as discussed in Chapter 1: it was originally coined by Alexander Conze in order to explain similar changes in Greek art, particularly vase painting and the transition from Geometric to Orientalizing motifs and decoration in it. The term was then applied to Etruria, understandably, given the philhellenism of nineteenth-century scholarship, and the momentous discoveries that by then had already taken place such as that of the monumental Regolini Galassi Tomb in 1836 in the Sorbo *necropolis* of *Caere*, as we saw in Chapter 1. This tomb, in fact, is not dissimilar from the Tumulus of the King, whose lavish objects were illustrated in an 1842 publication by the Vatican Museum.

In reality, the term Orientalizing was anything but neutral as intimated in Chapter 1: it carried a set of assumptions that were at the core of the intellectual arm of nation-building and colonialism, the twin political projects of nineteenth-century Europe in which antiquity was pressed into service in the construction of national identities. In particular, Orientalizing encapsulated an inherent opposition between east and west that contributed to an essentialist view of cultures; according to this view, the Orient was seen as a uniform entity, despite incorporating vast and very diverse regions of the Middle East (Riva and Vella, 2006). Under the drive of philhellenism, by contrast, the Classical past was employed to forge an identity for the west, that is, Europe, in stark opposition to the antiquity of the Orient, which was being discovered by European archaeologists at the same time as it was being subjugated by European colonial powers. Nineteenth-century European archaeologists explicitly posited the superiority of Greek art vis-à-vis the Oriental influences, from which it managed successfully to free itself; at the same time they pejoratively characterized those influences, dismissing certain aspects such as opulence, luxury or copying and imitation, as inherently Oriental, in stark contrast with the originality and dynamism of Greek art (Gunter, 2013; Nowlin, 2016, pp. 33–7).

This vision, which historians refer to as 'Orientalism', had particular traction for interpreting the eastern-looking material culture of seventh-century BCE Etruria for several reasons, not least because of the view that the genius of Greek art shaped Etruscan art and promoted its flourishing out of earlier Oriental influences. Those interpretations, in fact, belong to a much broader perspective that saw Etruria evolving out of external forces, whether Oriental, including Phoenician, or Greek; according to these views, Etruscan art grew from the imitation of the art of both. These views were clearly spelt out in the 1920s by Alessandro Della Seta (*Italia Antica*, 1922) and Pericle Ducati (*Storia dell' Arte Etrusca*, 1927). Twenty or so years later, Pallottino highlighted the role of local elites and their commercial networks, and recognized the Orientalizing period as crucial to Etruscan cultural formation. He nevertheless remained close to those Hellenocentric views: the introduction of Greek myth, for example, identified on the painted figured decoration of ceramic vessels, as we shall see later, was seen to usher Etruria into history. Ultimately, like Ducati's and Della Seta's, Pallottino's was a diffusionistic perspective that proved influential in the decades to come. Two aspects, in particular, were central to this perspective: first, the lavishness and monumentality of burials were seen as evidence of the adoption by Etruscan elites of a lifestyle suited to eastern kings and princes, a view encapsulated in the name given to the Tumulus of the King at Doganaccia; second and concurrently, that lifestyle pointed to Oriental-style, kingly forms of political power embraced by those elites in their rule over their local communities. This interpretation, in particular, not only effectively provided an explanation for the origins of Etruscan kingship which ancient authors such as Livy described but also contributed to the characterization of this period as the first historical period for Etruria (Riva, 2006; Nowlin, 2016, pp. 33–60).

Recent perspectives have pushed Pallottino's emphasis on Etruscan formation further as archaeologists have recognized the need to examine cultural change in terms of long-term processes since the second half of the twentieth century. The warrior burials discussed in the previous chapter demonstrate how it is no longer possible to see the seventh century BCE as a period of abrupt change; on the contrary, long-term indigenous sociopolitical transformations led to cultural change and the active embracing of a material culture afforded by growing contacts with the outside world. Pallottino's vision of an elite-centred Orientalizing culture has also broadened: it includes foreign and indigenous craftsmen providing new technologies, whether writing or ceramic innovations like *bucchero* or new techniques for decorating metal objects, as well as the presence of Phoenician traders, largely responsible for the earliest imported artefacts, and to whom scholars have given a far more central role than previously (Cristofani and Martelli, 1994)[1] (Figure 3.3).

Moreover, the growth of comparative approaches to the archaeology of the Mediterranean has stimulated a vibrant exchange among archaeologists working on this period in different regions of the basin (Riva and Vella, 2006): this exchange has interestingly resulted in two broadly distinct perspectives on Orientalizing Etruria. The first, stemming from Pallottino's own pan-Mediterranean views of what he defined as an 'international' Orientalizing style, is concerned with tracing the origins of this style: much of this work has entailed examining closely either the hand of craftsmen on locally manufactured artefacts such as the fine decorated *bucchero* vessels from the Tumulus of the King, or the cultural environment from which objects were imported, as well as searching for the eastern prototypes and their contexts, which inspired the making of a pan-Mediterranean Orientalizing culture (Naso, 2012; Sannibale, 2013). Key to this perspective is the assumption that Etruscan elites, active participants in this culture, emulated an eastern way of life and employed cultural models of

Figure 3.3 *Bucchero oinochoe*, *Caere* (Villa Giulia Museum), photograph by Sailko (CC BY-SA 4.0), from Wikimedia Commons.

eastern kingly courts for their own social and political needs. Thus, for example, scholars have sought parallels for the monumental *tumuli* in the enormous funerary mounds excavated in Phrygia and Lydia in central and western Anatolia respectively (Naso, 1998). The mouldings and carvings of the drums of some *tumuli* at *Caere*, where we find some of the earliest examples of monumental funerary architecture, have been likened to similar stone carvings in northern Syria; whether Syria is the origin of the craftsmen who worked on the *tumuli* at *Caere*, however, is more difficult to ascertain, but not far-fetched. Bronze vessels such as the ribbed shallow bowls called *paterae*, first imported from Assyria and then deposited in late eighth-century BCE elite burials, were later imitated and locally manufactured both in bronze and ceramic; of these, notable examples come from *Veii* (Sciacca, 2005). Likewise, parallels for bronze cauldrons, decorated with lion and griffin heads from the Regolini Galassi Tomb at *Caere* and a similarly lavish burial, the Circolo dei Lebeti at Vetulonia, have been found in similar cauldrons from central Anatolia and northern Syria. Although it is often difficult to identify exact parallels for specific styles and decorative motifs on Orientalizing artefacts, scholars embracing this approach are happy to accept that fuzziness as inherent to an Orientalizing culture, which derived from the medley characteristic of Levantine and Phoenician craftsmanship (Naso, 2012, p. 450).

The second approach has developed out of a critical reaction to diffusionism and a rejection of its assumption that the original eastern context of use of those imported styles and artefacts is key to the understanding of their presence in Etruria (Riva, 2010b, pp. 39–71). This approach has, on the contrary, shifted attention towards local processes of appropriation and use of artefacts, whether imported or locally made, and the ways in which the elites actively transformed their own material and visual world by selecting and incorporating eastern-looking styles, motifs and objects into that world. Important to this approach is a long-term view of change, the seeds of which, we now know, are to be found in the Iron Age, as previously explained. Nowadays, our greater knowledge of the early first millennium BCE has enabled us to assess more thoroughly these local processes (Iaia, 1999) and, at the same time, to see remarkably minute details of interaction and cultural contact with the outside world (Iaia, 1999, 2005). The recent reopening of the excavation at Doganaccia, for instance, has advanced our knowledge of what seems to be an elite family burial, the monumental *Tumulo della Regina*, and nearby chamber tombs

(Mandolesi and de Angelis, 2011; Mandolesi et al., 2015; Gleba, Mandolesi, and Lucidi, 2017). Ultimately, both perspectives acknowledge that Orientalizing culture provided Etruscan elites with a source to manipulate in order to assert and articulate, materially and visually, their power in ever more complex and growing urban communities (Figures 3.4, 3.5, 3.6 and 3.7).

Let us thus explore some key interrelated aspects of the seventh century BCE through what we know of the archaeology today: first, change and continuity in funerary customs leading to the adoption of inhumation as the largely, though not exclusively, predominant burial ritual across Etruria. The symbolism of the house explored in the previous chapter continued in monumental form for the expression of the elites' social and political power. Second, the escalation and visibility of banqueting and drinking in elite circles, whether at their tomb or residence, which went hand in hand with the demand for technological innovation afforded by an Orientalizing material and visual culture. Third, the role of cultural contact in fostering innovation as the central Mediterranean became the meeting ground between indigenous and the new Greek and Phoenician communities in Sicily, southern Italy and Sardinia. The seventh century BCE, ultimately represents the continuation, if not acceleration, of urbanization, detected in the settlement and funerary evidence, which, in turn, speaks of a remarkable accumulation of wealth that this very

Figure 3.4 *Tumulo della Regina* under excavation, Doganaccia, Tarquinia, photograph by Università degli Studi di Torino.

Figure 3.5 *Tumulo della Regina* under excavation, tomb entrance, Doganaccia, Tarquinia, photograph by Università degli Studi di Torino.

Figure 3.6 *Tumulo della Regina* under excavation, monumental staircase leading to tomb entrance, Doganaccia, Tarquinia, photograph by Università degli Studi di Torino.

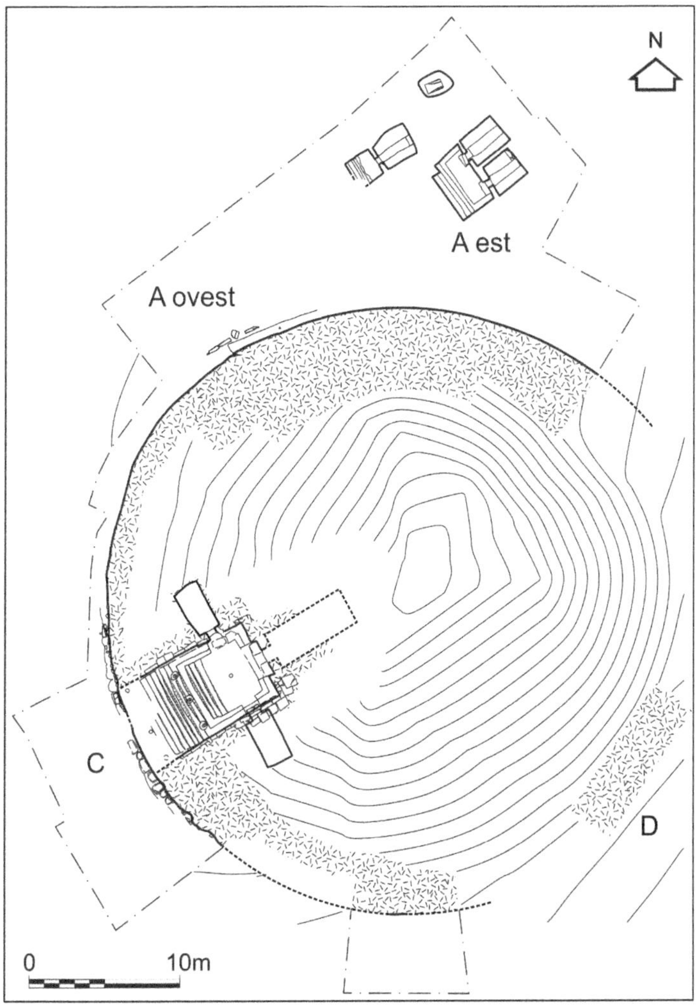

Figure 3.7 *Tumulo della Regina* and nearby tombs, plan, Doganaccia, Tarquinia, photograph by Università degli Studi di Torino.

acceleration afforded; indeed, there is no doubt that such an urban growth went hand in hand with the control of resources and innovation by the elites of these towns, as I shall examine next. Such a growth and its consequences then culminated in the following century, as the next chapter will show.

FUNERARY SYMBOLISM AND BURIAL RITUAL: OSTENTATION AND SOCIAL POWER

As indicated in the previous chapter, the aristocratic family group came to be at the centre of the elites' burial ritual. Although distinctive groupings of single or double cremation burials are found in some Iron Age cemeteries and may be evidence of the intentional display of family ties, it was not until the seventh century BCE that the tomb acted as an architecturally constructed physical space where those ties were exhibited through the monumental tomb chambers, in some cases multiple chambers underneath a single tomb where more than one deceased was placed; this change went hand in hand with the adoption of inhumation (Prayon, 1975). The transition, however, between the cremation and inhumation ritual was not immediate, and varied from cemetery to cemetery in the modes and timescale in which it occurred. The earliest chamber tombs holding inhumation burials were constructed at Populonia towards the end of the ninth century BCE: here, these chambers were circular and had a false dome under a small *tumulus* (ten Kortenaar, Neri, and Nizzo, 2006). In southern Etruria, we can trace the transition from late eighth-century BCE cremations placed in burial pits and trenches, where distinct sets of grave goods were deposited in discrete areas of the burial space, to increasingly larger burial trenches that came to be signposted by small mounds above ground. The cemetery where we see most clearly the early development of these mounds into monumental *tumuli* is *Caere* (Naso, 2007; Naso and Botto, 2018), but the best examples of burials that show the beginning of this transition are the warrior graves from *Veii* and Tarquinia, as well as some inhumation burials at the Olmo Bello *necropolis* at Bisenzio (Iaia, 2006). The soft *tufa* stone that characterizes the southern Tyrrhenian landscape lent itself well to the carving out of tomb chambers into the rock. Elsewhere, most notably, in inland northern Etruria, the use of limestone blocks for the construction of the tomb distinguishes the local funerary architecture here from that seen further south, exemplified by the so-called *tholos* tombs of Montagnola, Mula and Montefortini near Sesto Fiorentino (Florence) (Cianferoni, 1999; Poggesi, 2011, pp. 34–7).

The transition also took different forms in the burial ritual employed and the tomb where this took place: this is notable at Chiusi and its hinterland where the use of cremation for single burials persisted (Minetti, 2004). Deposited in pits known as *ziro* tombs, to refer to the sizeable terracotta container (*ziro*) that held it, the cremation urn, made of *impasto* ware and of the biconical type with its lid, was increasingly made to resemble a human body as the potter sometimes added hands and arms to the body of the vessel and shaped the lid into a human head (Paolucci, 2010): these anthropomorphic so-called canopic urns, which were often seated on a chair in front of banqueting tables inside the tomb, may have been a sign of social distinction prior to the mid-seventh century BCE, but their widespread use continued after that date. From the late seventh century, that is around 630 BCE, we begin to see the earliest chamber tombs dug into the soft *tufa* rock, and the beginning of decorating the interior of the chamber with wall paintings (Minetti, 2004, pp. 511–29), a custom which we see in southern Etruria as early as the first decades of the seventh century at *Veii* in the *Tomba dei Leoni Ruggenti* and the *Tomba delle Anatre*, and at Tarquinia, in the *Tumulo della Regina* (Rizzo, 1989; Naso, 1996; Boitani, 2010; Mandolesi and de Angelis, 2011). A particular type of chamber tomb found at Chiusi and further north is the so-called *tomba a tramezzo*, which was, in some cases, surmounted by the monumental *tumulus* (Minetti, 2004, pp. 514–17). The custom of the incineration rite, however, persists in these chamber tombs as does the *ziro*-type tomb, although there are cases, recently investigated, of inhumation burials in some cemeteries near Chiusi, such as the cemetery at Tolle not far from Chianciano (Paolucci, 2015). In any case, while the canopic urn is typically Chiusine, the preoccupation with maintaining the corporeality of the cremated body of the deceased is not exclusive to the area: in some elite tombs at Vulci, most recently the Tomb of the Silver Hands, and two other burials at Marsiliana d'Albegna, north of Vulci, anthropomorphic simulacra of different styles and made of different types of material were found, from sheet bronze to sheets of precious metal such as silver and gold as well as ivory and wood (Morandi, 2013; Arancio et al., 2014). Although some examples of these simulacra belonged to inhumation burials, those that were associated with the cremation rite, of which an example comes from the *Tomba del Carro* at Vulci (see this section, below), suggest the need to highlight the deceased's body lost to incineration (Figure 3.8).

Chiusi, in fact, demonstrates the remarkable regional variation in the choice of tomb and ritual adopted across Etruria in the seventh century BCE. At Pisa, for instance, underneath the modern town, recent excavation brought to light a monumental *tumulus*, dated between the end of the eighth and the beginning of the seventh centuries BCE, with no human burial, but evidence of ritual activities, which may be read as a cenotaph (Bruni, 2000). Bologna and its region, where we do not see the monumental funerary spaces that distinguish Tyrrhenian Etruria, provide

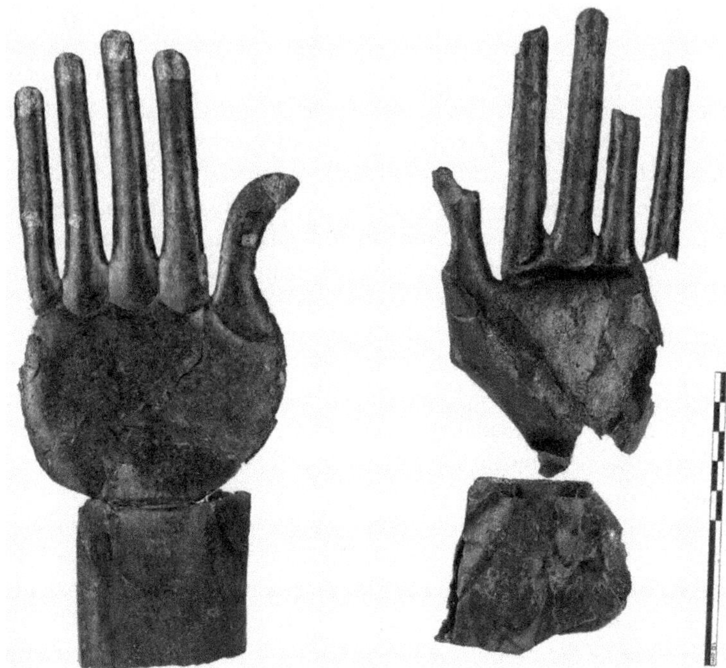

Figure 3.8 Couple of hands in laminated silver and gold leaf, Tomb of the Silver Hands, Osteria *necropolis*, Vulci, photograph courtesy Parco Archeologico di Vulci (Fondazione Vulci).

another example (Morigi Govi and Dore, 2005). In some instances, both cremation and inhumation rites were used inside the same tomb: we see that at Chiusi and in southern Etruria where the coexistence of both rites in particularly wealthy tombs where the grave goods highlighted heroic warriorhood as an expression of status suggests that cremation was part and parcel of this expressive symbolic process.

Dated to *circa* the mid-seventh century BCE, Tomb 5 at Monte Michele near *Veii* is exemplary in this respect. North-west of *Veii*, the hill of Monte Michele sits opposite the city gate known as Porta Capena; here, in 1842, a chance discovery led to the unearthing of the famous Campana Tomb, a frescoed chamber tomb described by George Dennis in his 1848 *Cities and Cemeteries of Etruria*. After that discovery, the area was intensively investigated at the beginning of the twentieth century by the brothers Benedetti who sold several excavated artefacts to the *Museo*

Archeologico of Florence in 1903. While the area had been subjected to ancient and modern looting and the poor documentation of those early excavations did not allow a clear picture of the spatial distribution of the tombs, the grave goods in the *Museo Archeologico* were studied before the great flood of Florence by Mauro Cristofani who published them, noting the different types of tombs there, from the pit or trench tombs to the chamber tombs (Cristofani, 1969) (Figure 3.9).

Unearthed in 1980 together with five other chamber tombs, Tomb 5 is a large single chamber tomb with two small rooms on either side of the corridor that led to the chamber (Boitani, 2001). It hosted the burial of four individuals, probably belonging to the same family, among whom was an infant buried in one of the small side chambers. The other side chamber hosted a young male cremation inside an Italic–Geometric so-called stamnoid *olla*; the main chamber held a female inhumation, recognized as such by its associated grave goods, and a male cremation wrapped in a cloth and held inside a laminated bronze house-shaped urn. The urn was placed on a four-wheeled iron and wooden chariot that was decorated with repoussé-worked bronze sheets. On the chariot was placed the accoutrement of the cremated warrior: iron arrow heads

Figure 3.9 Tomb 5, Monte Michele, *Veii*, the grave goods ©Museo Nazionale Etrusco di Villa Giulia. Archivio fotografico.

and a dagger along with a 'sceptre', a wooden pole decorated with silver elements and surmounted by a bronze head with iron inlay decoration, as well as two red *impasto* shields. Associated with the chariot were also a pair of iron horse bits and javelin heads. An entire banqueting set was placed in the chamber and included ceramic vessels to draw, pour and drink wine or other similar alcoholic liquids, equipment for roasting meat and a bronze grater, an object found in other similar banqueting sets of other comparable elite burials that has been interpreted as an instrument to grate flavoured additives into wine. Included with the objects was also a laminated bronze fan, a so-called *flabellum*, decorated with guilloches and palmettes, motifs that are also found on the bronze laminate of the urn and on the long side of the chariot. The function of the fan within a banqueting and funerary context is confirmed by a contemporary depiction of a seated banquet, sculpted in terracotta on a cinerary urn from Montescudaio near Volterra, in which an attendant is holding a fan. The Veian tomb's recent excavation and documentation have enabled archaeologists to carefully reconstruct the objects inside the tomb as well as provide a virtual reality of the tomb and its content thanks to a European-Union-funded project for the development of digital visualization at the Etruscan National Museum of Villa Giulia in Rome.[2] This project has also virtually reconstructed the objects and provided a 3D model of some of them; among them is a truncated ivory cone sculpted in relief with a series of winged sphinxes, a fabulous animal that, like the palmettes and guilloches of the bronze fan, belongs to the figurative repertoire found in the decoration of seventh-century BCE imported and locally manufactured objects.

There are a few features that this tomb and its artefacts highlight. First, the cinerary urn, a bronze rectangular receptacle surmounted by a sloping roof, decorated on its long side and, on one of its short sides, with an engraved face perhaps belonging to a gorgon, demonstrates the continuity of the symbolic association of house and warrior discussed in the previous chapter. The combination of the house-shaped urn and chariot is known elsewhere, namely at Marsiliana d'Albegna, in the tomb known as *Circolo della Fibula* inside the Banditella *necropolis*, and at Vetulonia where we have a particularly high concentration of seventh-century BCE chariot burials. Among these is the contemporary *Tomba del Duce*, excavated by Isidoro Falchi in 1886, and containing a silver-laminated bronze urn of similar rectangular shape with a sloping roof. This tomb was located on a hilltop at Poggio Bello, namely in a high, visible and distinctive location. A recent revision and re-study of the seventh-century cemeteries of Vetulonia has shown that these cemeteries developed both near the earlier Iron Age burial grounds and in new high places (Colombi, 2018) (Figure 3.10).

The *Tomba del Duce*, like many other contemporary tombs at Vetulonia, was a large trench surrounded by a continuous stone circle of 17 metres in diameter (Camporeale, 1967; Cianferoni and Celuzza, 2010, pp. 125–44). Although the trench had been looted, five distinct burial groups that functioned as ritual spaces were identified inside it, probably belonging to four cremation graves. Some of these spaces contained banqueting and drinking equipment, including several types of bronze vessels, fine *bucchero* and *impasto* vessels as well as other ceramic imported vessels, preparation equipment such as iron spits and a bronze grater, as well as elements of warrior accoutrement including a bronze helmet and shield; remains of a chariot were also identified. In one of the group the deceased's cremated remains were similarly wrapped in a cloth and placed inside the urn, which was itself associated with bronze shallow ribbed bowls, silver brooches and a small bronze Nuragic boat imported from Sardinia (Lo Schiavo, 2008). The silver laminate covering the urn was also decorated in repoussé work with the Orientalizing

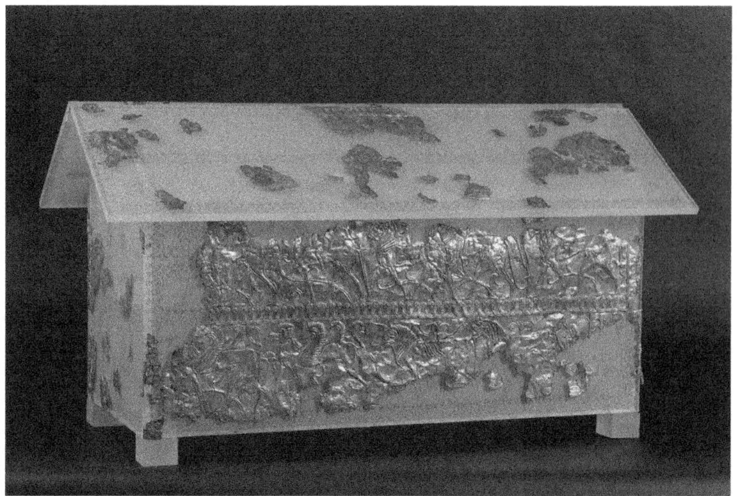

Figure 3.10 Silver-laminated urn, *Tomba del Duce*, Poggio Bello *necropolis*, Vetulonia, photograph of Archivio fotografico ex SBAT, from Cygielman, M. and S. Rafanelli (eds) 2004 *Io sono di Rachu Kakanas. La Tomba del Duce di Vetulonia.* Catalogo della mostra, Grosseto.

figurative repertoire: animals such as lions, horses, panthers as well as similar animals with wings, as well as the so-called Phoenician palmettes.

The symbolism of the house is also suggested by the interior decoration of the tomb chamber. At the Banditaccia cemetery of *Caere* some multi-chamber tombs displayed, in the remarkably detailed stone-carved decoration of their interior, architectural elements that were probably employed in residential architecture (Prayon, 1975). We see this development flourishing in the sixth century BCE there, but the earliest example dates to the seventh century, as exemplified by the Tomb of the Five Chairs, a monumental tomb excavated in 1865 and composed of three funerary chambers and a long corridor (Prayon, 1974). Its name comes from the five chairs that were carved into the *tufa* rock inside the left-hand-side chamber adjacent to the corridor, immediately before one enters the main funerary chamber, that was probably conceived as a cult space for the deceased members of the burying group. Contemporary or slightly earlier tombs with an architecturally less complex interior, such as Tomb 5 at Monte Michele, may hint at a similar symbolic association of house and warrior through the monumentalization of the chamber itself on the one hand, and the deposition of the chariot on the other (Figures 3.11 and 3.12).

Figure 3.11 Banditaccia *necropolis*, *Caere*, photograph by Lisa Pieraccini.

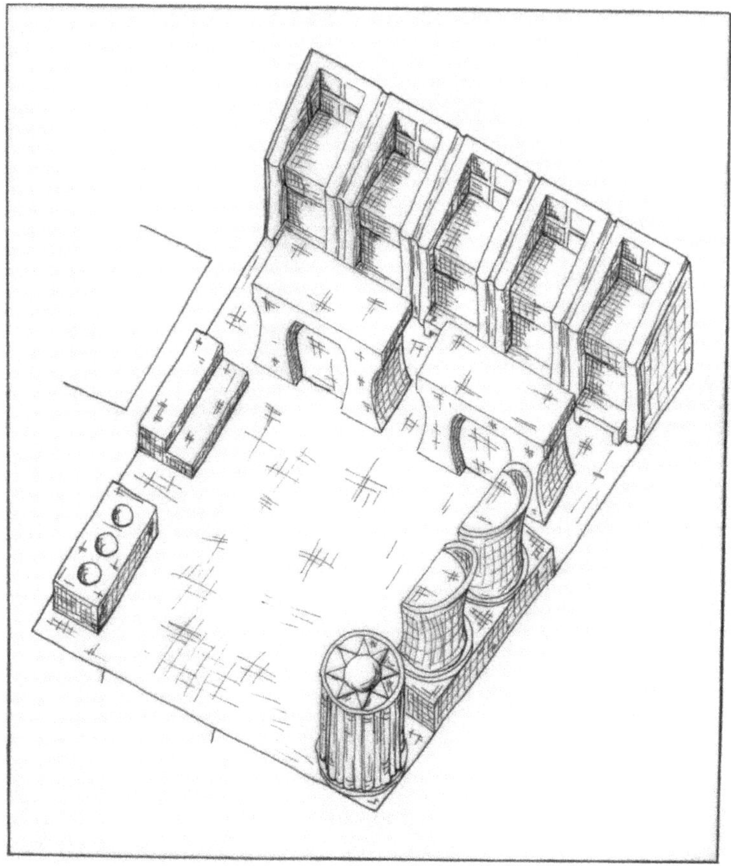

Figure 3.12 Tomb of the Five Chairs, *Caere*, reconstruction of side-chamber interior adapted by L. de Camillis from Tuck, A. S. 1994 The Etruscan Seated Banquet: Villanovan Ritual and Etruscan Iconography, *American Journal of Archaeology* 98, 617–28.

One may see this in the early seventh-century BCE *Tomba del Carro* at the Osteria *necropolis*, mentioned above, one of the main urban cemeteries of Vulci just north of the city (Sgubini Moretti, 1998). It was identified in 1965 through magnetic prospection but poorly documented and awaits new investigation: the tomb's monumental architecture stood out among other contemporary tombs within Osteria that consisted of deep burial trenches. Composed of a short corridor leading to the main chamber with a small niche adjacent to it and surmounted by an ogive vault, the tomb held three cremation burials each deposited in laminated bronze urns; a fourth cremation was held in a bronze cauldron. The tomb group was composed of a rich banqueting and drinking service, which included bronze, ceramic, locally manufactured and imported vessels, as well as meat-roasting equipment. Unlike the four-wheeled chariot at Monte Michele, most likely utilized as a funerary parade chariot, the chariot deposited in the main chamber of the *Tomba del Carro* was a two-wheeled war chariot. But war equipment it was not: the front railing of the chariot was covered by bronze laminate decorated in repoussé work with Orientalizing motifs such as guilloches and processions of horses, comparable to what we see on the bronze sheets of the chariot at Monte Michele. In other words, although we have evidence of the use of the chariot prior to its deposition in the *Tomba del Carro*, the bronze sheets turned a war chariot into a parade item probably used on ceremonial occasions only. We may thus see in this object and its funerary context, at one and the same time, the continuity of the symbolic house–warrior association and its translation onto a new level where ostentatious display of the elite family's or burying group's social power took a monumental form. But what did this social power consist of?

CONTROLLING RESOURCES AND TECHNOLOGICAL INNOVATION

Several clues point towards the control of natural and agricultural resources, on the one hand, and the control of technological innovation, on the other, which new contacts with the outside world facilitated. As argued in the previous chapter, the new urban settlements that were much larger than previous Bronze Age sites were strategically located closer to the sea or on key communication routes, and surrounded by an environment rich in natural resources, particularly agricultural and mineral ones. The elite tomb flaunted the control of these resources in the very rich banqueting services that were deposited, not just in the vessels that composed these services, but also in the offerings to the dead contained in these vessels (Bartoloni, ten Kortenaar, and Acconcia, 2012). Belonging to these services were also large terracotta containers of agricultural produce, whether solid or liquid, from the heavily decorated so-called *pithoi* at *Caere* to very large *ollae* that were plain or decorated with vertical ribs (Serra Ridgway and Pieraccini, 2010). The deposition of bronze and precious metal objects, from vessels and personal ornaments such as brooches and pectorals, to richly decorated parade military equipment such as chariots and shields, also speaks of the ability of elite groups to own the metal supply, of which Tyrrhenian central Italy was particularly rich, as well as to have access to craftsmen for the production of fine metalwork displaying new decorative techniques such as filigree and granulation used on gold jewellery.

Access to new techniques and craftsmanship was not limited to these objects: indeed, what is striking about seventh-century BCE Etruria is the overall technological innovation, whether in the craftsmanship of different materials, from terracotta to metal and ivory, or in new monumental architecture, modes of drinking and eating and novel forms of communication such as writing (Riva, 2010b, pp. 59–71). The very location, furthermore, of the tombs just outside the settlement, in the earlier Iron Age cemeteries and in isolated positions, or distant from it along communication routes, either towards the sea or inland, suggests that these tombs owned the very landscape and the cities' hinterlands, out of which came the resources of wealth: in doing so, they transformed it into a 'landscape of power' (Zifferero, 1991). The Doganaccia cemetery is, in this respect, exemplary: belonging to an elite family, it was established according to a plan, as the most recent excavation of the site has made clear, that focused on the two monumental *tumuli* overlooking the sea and linking the route from Tarquinia to the sea (Mandolesi et al., 2015). We may similarly interpret the small group of tombs, of which Tomb 5 was the first to be built, at Monte Michele, where the planned arrangement of the tombs may have been determined by the choice of location at one of the main entrances to *Veii*.

Access to new craftsmanship and therefore technological innovation was only possible through establishing and maintaining relations with the outside world that could provide it. The object and its context that best exemplify this is a small *bucchero* jug, dated to *circa* 630 BCE, known as the San Paolo Olpe, and found in one of the two tombs probably belonging to the same monumental *tumulus* excavated in 1988 at *Caere* (Rizzo, 2015). Although looted, Tomb 1 and Tomb 2 contained overall more than 400 objects. Located on the western slopes of Monte Abatone, the *tumulus* was in an isolated position along the route that linked *Caere* to the port of *Alsium*, marking the surrounding landscape similarly to another monumental *tumulus*, Montetosto, located on the road leading to *Pyrgi*, another coastal port that developed in the sixth century, as we shall see in the next chapter. The structure of both tombs at San Paolo was similar to that of the renowned Regolini Galassi Tomb excavated more than a century earlier and located on the nearby Sorbo hill overlooking *Caere*: a long corridor led to the funerary chambers built with large stone blocks and surmounted by an ogival vault. Slightly earlier than Tomb 2, Tomb 1 contained almost 200 vessels including storage jars, imported transport *amphorae* from Attica and Chios in the Aegean, local fineware, *impasto* and *bucchero* banqueting vessels and plates, and several imported, mostly proto-Corinthian, banqueting vessels and oil containers; other imported objects, among which was a faience ribbed bowl as well as several fragments of ivory, amber, silver sheets; bronze objects such as a shield and a grater; and remains of a chariot, all attest to the wealth of the burial. The main funerary chamber of Tomb 2 contained proto-Corinthian and *bucchero* vessels, among which was the *olpe*, while the side chamber, the only intact room found sealed with a stone block, also contained among the grave goods the remains of a chariot. Made of thin *bucchero* (*bucchero sottile*), the *olpe*'s shape is similar to other jugs of proto-Corinthian manufacture, of which the most famous is the Chigi vase found in 1881 at Monte Aguzzo near *Veii* (Figure 3.13).

Two figured friezes in relief and incision decorate the body of the *olpe* (Riva, 2010a): the upper frieze shows feline animals devouring humans, a rather typical seventh-century BCE decorative motif of *bucchero* pottery; the lower frieze is filled with three groups and an isolated winged figure identified as *Taitale*, that is, Daidalos, the skilled craftsman of Greek mythology. Of these three groups are, first, a figure identified as Medea by its inscription transliterating the Greek name and standing in front of a man coming out of a cauldron; second, a group of six youths carrying an object identified by the word *kanna* of uncertain meaning; third, a group of two facing boxers. That the man in the cauldron is identified as Jason and that the rest of the figures allude to the Greek saga of the Argonauts is not in doubt; the myth, though rare in Etruria, also recurs on two other locally produced vessels, two unfortunately unprovenanced *amphorae* with painted decoration, now in Amsterdam and Würzburg respectively. The figured decoration of the *olpe*, in fact, belongs to a considerable number of other images that refer to other Greek myths and that occur on vessels of different shape and type, from painted fineware, to *bucchero* and ivory (Bellelli, 2010; Krauskopf, 2016). Among these are the two renowned so-called Pania *pyxides*, two ivory vessels coming from two *tramezzo*-type chamber tombs excavated in the latter part of the nineteenth century at Chiusi and Montepulciano respectively. In the cut frieze decoration, these vessels depict the escape of

Figure 3.13 San Paolo Olpe, San Paolo Tumulus, *Caere* (Villa Giulia Museum), photograph by Sailko (CC BY-SA 4.0), from Wikimedia Commons.

Odysseus and his companions from the cave of the Cyclops Polyphemos narrated in Homer's Odyssey, and Geryon's cattle, a reference to one of Herakles' twelve labours narrated in the *Geryoneis*, a poem by Sicilian Greek poet Stesichorus (Menichetti, 1994, pp. 45–89). Closer to the San Paolo Olpe is another *bucchero olpe*, found near a recently excavated but looted monumental *tumulus* in the Banditaccia cemetery of *Caere* in the area of Campo della Fiera. This *olpe* depicts, with similar relief and incised decoration, the *prothesis* (lying in state) of Achilles, another episode in Homer's Odyssey (Cosentino and Maggiani, 2010). Here too, an inscription, which may have been engraved by the same hand that inscribed the San Paolo Olpe, identifies the body on the funerary bed as that of Achilles; the name *Achilleus* is also a transliteration from Greek.

Returning to the San Paolo Olpe, the fact that the Argonauts' saga was depicted on an Etruscan vessel inscribed with names transliterated from Greek suggests that the myth was understood in Etruria and may have functioned as a means to promote cultural contact and dialogue between Etruscans and Greeks. Choosing the Argonauts' saga for this particular *olpe* was not random: the saga was, in fact, concerned with the Greeks' maritime explorations for the acquisition of mineral sources as well as the discovery of technical knowledge for the production of metal. Combining the saga with the figure of Daidalos, the artisan inventor who, in Greek mythology, was associated with Hephaistos, the Greek god of the forge, cannot have been random either: these images were placed upon an early example of *bucchero sottile*, a ceramic ware that was 'invented' by Etruscan potters as they perfected their firing techniques in order to produce metal-like black vessels out of increasingly refined *impasto* ware.[3] Adding material to the *bucchero* vessel's surface such as silver coating or ochre and cinnabar onto the existing engraved decoration made *bucchero* particularly prized. Given that the earliest and finest *bucchero sottile* comes from elite tomb groups at *Caere*, among which are the San Paolo tombs, it is reasonable to assume that this invention took place there prior to the middle of the seventh century BCE before the technology spread to other workshops across Etruria (Rasmussen, 1979; Naso, 2004).

The figure of Daidalos, therefore, may have alluded to the role of the craftsman in technological innovation and virtuosity. It also hints at the close relationship between the artisan and the elites whose mobility, confirmed by the epigraphic evidence as mentioned earlier, gave them access to reciprocity relations across Etruria and beyond that brought them new craft skills, including writing, and thus promoted their own role in innovation (Smith, 1998; Bonaudo, 2008–9). Indeed, the inscriptions on the *olpe* may have been functional to displaying the technique of writing first introduced in the late eighth century BCE. That writing was a technical innovation that was exhibited at the tomb is confirmed by the famous ivory writing tablet accompanied by writing tools, a bronze stilus and two ivory *spatulae*, found among the grave goods of the *Circolo degli Avori* at Marsiliana d'Albegna, a wealthy tomb containing a chariot among other objects (Minto, 1921, pp. 122, 127, 236–45). The San Paolo tombs and their content further support this interpretation: the quantity of the imported objects there, from across the Mediterranean, combined with locally produced fineware and bronze objects, is unprecedented; the intact side chamber of Tomb 2, which probably held more than a single burial given the finding of two cremated adults inside an *olla*, contained about 200 objects, including two inscribed *ollae* with the name of the male owner of the vessel and possibly of the tomb, and a rare imported object, a Greek bronze gorgon mask.

While the imports, particularly those from Corinth, hint at the far-flung relations of the owners of the San Paolo tombs, locally produced objects speak to the reciprocity relations and alliances of a political and economic nature between elite families across Etruria that were forged through the exchange of gifts. Among the *bucchero sottile* pottery of Tomb 1 is a *kyathos*, a drinking vessel with a single high handle, decorated with excision and relief decoration that is comparable to two other *kyathoi* coming from two other Caeretan elite burials, the Calabresi Tomb at the Sorbo cemetery and the already mentioned Montetosto Tumulus on the way to the coast. The conical foot of the *kyathos* carries an Etruscan inscription that is similar to those from the *kyathos* of the Calabresi Tomb and two others coming from *Tomba del Duce* at Vetulonia and Tomb 150 at the Casone cemetery near Monteriggioni north of Siena. All these inscriptions carry a linguistic formula that turned them into so-called 'speaking objects': the formula consists of a first person-object (*mi*) followed by a verb indicating the act of gift-giving (*muluvanice* = gave) and the personal name and family name of the gift-giver, the subject of the verb (Maras and Sciacca, 2011). The inscription of the San Paolo *kyathos* may thus be translated as 'Venel Paithinas gave me' recording an act of gift exchange. Indeed, the family name *Paithina* is attested on another *bucchero kyathos* from Santa Teresa di Gavorrano near Vetulonia and probably on one from Casale Marittimo in northern Etruria, indicating the network of gift exchange between southern and northern Etruria (Cappuccini, 2007).

These *muluvanice* inscriptions are also found on sixth-century BCE votive objects at one of the main sanctuaries of *Veii* at Portonaccio, which I will examine in the next chapter (Maras, 2013). Suffice it to say that *muluvanice* inscriptions on these objects indicate a very tight elite network of alliances and relations that made possible the exchange of resources, new technological skills and materials that we see in the archaeological record. Importantly, the network was permeable to elites of equal social status and of non-Etruscan origins. This is attested, again epigraphically, by the Etruscan inscription, mentioned before, from the *Tumulo del Re* at the Doganaccia *necropolis* of Tarquinia.

Hipukrates of the inscription is an individual of Greek aristocratic origin that becomes, in Etruscan, a gentilicial name. We have, in other words, a Greek aristocrat fully integrated into the structure of Etruscan society (Ampolo, 2017, pp. 68–70, 80–2). Another example comes from Vetulonia: the Caeretan script recognized in an inscription claiming ownership by a certain *Rachu Kakanas* and placed on a silver laminate cup, recently identified among the grave goods of the *Tomba del Duce*, may hint at the presence of itinerant craftsmen, or even the owner of the very cup (Cygielman and Rafanelli, 2004). We will see more, in the next chapter, of the materialization of the close relationship between elites and workshops in the sixth century BCE detected in the building and decorative programmes of private and public religious structures. The *olpe*, however, demonstrates that this kind of relationship had already been established a century earlier, and that gifts did change hands within the society of the living before they were deposited in the grave as part of the tomb furnishings. Ultimately, this archaeological evidence fits nicely with the legend, transmitted by ancient literary sources, of Demaratus, a Corinthian aristocratic exile and trader who fled his city of Corinth at the fall of his family dynasty in the middle of the seventh century BCE and travelled to Tarquinia (Ampolo, 2017). Here, he settled, bringing with him craftsmen who taught his fellow Etruscans the skills in clay modelling for architectural terracottas and roof tiles, an innovation linked to Corinth, as we shall see in the next chapter.

In fact, ostentation in the deployment of resources, technological innovation and conspicuous consumption was not limited to the tomb. While the history of discoveries predominantly showcases funerary sites, the few seventh-century BCE houses and residential structures that have been excavated do give us a glimpse of elite social practices above ground, so to speak. A clutch of elite residences established in the second half of the seventh century are known in northern Etruria: at Casalvecchio near Casale Marittimo, 15 kilometres away from Volterra, Castelnuovo Berardenga near Siena, and Poggio Civitate (Murlo) south of Siena (Talocchini, 1980; Esposito and Burchianti, 2009; Tuck, 2017). These residential complexes were located outside towns and associated with small *necropoleis* (Esposito, 1999; Tuck, 2009). Other elite houses existed inside urban centres, although our knowledge of the seventh century BCE is limited, partly because of poor preservation; the other problem is that the findings of roof clay tiles, a new building material introduced at around the middle of the century that revolutionized domestic and religious architecture along with stone foundations and mudbrick walls, are not exclusive to such residences. The evidence from Acquarossa near Viterbo, one of the few settlements for which we have extensive knowledge of domestic architecture, shows that tiles were used for all the excavated houses there (Wikander, 1993) so we can reasonably assume that this picture must have applied to larger towns.

On the other hand, once this architectural revolution was under way, elite families capitalized on this technological innovation: their houses are distinguished by the complex decorative programmes of their roofs and by their monumentality (Meyers, 2013). I will return to this innovation in the next chapter. Although so far limited, the evidence, on the other hand, of ostentation in the form of banqueting and drinking ceremonies inside urban elite houses is remarkably early. We see this at Poggio del Telegrafo, a prominent area of Populonia where a rectangular structure with thatched roof and wooden posts has been recently excavated (Bartoloni and Acconcia, 2007). The building, according to the excavators, was restored three times before its intentional abandonment in the first quarter of the seventh century BCE. The abandonment is contemporary with a pit filled in with almost 100 *kyathoi* and organic material in the earth fill: this suggests a single event involving eating and drinking, a rather strong manifestation of competitive social behaviour. The evidence from Poggio del Telegrafo also prompts questions with regard to the public nature of these ceremonial events: its excavators have proposed that a 100 people attended a ceremony that may have marked a change in the exercise of political power among Populonia's high-status groups. The plan of some of these elite houses did include spaces that may have been appropriate for collective ceremonies; this has been suggested, for example, for a house found at Roselle near Grosseto. The house was encircled by a large precinct and characterized by an external rectilinear plan and an internal oval plan, although this peculiarity and the small size of the interior space may, in fact, indicate the cultic function of this structure (Donati, 2000).

The residential complex of Poggio Civitate, located on a hill adjacent to Murlo, is perhaps the site that best illustrates all of the above, thanks to the continuous attention and field investigation that the site and its surroundings have received since the 1960s after its initial discovery in 1926. As such, Murlo offers the archaeologist an unmatched in-depth view of three phases of life of an Etruscan elite residential complex, starting with the first half of the seventh century BCE, when the earliest structure, unearthed as recently as 2015, was in use (Tuck, 2017) (Figure 3.14).

Figure 3.14 Earliest structure (EPOC 4 from south-west), Poggio Civitate (Murlo), photograph Anthony Tuck.

According to the preliminary and therefore still provisional account of such a recent find, the 20-metre-long structure, named early phase Orientalizing complex 4 by the excavators, had a rectilinear plan with a deep open portico, not unlike the plan of other houses known from Roselle and San Giovenale; the roof may have been covered by roof tiles and architectural decoration, a feature of the later Orientalizing complex. That it was a house of not just anybody is confirmed by the fine banqueting vessels recovered and the textile-making equipment located in the portico area. The second phase of life of the site has been known since the 1970s.[4] Ongoing excavation since then has revealed an Orientalizing complex consisting of a much larger rectangular residential building, *circa* 36 metres in length, covered with roof tiles and extensive architectural terracotta decoration, a smaller tripartite structure perpendicular to the residence and interpreted as a religious space, and, finally, an open-air workshop further south; both the tripartite and workshop buildings also had a tiled roof and roof terracotta ornaments such as cut-out *acroteria*. Feline head waterspouts and female head antefixes further decorated the edge of the workshop's roof. The presence of a large banqueting service, cooking and storage vessels in the large residential building hints not simply at the wealth of its owners, further confirmed by gold and silver jewellery, carved bone, antler and ivory fragments that probably decorated wooden furniture; it also points to the occurrence of large-scale lavish banquets for more than 200 participants (Berkin, 2003) (Figure 3.15).

The workshop, on the other hand, gives us a remarkable insight into the ability of the house owners at Poggio Civitate to capitalize on manufacturing activities of all kinds, from the working of hard material such as antler and bone to metallurgical activities, textile making, food production and the making of the very clay tiles and architectural terracottas that covered the buildings. The evidence at the workshop also tells us something about those involved in these activities: the occurrence of alphabetic letters on roofing material placed before firing and an inscribed ceramic spool suggests a certain level of skill in reading and writing by the producers and users of these objects. The writing of both single letters and signs on the roofing material, in particular, may have marked batches of production in relation to the enormous volume of tiles required for the roofs, which, according to the excavator's calculations, amounted to *circa* 28,000 kilograms just for the tiles of the workshop (Tuck and Wallace, 2013). Interestingly, while the owners of the house imported goods from Etruria, such as *bucchero* vessels with *muluvanice* inscriptions, and from outside the region as far away as the

Figure 3.15 Orientalizing complex, reconstruction, Poggio Civitate (Murlo), photograph Anthony Tuck.

Figure 3.16 Archaic complex, reconstruction, Poggio Civitate (Murlo), photograph Anthony Tuck.

Aegean (Wallace, 2008), the material produced at the workshop never left the site.

And yet, Poggio Civitate was not isolated: recent research has ascertained seventh- and sixth-century BCE occupation of the hills surrounding the site leading to the interpretation of the complex as an elite centre controlling a dispersed population inhabiting the surrounding hills that would have contributed to the building and maintenance of the Orientalizing complex and perhaps frequented the centre for religious purposes (Tuck, 2017). But what kind of control did Poggio Civitate exercise over its surrounding population? This is not an easy question to answer and one that has provoked much debate among Etruscologists. Like other elite residential complexes, Poggio Civitate thrived among much larger settlements and towns that were, by the late seventh century BCE, able to maintain and produce the wealth that elite groups displayed in their tombs. Only a view into the sixth century BCE, however, can help answer this question vis-à-vis urban growth, when the site was rebuilt following destruction by fire towards the end of the seventh century. The early sixth-century BCE complex, a square building enclosing a courtyard measuring *circa* 61 by 60 metres, was built on a much larger scale, mirroring the growing investment in building, production and technology of the largest cities. Indirectly, therefore Poggio Civitate shows us what urban growth meant for Etruria between the seventh and sixth centuries BCE: we turn to this very topic next (Figure 3.16).

4

THE ETRUSCAN NON-*POLIS*

URBAN GROWTH IN THE ARCHAIC PERIOD

PIAZZA D'ARMI AT *VEII* AND THE EARLIEST ARCHITECTURAL TERRACOTTAS

During the nineteenth and the beginning of the twentieth century, some archaeologists believed that the high terrace to the south of the main plateau of *Veii* known as Piazza d'Armi was the *acropolis* of the Etruscan city; George Dennis and eminent scholars Luigi Canina and Rodolfo Lanciani were of this opinion, but not everyone agreed. Its high position, naturally defended on three sides, was notable, but the terrace was separated from the plateau of the city by the gorge of the Fosso della Mola. To Ettore Gabrici, Neapolitan archaeologist then working at the Villa Giulia Museum, the area looked like an uncultivated patch with a few traces of ancient remains. In 1913, he went on to conduct the first ever stratigraphic excavation in the middle of the terrace, and brought to light painted tiles, parts of drystone walls and an elliptical structure dressed with *tufa* blocks, which he assumed belonged to a very early date prior to the flourishing of the Etruscans, but which we now know to be a cistern. Less than ten years later, field investigation in the area continued under the direction of Enrico Stefani who subsequently published the finds in 1944 (Stefani, 1944, p. 143). Among them were Iron Age huts, a series of buildings with stone blocks arranged according to an almost orthogonal plan, the remains of the ancient walls related to a large gate that, he saw, connected the terrace to the ancient city to the north (Figure 4.1).

Figure 4.1 Piazza d'Armi, *Veii* © Sapienza Università di Roma, Scienze dell'Antichità.

Stefani also identified a rectangular building of stone blocks sitting above some of the huts, just above 15 metres long and 8 metres wide, which he interpreted as an Italic sanctuary. The finds of this structure included clay tiles, found all around it, antefixes, that is, terracotta heads decorating the edges of roofs, painted eaves and over 400 fragments of terracotta friezes, decorated in relief with processions of armed men, riding on horses or on chariots, and a few traces left of polychrome paint. Because they were found on the front of the building, Stefani saw these friezes as belonging to the decoration of the entablature. These kinds of artefacts were not unknown in central Italy: similar roofing decorated material had been discovered as early as 1784 at Velletri, in *Latium*, near the Church of Santa Maria della Neve, and ended up in the National Museum of Naples. Others had been excavated at Poggio Buco, southern Tuscany, and the central Italian and Etruscan provenance of yet other pieces belonging to museum collections was identified. At the end of the nineteenth century, a comprehensive study by Giuseppe Pellegrini had been published and the terracottas interpreted as architectural decoration of religious buildings (Pellegrini, 1899). Unlike these others, however, the roof at Piazza d'Armi was found in situ and excavated stratigraphically. Stefani, in fact, recognized two distinct phases of the decoration of the

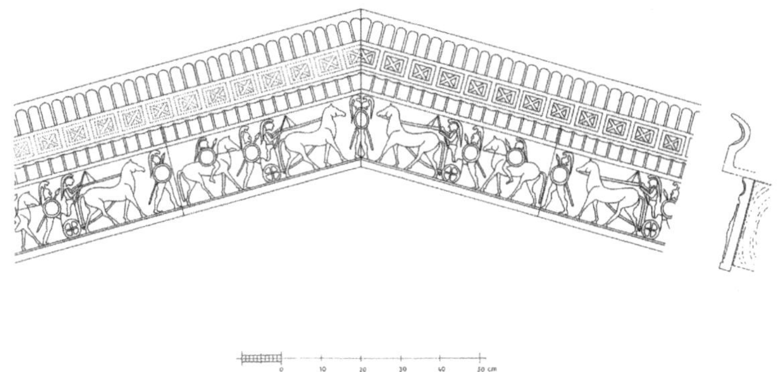

Figure 4.2 So-called *oikos*, reconstruction, Piazza d'Armi, *Veii*, drawing by Renate Sponer Za for Winter, N. 2009 *Symbols of Wealth and Power: Architectural Terracotta Decoration in Etruria and Central Italy, 640-510 B.C.* MAAR Suppl. 9, Ann Arbor.

building in the two different styles of the terracottas and antefixes. He thus offered a hypothetical reconstruction of the façade and front entablature of the temple as well as reporting on the plan of the building (Figure 4.2).

Since Stefani's publication, later excavations have partly confirmed and added to his interpretation of what is now known as the *oikos* temple; the building, for example, was found to have been enlarged before its abandonment, and a different reconstruction proposed from that suggested by Stefani (Bartoloni et al., 2006). There is no consensus, however, on the dates of the architectural terracottas, nor on their religious function. The current excavators see two distinct phases, as Stefani did, the first at the beginning and the second at the middle of the sixth century BCE (Bartoloni et al., 2006, pp. 63–8). Others date the roof to *circa* 580 BCE altogether, comparing it to other similar roof decoration from the so-called Regia, a building complex in the Roman Forum in Rome that has also been interpreted as having a religious function (Winter, 2009, pp. 224–8, 568). Further domestic structures and a road network between these structures have also been identified over the decades since the Soprintendenza continued the excavation from the 1960s. The so-called *oikos* temple itself was skirted by the main road, and facing onto this road, on the other side, was an elite house, interpreted as such by fine *bucchero* and other fineware, and by the monumental appearance of the building that included a portico. That different phases pertained to this road network importantly suggests that an urban plan of orthogonal roads was established as early as the second half of the seventh century although it is not until the middle of the sixth century BCE that we see the architectural monumentalization that characterizes Tyrrhenian cities in this century (Bartoloni et al., 2005; Acconcia, 2019). The *oikos* temple, we now know, was no longer used beyond the second half of the sixth century BCE and thus never became a large sanctuary if it ever had this original function. The emergence of increasingly larger sanctuaries dedicated to the worship of deities that we see at *Veii* with the development of the Portonaccio sanctuary, is found across Central Tyrrhenian Italy, as we shall see later. This has led some to doubt the *oikos* temple's cultic function; in fact, the current excavators of Piazza d'Armi view the area as belonging to a prominent elite family who performed cultic activities at the *oikos* temple and continued to live there after these activities ceased and the building was subjected to spoliation of its terracottas in a phase of change and urban growth.

A BUILDING REVOLUTION?

As mentioned in the previous chapter, the introduction of roof tiles replacing the use of thatched roofs, and of stone foundation and mudbrick walls was revolutionary in building technology, and as such its impact on urban living cannot be overemphasized enough. Not only did it enable the construction of much larger buildings, thus spearheading other innovations in architectural technical knowledge necessary for ensuring a long life for these buildings, whether they were used for residential or religious purposes, but it also allowed a more rational organization of urban space and the realization of monumental infrastructure and public buildings, from walls and roads to sanctuaries, even though thatched roofs did not completely go out of use (Brandt and Karlsson, 2001; Izzet, 2007, pp. 143–64; Thomas and Meyers, 2013; Wikander and Tobin, 2017).[1] At Acquarossa, the extensively excavated areas have revealed tile-roofed houses of one to four rooms, all arranged in a row, often with a portico in front, and a building, known as House E in zone F, that enclosed a walled courtyard (Strandberg Olofsson, 1989). The so-called courtyard house, in fact, is a house type found elsewhere in Etruria and *Latium*: it may have originally had a special, if not religious, function before becoming a standard feature of domestic architecture from Rome to Spina on the Adriatic as we shall see in the next chapter. An orthogonal plan at Acquarossa is detected only for the last phase of the town's occupation before its abandonment at *circa* 550 or 525 BCE, as the earlier houses were built around communal open spaces, some of which had a well. Only a fraction of Acquarossa's plateau of *circa* 32 hectares has been excavated, and the settlement itself, probably comprising a few thousand inhabitants, was small when compared with the much larger cities in Tyrrhenian southern Etruria. The site nevertheless does give us an idea of what innovation in architecture meant from the middle of the eighth to the late sixth centuries BCE for a sizeable settlement (Pallottino and Wikander, 1986). This is particularly because none of these larger cities have survived in such a well-preserved state. Detailed studies of the roofs at Acquarossa have furthermore demonstrated that it hosted some of the earliest workshops of clay roofs in southern Etruria, beginning between 640 and 620 BCE. Other very early workshops have been identified at *Caere*, but the roofing material there comes from large pits which were probably originally quarries and were later reused as dumps following the reorganization of the urban space (Winter, 2009, pp. 539–46).

Since the earliest excavation at Piazza d'Armi, much scholarship has developed around the origins of this roofing innovation and its integration into existing earlier architecture, particularly because, as indicated before, this innovation spread beyond Etruria into *Latium*, including Rome. The early rooftop terracotta decoration of the workshop of the Orientalizing complex at Poggio Civitate is similar to the roof ridge decoration of contemporary terracotta house-shaped urns coming from *Caere*, but the feline head waterspouts and female head antefixes were mould-made with no indigenous precedent. Likewise, the late seventh-century BCE roofs at Acquarossa were decorated with white-on-red painting that was also employed on local ceramic vessels. At the beginning of the sixth century BCE, however, new elements and decorative motifs were introduced to roofs from Acquarossa to *Caere*.

A broader view on the origins of new architectural forms and techniques points to Greek Corinth, where the early seventh-century BCE temple of Apollo and the later Temple of Poseidon at Isthmia displayed tiles that are comparable to those found in Etruria. The use of female heads and feline head waterspouts on the temple of Hera at Corfu, another Greek temple under the control of Corinth, further suggests that Corinthian craftsmen may have been responsible for introducing the new roof construction technology to central Italy. That Etruscan cities like *Caere* had preferential trade relations with Corinth is confirmed by the volume of Corinthian imported pottery as known from elite tomb groups such as the San Paolo tombs mentioned in the previous chapter. But *Caere* was not the only city with these trade connections: Rome's early sixth-century BCE roofs, such as that of the Regia in the Forum, mentioned earlier, reveal a similar Corinthian connection in the mould-made reliefs that would be adopted across Etruria in the sixth century (Winter, 2017). Poggio Civitate, too, reveals stylistic and iconographic links with Corinth in the lavish decoration of the roof that covered the new monumental courtyard building: terracotta friezes displaying images of a horse race, a banquet and a procession following a cart have their comparable counterparts in Corinthian vase painting; so do some of the *acroteria* statues that decorated the roof ridges and that included animals such as horses, bulls, mythical figures such as sphinxes and a griffin, and seated figures interpreted as the ancestors of the owners of the new residential complex (Winter, 2017, pp. 134–5).

This is a scenario of technological innovation not unlike the one I described in the previous chapter. However, sixth-century BCE innovation did not simply benefit elites, a phenomenon we often associate with the seventh century BCE as argued previously, but it was also promoted by a growth in mobility and trade at this time across the central-west Mediterranean. This is confirmed by a wide and diverse range of evidence, archaeological and literary as well as epigraphic, which I will explore in this chapter. Scholars have recently argued that this evidence, in turn, throws light upon increasing mobility and exchange as one of the main drivers of urban growth. One example should suffice to illustrate this particular point: after *circa* 560 BCE roof ornamentation that up until then had been used on both elite houses and religious buildings in Etruria became restricted to the latter only; shortly thereafter, from *circa* 550 BCE, we see a further innovation in roof decoration and roof-building techniques. This shift in tradition had implications for the craft environment and, at the same time, coincides with the displacement, recounted by Greek historian Herodotus (1.164–68), of populations from Greek cities in Asia Minor, in the eastern Mediterranean; some of those displaced from the Greek city of Phocaea moved to Corsica. This led, as Herodotus tells us, to a military conflict in 540 BCE, the so-called Battle of the Sardinian Sea, between a Carthaginian and Etruscan alliance and the Greek Phoceans who won in the end and abandoned Corsica to settle in Campania (Winter, 2017, pp. 147–8). Since historical sources can never be taken at face value, scholars have interpreted the Greek historian's account in different ways, but that Ionian Greeks from Asia Minor were present in substantial numbers in the central Mediterranean in the sixth century BCE is confirmed by the archaeological evidence. With the establishment of Massalia, at *circa* 600 BCE, a Greek settlement today underneath modern Marseilles in southern France, we see the impact of a Greek Ionian style and iconography on material culture, both imported and locally made, from pottery decoration to the very roof ornamentation mentioned above. The impact is detected not only in Etruria but also across the broader central Italian region and further afield in the central-west Mediterranean (Cristofani, 1976a; Spivey, 1997, pp. 53–76; Bonaudo, 2004; Hemelrijk, 2009). The closest comparison of the new chariot races depicted on architectural terracottas and other decorative motifs such as floral patterns on roofs after 550 BCE are with motifs found in Greek cities in Ionian Asia Minor (Winter, 2017); it is not therefore far-fetched to suggest that Ionian Greek craftsmen were responsible for this further innovation at a time when we see a greater investment in communal cult sites inside and outside cities.

BUOYANT TRADE AND THE PRODUCTIVE ECONOMY

Growing mobility and exchange also meant the greater opening of Etruscan communities to increasingly buoyant trade links near and far across the central-west Mediterranean from the Tyrrhenian to the Adriatic Sea. There are several lines of evidence pointing to this. I shall focus on three broad themes: first, itinerant craftsmen, as noted earlier, point to interregional contacts; second, the establishment of ports and coastal settlements as trading centres; and third, the movement of goods to and from Etruria. The restriction of innovative roof decoration to religious buildings probably led to a decline in the demand of the craft and therefore in the number of local workshops, and to the corresponding rise of incoming craftsmanship from outside. That some craftsmen were itinerant is implied in the ancient written sources: Pliny the Elder (*HN* 35.157) tells us that according to Varro an Etruscan artist from *Veii*, Vulca was called to Rome by Tarquinius Priscus to create terracotta sculpture for the Capitoline temple in Rome dedicated to Jupiter, Juno and Minerva. Plutarch (*Poplicola* 14), on the other hand, points to the later Tarquinius Superbus as the ruler that commissioned the temple, leaving Vulca to belong to this phase of heightened mobility.

Iconographic and stylistic examination of the actual architectural terracottas has been combined, where possible, with scientific analysis, and this has corroborated our views on interregional exchange. This is the case with the mould-made painted terracotta female head antefixes belonging to the so-called Etrusco-Ionian roof of a small temple dated to *circa* 540–530 BCE and dedicated to an Italic goddess, Mater Matuta, at *Satricum*, a Latin settlement south-east of Rome (Knoop, 1987). Petrographic analysis of the clay of these antefixes has identified this clay as originating in the Tolfa Mountains just north of *Caere*, and the fabric to be the same as that of the products of *Caere*'s workshops. The suggestion that the roof may have been imported from *Caere* has been repeatedly made (Lulof, 2006; Winter, 2009, pp. 436, 537), and sits well with the evidence we have of Etruscans making votive offerings to the sanctuary at *Satricum*. This is startlingly documented by a seventh-century BCE Etruscan dedicatory inscription engraved on a *bucchero* cup by a certain *Laris Velchaina* whom we also find at *Caere*. Further evidence of the lively itinerant craft environment at *Caere* comes from Marzabotto, a town over 400 kilometres away: here, a later fifth-century BCE temple dedicated to *Tinia/Tina* (Greek Zeus) was decorated with mould-made terracottas that are stylistically close to those found at *Caere* (Sassatelli and Govi, 2005). We shall return to Marzabotto in the next chapter.

The broader context of this exchange is also strongly political: the iconographic programme of the roof's decoration of religious buildings was chosen carefully by the ruling classes of these cities who exploited the mythical figures and narratives represented on the roofs in order to send political messages that would have been understood by some, though not all, social segments of the community. Thus, the roof of the temple at *Satricum* was notably decorated with a central life-size terracotta statue group placed on the ridge pole and representing Herakles and a female figure with drapery, perhaps Athena; we find similar statue groups adorning coeval temples' roofs elsewhere, from Etruria to Campania. In particular, statue groups of Herakles (Etruscan *Herkle*) and Athena (Etruscan *Menrva*, or another female deity), illustrating the ascension of the hero to the Olympus with the help of the armed female goddess who ensured his protection, have been found in the following locations: in Rome at the *Forum Boarium*, a commercial and port area near the Tiber, underneath a pair of fourth-century BCE twin temples dedicated to the Italic goddesses of Fortuna and Mater Matuta, in the so-called sacred area of Sant'Omobono; at *Veii* at the Portonaccio sanctuary where the statue group is coeval with the earliest monumental building; at *Caere*, at the site of Vigna Parrocchiale within the city where the statue group, found in fragments in a votive pit, must have adorned a temple in the vicinity, possibly similarly dedicated to a female goddess; at *Pyrgi*, *Caere*'s coastal port, where again a fragmentary statue group inside the sanctuary is associated with the worship of female fertility deities; finally at Velletri and Caprifico in *Latium*, and *Pompeii* (Lulof, 2000, 2016; Potts, 2018). We shall return later to the political significance of these figures, but here it is sufficient to note that while these statue groups are all in cities near Rome they are also all associated with places of intense cross-regional interaction and, notably, ports of trade or *emporia*, from Rome's *Forum Boarium* to *Pyrgi* and *Satricum* (Potts, 2018, pp. 119–21).

It is to these ports that I would like to turn to as the second line of evidence of Etruria's greater opening up to the outside world.[2] *Pyrgi* is one of a series of such settlements linked to, and controlled by, the cities located inland, that flourished on the Tyrrhenian coast in the sixth century BCE as a result of this opening (Michetti, 2016). Not all have been excavated; in fact, sporadic findings along the coast suggest that several landing sites must have existed, some smaller than other, with not much infrastructure, but taking advantage of secure mooring points along the northern Tyrrhenian coast that was characterized by lagoons until the end of the nineteenth century of our era. These are, however, difficult to locate archaeologically unlike those harbour sites that hosted a monumental sanctuary and significant infrastructure. Like *Pyrgi*, Gravisca, less than 10 kilometres away from Tarquinia, is particularly notable in this respect, largely thanks to the forty-year-long investment in field research there: this gives us a fairly accurate picture of the function and transformation of this type of site from its earliest structures dated to *circa* 580 BCE to its destruction in 280 BCE that was followed by the establishment of a Roman *colonia* (Fiorini, 2005; Fiorini and Torelli, 2010; Mercuri and Fiorini, 2014) (Figure 4.3).

Sitting on what used to be a narrow coastal lagoon, belonging today to a protected nature reserve, Le Saline, the excavated area of Gravisca consists of the religious buildings that formed the sanctuary of the harbour. The harbour itself was probably located just south of these buildings, as suggested by recent investigations that partially brought to light, west of the buildings, fourth-century BCE rectilinear structures with an east–west orientation, and which the excavator, Lucio Fiorini, has interpreted as belonging to slipways for the movement of boats (Fiorini and Materazzi, 2017, pp. 10–11). The sanctuary itself went through several phases of

Figure 4.3 Gravisca, aerial view of the sanctuary, from Bagnasco Gianni, G. and L. Fiorini 2018 Between Tarquinia and Gravisca, in É. Gailledrat, M. Dietler and R. Plana-Mallart (eds) *The Emporion in the ancient western Mediterranean. Trade and colonial encounters from the Archaic to the Hellenistic period*, 155–66, Montpellier.

construction and refurbishment, which denote significant changes in the type and nature of religious cult activity at the site over time. The earliest shrine, dedicated to Aphrodite, was followed by the reorganization and enlargement of the sanctuary, which included a shrine dedicated to another Greek female deity, Hera, during the middle of the sixth century BCE. Yet other later renovations were made, including a road linking Tarquinia to the port, constructed at the beginning of the fifth century BCE, thus highlighting the control of the site by the city. Aimed at Greek deities, the earlier cult activities took place in what is known as the Southern Area of the sanctuary: here, furnaces and implements point to metalworking activities and the processing of copper and iron, which we find in other contemporary coastal sanctuaries, most recently at *Regae*-Regisvilla, the partially excavated port of Vulci (Regoli, 2017). To the north of this Southern Area is the so-called Northern Area, that was monumentalized as it became the focus for the worship of two chthonic Etruscan deities, perhaps *Suri* and *Cavatha* (see Religion and the city), to which two monumental altars were dedicated (Fortunelli, 2007).

That the sanctuary was a meeting ground for worshippers coming from different regions of the Mediterranean is confirmed by the very deities worshipped there, the votive objects offered to them, many of them ceramic drinking vessels imported from Attica in the Aegean, and the inscriptions placed on some of these objects. The inscriptions are particularly valuable because they sometimes allow us to determine the provenance of non-Etruscan worshippers (Johnston and Pandolfini Angeletti, 2000). Several came from the Greek city of Samos, in Asia Minor, and were probably responsible for introducing the cult of Hera; some of them practised this cult at *Naukratis*, another sanctuary frequented by Samians on the Nile Delta in Egypt, as confirmed by contemporary epigraphic evidence from both *Naukratis* and Gravisca (Johnston, 2019). This significantly adds to the scenario of an increasingly more mobile trading Mediterranean in which Etruscan cities played no insignificant role. The most famous Greek inscription at Gravisca, however, was engraved on a stone anchor by a certain *Sostratos* (Harvey, 1976; Fiorini, 2015): this fragmentary inscription mentions *Sostratos* himself and 'Aeginetan Apollo', to whom the anchor was dedicated, revealing Aegina, an Aegean island in the Saronic Gulf opposite Attica, as the provenance of the dedicant. Whether *Sostratos* at Gravisca, as has been suggested, is the descendant of another Aeginetan *Sostratos*, whom Herodotus mentions (Herodotus IV, 152) as a successful merchant, is difficult to establish. If that correspondence were true, however, it would not simply hint at the extraordinary success of the trading ventures of *Sostratos'* family; it would also demonstrate the role of Gravisca as a key stop-over in these ventures (Figure 4.4).

The benefits that a harbour sanctuary like Gravisca could offer, however, were reciprocal: Etruscan worshippers mixed and mingled with Greek visitors there, and this interaction provided trading opportunities for both while leading to changes in local religious worship habits, as shown by Etruscan inscriptions on votive offerings. I will return to these changing habits below; for now, it is sufficient to emphasize the multiculturalism that denotes Gravisca as well as other harbour sites not only on the Tyrrhenian coast, at *Pyrgi* for example, but also at other later Etruscan coastal settlements and other sanctuaries much further afield (Johnston, 2001). An Etruscan dedicatory inscription on a Greek Laconian cup dated to the third quarter of the sixth century BCE comes from Aegina itself and its extra-urban sanctuary of Aphaia whose cult was as open to outsiders as were the ones at Gravisca (Cristofani, 1993b). Closer to home, in the Po Valley and south of it

Figure 4.4 Inscribed stone anchor with *Sostratos* dedication, Gravisca © Museo Nazionale Etrusco di Villa Giulia. Archivio fotografico.

in the area known as Etruria Padana, are the harbour settlements of Adria and Spina, established in the course of the sixth century BCE in the wetland environment of the delta of the river Po along the northern Adriatic coast. These settlements reveal equally lively relations among Greeks, Etruscans and local populations. Their expansion, along with other smaller satellite sites nearby, as a result of the flourishing trade in the region from the late sixth century, is documented by the arrival there of imported Greek transport *amphorae* and Greek, mostly Attic, painted fine ware, several fragments of which carry Greek inscriptions.

Of these inscriptions, many consist of trademarks, that is, painted or engraved marks or letter tags that referred to the commercial transaction of the imported vessels themselves and that are also documented across southern Etruria; the surviving majority, in fact, comes from Vulci. Indeed, most Attic vessels bearing these trademarks originate from southern Etruria and, in lesser quantities, from Greek colonial sites in southern Italy (Johnston, 1979, 2006). From Adria, established before Spina in the early part of the sixth century BCE on the northern branches of the Po river, comes an Attic Black-Figure painted cup dated to *circa* 540–530 BCE and carrying a painted inscription that greets the reader and says to him/her 'buy me' (Gaucci, 2010, 2012; Baldassarra, 2013, pp. 33–9). This type of inscription painted on other contemporary similar cups known as little-master cups that are found elsewhere in Italy, from Etruria, including Gravisca, to Sicily, and across the Mediterranean basin, indicates clearly the dynamic commercial network that moved these drinking vessels from Athens across the sea. The presence at Adria of trademarks written in Etruscan rather than Greek script, which we also see at Vulci between the late sixth and first decade of the fifth century BCE, further confirms the commercial entanglement between Greek and Etruscan traders, and the control, by Etruscan traders and middlemen, of the movement of batches of imported vessels in different directions across Etruscan Italy between the Tyrrhenian and the Adriatic (Baldassarra, 2013, pp. 262–3). Recent epigraphic studies have moreover shown that the extant types of Greek trademarks found at Adria are also found at nearby Spina, located in the southern branches of the Po, Bologna, and across southern and inland Etruria, as well as Campania and Greek settlements in Sicily and southern Italy. Just as interestingly, local types of trademarks identified at Adria, which is probable evidence of Greeks living locally, have been found in the east Mediterranean, from the Aegean to Rhodes and Cyprus (Baldassarra, 2013, pp. 269–70).

I will return to Adria, Spina, and other 'new towns' established in the northern Adriatic in the following chapter in order to examine the broadening of trade contacts from the Italic peninsula to continental Europe via the Po Valley. Here, it is sufficient to highlight the dynamism, which all this epigraphic evidence demonstrates, of these Adriatic harbour sites, which grew into commercial hubs from the late sixth century BCE, and followed the dynamism of Tyrrhenian coastal sites in the earlier decades of the century. It is also, however, worth reminding the reader that, while offering us a direct and attention-grabbing glimpse into the involvement of individual traders or middlemen, this evidence may very well reflect the tip of the iceberg of the volume of goods that moved in and out of Etruscan Italy. It also gives us a very partial view of what types of goods were traded.

Indeed, if Greek painted fineware appears prominent in the archaeological record this is so for two reasons: first, the high survival rate of pottery vis-à-vis other materials, from organic ones such as wood, leather or textiles, which barely survive in the record, to metals, some of which were recyclable and recycled. This unfortunately fails to offer a precise accuracy of what was traded where. Second, unlike coarseware, painted fineware, even when found in small fragments and especially when carrying figured decoration, is easily recognizable according to type, and therefore datable and traceable to specific contexts of production. Greek pottery with painted figured decoration has ultimately received the lion's share of scholarly attention since the large-scale excavation of tomb groups at Vulci that flooded the art market with it in the nineteenth century. It is only relatively recently that other types of ceramic fineware, especially those produced in Etruria, from *bucchero* ware to painted pottery imitating Greek decorative techniques (Etrusco-Corinthian and Etruscan black figure pottery), have received comprehensive attention in studies of Etruscan trade (Martelli, 1987; Spivey, 1987; Szilágyi, 1992; Naso, 2004; Paleothodoros, 2010; Bellelli, 2011a; Benelli, 2017). Similarly, coarseware, either imported or locally produced and then exported, has only relatively recently received scholarly attention despite its fundamental importance in the study of ancient trade. Coarseware, in the form of transport *amphorae* and *pithoi* or storage jars, was used for the transport and storage of agricultural produce from olive oil to wine and cereals, that is, the range of products of the agricultural economy that characterized pre-Roman Italy and the Mediterranean more broadly, and is therefore particularly helpful when addressing the nature of the Etruscan economy and the movement of trade goods, the third and final theme of this section.

Our current knowledge of archaic imported transport *amphorae*, which are mostly but not exclusively Greek from across the Mediterranean, is largely known from funerary contexts in southern Etruria. Here we have the earliest presence of these *amphorae* from *circa* the middle of the seventh to the end of the sixth century BCE, with a particular concentration of these transport vessels at *Caere* (Rizzo, 1990). Fewer and mostly fragmentary examples come from settlements, from the larger cities such as Tarquinia (Chiaramonte Treré and Bagnasco Gianni, 1999, pp. 262–77) to smaller communities such as Poggio Civitate, the Tyrrhenian harbour sites of Gravisca, *Pyrgi* and *Regae*-Regisvilla, and discovered in an underwater shipwreck site off the coast of the Giglio Island opposite the Tuscan coast (Cristofani, 1985). Rather than reflecting an ancient reality, however, the paucity of *amphorae* outside tombs is a result of the incomplete study of this material as well as the genuine difficulty in identifying *amphora* fragments from stratigraphic excavations. Fragments from Greek *amphorae*, for instance, have been identified from coarseware fragments collected during the archaeological survey of the Albegna river valley, but this identification is not certain (Perkins, 1999, p. 143). A more thorough state of the published evidence and therefore of our view over the importation and movement of Greek *amphorae* is from inland and coastal sites of Etruria Padana, including Adria and Spina, where these *amphorae* have been excavated from later tomb groups and settlements (Sacchetti, 2012); we will return to the Adriatic in the next chapter.

To complicate matters further, like many other coarseware and fineware ceramics, specific types of imported transport *amphorae* were copied and manufactured outside their original place of production. This generates tremendous challenges to our attempts at tracing trade routes, and can only be properly assessed through an archeometric analysis of the vessels' clay. This is the case, for instance, with the early Sardinian manufacture of Phoenician Levantine-shaped *amphorae*, known as 'Sant'Imbenia-type' *amphorae*, only very recently identified, and so-called from the early first-millennium BCE trading centre at Sant'Imbenia, north-west Sardinia, where these *amphorae* were produced (Roppa, 2012). We now know that these *amphorae* were widely distributed from the eighth century BCE in the central western Mediterranean. Although only a few finds are so far known from Italy, future studies may well change this picture and demonstrate that not only more of them reached Tyrrhenian central Italy, but that they inspired the very early local manufacture of *amphorae* in Etruria (Tronchetti, 2015, p. 273). Indeed, this scenario is not far-fetched given that, by the end of the eighth century BCE, the earliest Phoenician and Greek settlements had been established in the central Mediterranean from Sardinia and Sicily to the north African coast with Carthage, and Phoenicians were travelling even further west all the way to the Iberian peninsula.[3] A final aspect to bear in mind is that, as with Attic fineware or indeed any other traded goods, the actual traders may not have been the producers of the goods: a striking example of this is a type of Attic *amphora* known as SOS *amphora* that circulated throughout the Mediterranean basin from the second half of the eighth to the beginning of the sixth century BCE, and reached south Etruscan cities such as Vulci and *Veii* with a particular concentration at *Caere*. The presence of these *amphorae* at Phoenician sites and along Phoenician routes across the basin suggests that they reached southern Etruria in the seventh century BCE through Phoenician trade (Pratt, 2015).

The last quarter of the seventh century BCE is also the date of our earliest secure finds of Etruscan transport *amphorae* documented at Doganella, a newly established site near Marsiliana d'Albegna, and from eastern Languedoc in southern France. These finds mark the beginning of a flourishing trade of Etruscan products aimed at indigenous and Greek communities in southern France after the establishment of Greek Massalia (Dietler, 2005; Gori and Bettini, 2006). This trade is documented by the wide-ranging distribution of *amphorae* and other Etruscan exports such as *bucchero kantharoi* (drinking cups with two high handles) and, in much lesser quantities, metal vessels across the region, from coastal and inland sites to underwater shipwreck sites off the French coast (Long, Pomey, and Sourisseau, 2002). That the content of these *amphorae* was also wine is extraordinarily confirmed by the most noteworthy of these underwater sites: this is the so-called Grand Ribaud F sunken ship dated to the end of the sixth or beginning of the fifth century BCE, and found by the island of Grand Ribaud, east of Marseilles. The cargo of this ship contained about 1,200 to 1,400 Etruscan *amphorae* associated with vine shoots and grape pips, and estimated to have carried 300 hectolitres of wine (Long, Gantès, and Rival, 2006). Although this exceptionally large cargo is not comparable to those of other much smaller ships also carrying Etruscan *amphorae* and sunken off the French coast, it nevertheless gives us an idea of the buoyancy of the Etruscan agricultural economy and its export market towards the end of the sixth century BCE.

Testimony to this buoyancy is the concurrent growth of sites in the course of the sixth century BCE in the southern Etruscan countryside, detected through archaeological field survey. In the Albegna river valley, perhaps the most thoroughly archaeologically investigated valley in Etruscan Italy, the increase of rural sites in this century is twofold and follows the foundation of Doganella, which has been interpreted as a centre for the production and distribution of transport *amphorae*, and from which comes the only archaic *amphora* kiln known so far (Perkins and Walker, 1990). Towards the end of the century and contemporary with the Grand Ribaud F shipwreck, is the emergence of sizeable farms, of which only a few have been excavated. One of these, only very recently excavated near Marsiliana and aptly called the House of Amphorae, held *amphorae* and *pithoi* that contained wine, oil, some kind of resin and bee's wax or honey according to the scientific analysis of their content's organic residues (Zifferero, 2017). Whether honey was, in fact, used as an additive to wine is not unreasonable. But it is not surprising that Etruscan *amphorae* such as these transported food produce other than wine; analysis of the cargoes of other sunken ships has detected traces of fish bones and olive pips among the contents of the *amphorae* (Figures 4.5, 4.6 and 4.7).

Archaic Etruscan trade went much further afield than southern France: transport *amphorae* and other Etruscan goods, from *bucchero* to other types of fine ware such as Etrusco-Corinthian pottery reached several other southern regions of the central Mediterranean, from *Latium* and Sardinia to Campania and Sicily. However, the northern littorals, from the Ligurian coast to southern France, were undoubtedly the prime destination of Etruscan goods and were frequented by Etruscan traders directly. It is the epigraphic combined with the archaeological

Figure 4.5 House of Amphorae, the site under excavation, Marsiliana d'Albegna, photograph Archivio UNISI by Andrea Zifferero, courtesy Andrea Zifferero.

Figure 4.6 House of Amphorae, plan, Marsiliana d'Albegna, author Duccio Calamandrei, photograph Archivio UNISI, courtesy Andrea Zifferero.

Figure 4.7 House of Amphorae, virtual reconstruction, Marsiliana d'Albegna, author Duccio Calamandrei, photograph Archivio UNISI, courtesy Andrea Zifferero.

evidence, once again, that points to this scenario. A corpus of Etruscan short inscriptions or graffiti engraved on Etruscan ceramics comes from two indigenous settlements on the southern French coast: these are Saint Blaise, a flourishing trading site not far from Massalia and one of the best-known and well-excavated sites of the Lower Rhone basin, and Lattes, a fortified well-planned port town established at around 500 BCE in eastern Languedoc. At Lattes, excavations near the southern gate of the town's fortification have brought to light three houses, built at the beginning of the life of the town, and probably inhabited by Etruscan residents to judge from the predominance of Etruscan pottery, some of which bore Etruscan inscriptions; the destruction of these houses by fire around 475 BCE marks the moment when this Etruscan presence disappears from the site, which goes hand in hand with the decline of Etruscan imports to southern France more broadly from the middle to late sixth century BCE (Gailledrat, 2015).

The date 475 BCE is also the most probable date of another tantalizing epigraphic document, a lead tablet, rolled up in a cylinder, discovered in 1950 at Pech Maho, one of several so-called *oppidum* sites located on a lagoon, just south of Narbonne in western Languedoc. Used as a lead weight for fishing nets, more than twenty years passed before the little cylinder of lead was unrolled, restored and its two inscriptions, one in Etruscan, the other in Ionian Greek, discovered (Pébarthe and Delrieux, 1999). Both inscriptions give details of commercial transactions between parties, but they were not engraved at the same time: the earlier Etruscan one is also the more fragmented and hence difficult to read, but we can easily make out the personal names of two individuals involved in an exchange occurring at Massalia. The later, better preserved Greek text also records a transaction of goods, one of which is a small boat, between partners associated with the inhabitants of *Emporion*, a coastal Greek–Iberian settlement, located near modern-day Empúries in northern Catalonia. While the reuse of a written text is intriguing, both texts demonstrate the sophistication of commercial transactions, in the formal recording of these (Wilson, 1997–8). They are also not alone in doing so, since more such commercial letters written in some Iberian language have been found in the region, at Pech Maho itself and *Emporion* (Demetriou, 2012, pp. 40–2, 231) (Figure 4.8).

Writing, in fact, had already been put to use for other types of contracts or bonds of reciprocity less than a century earlier: a few minute ivory plaques in the shape of animals and inscribed with the personal and gentilicial names of individuals have been interpreted as hospitality

Figure 4.8 Pech Maho lead tablet, Greek text (above), Etruscan text (below) © Centre Camille Jullian.

letters on the basis of the later Latin *tesserae hospitales*: these latter, as we know from archaeological and literary sources, were formed of two identical matching pieces that two parties exchanged in the formal act of forging a relationship of reciprocity. One of these plaques, found at the site of Sant' Omobono in Rome, is written in the Etruscan of Rome: the text mentions a well-known Etruscan gentilicial name, *Spurianas*, and another name spelt as if it was a gentilicial name, that may refer to the Phoenician city of *Sulkis*, in south-west Sardinia. Another comes from the S. Monica *necropolis* at Carthage and may have been written at Tarquinia or Vulci according to the palaeographic analysis of its text, which mentions a Punic individual from Carthage. A few others come from the Orientalizing building at Poggio Civitate where they may have been manufactured (Maggiani, 2006). Dating to the earlier part or middle of the sixth century BCE, these plaques may be read as evidence of the evolution of the mechanics of trade towards the middle of the first millennium BCE, when the earlier network of elite alliances expanded as a result of urban and economic growth across the central and west Mediterranean, a situation epitomized by the Pech Maho lead letter.

RELIGION AND THE CITY

As has been noted earlier, the rise of monumental sanctuaries both inside and outside cities is part and parcel of this regional growth. These sites are, in fact, absolutely crucial to understanding the multiple levels of engagement in religion by urban communities, from the political use of these sanctuaries by local rulers to the actual votive habits of individual worshippers (Colonna, 1985).[4] They illustrate at once the tremendous cultural and economic vivacity of archaic Etruscan society already outlined, and the political competition and instability within and among cities in the context of an increasingly unstable wider central Mediterranean region. The Battle of the Sardinian Sea, noted earlier, was the first in a series of sea battles which saw cities in the region jostling for dominance and economic control. The sanctuary at *Pyrgi*, one of *Caere*'s coastal harbours, exemplifies this magnificently: here, first one, then a second monumental temple, was constructed in the space of about fifty years, following the earliest shrines known largely from decorative terracotta fragments, at a time when inside *Caere* the renovation of the urban infrastructure, from roads to hydraulic works, went hand in hand with the construction of other sanctuaries at the heart of the city (Bellelli, 2016)[5] (Figure 4.9).

At *Pyrgi*, the earlier temple was erected in the last decade of the sixth century BCE along with a stone precinct which led to the sanctuary via a monumental entrance, together with other ancillary buildings and

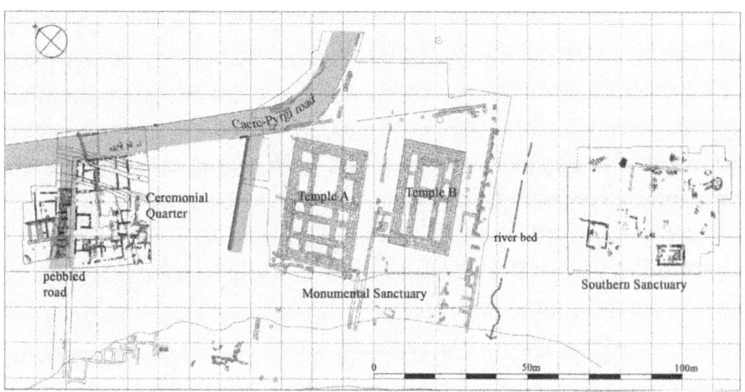

Figure 4.9 *Pyrgi*, the plan of the site © Sapienza Università di Roma, Missione Archeologica di Pyrgi.

structures that included altars, pits, a cistern, and a series of twenty small rooms of equal size running along the southern side of the temple and facing a series of altars. While the function of these rooms is still debated, their position and the terracotta antefixes that decorated them clearly point to a religious use, perhaps for ritual dining. Contemporary with this imposing building programme was the renovation of a cult area south of this first temple separated by a channel linked to a fresh water source: here, votive objects, mostly in the form of pottery, much of which imported from Athens, were offered at shrines to cults connected to *Fufluns*, the Etruscan deity who was merged with Greek Dionysos. Demeter was also worshipped here, as we know from the inscribed dedications to *Cavatha*, an Etruscan female goddess corresponding to *Kore* (later *Persephone*), Demeter's daughter, and *Śuri*, corresponding to Greek Hades, Kore's husband (Baglione and Gentili, 2013; Michetti, 2016).

This first temple at *Pyrgi* was decorated with the sculpture group of Herakles and a female deity, which Etruscologists have interpreted as Hera, and which, in the Etruscan pantheon, corresponded to *Uni*, whose cult is well-attested across southern Etruria. Etruscologists seem to agree that here, as at other sanctuaries where a similar group was placed on the temple roof, as noted earlier, the decorative programme was intended to represent Herakles' ascension to Mount Olympus following the successful outcome of the hero's labours, and hence his transition from hero to god (Colonna, 2000; Lulof, 2000; Winter and Lulof, 2016; Lulof and Smith, 2017). Several of these labours have also been identified in the rest of the terracotta decoration of this first temple, much of which has been found in fragments, thus making the accurate identification of many of the mythical figures represented difficult. It is, however, clear that, at *Pyrgi* as elsewhere, these figures were not simply borrowed from Greek mythology. They were rather the result of a local adoption and adaptation of a variety of source material, which Etruscan rulers and whoever commissioned these buildings used in order to express and communicate specific religious and political messages.

At *Pyrgi* luckily we know who commissioned this first temple thanks to a dedicatory inscription engraved on three golden leaves, which were discovered in 1963, as noted in Chapter 1. The leaves were carefully deposited, along with the nails used for hanging them, when the temple was dismantled in the early third century BCE, in an area (Area C) where the most important altars were located, just north of the temple. Two leaves contain the Etruscan text of the dedication, and the third is a close Phoenician translation of the main Etruscan text (Bellelli and Xella, 2016;

Wallace, 2016, pp. 45–7). In the dedication, a certain *Thefarie Velianas*, is self-proclaimed ruler or supreme magistrate of *Caere*, holding, that is, *zilac selaita*, a political office named in the Etruscan text (Maggiani, 1996, pp. 102–5); he also states that he built a house to goddess *Uni-Astarte* as she requested. In the Phoenician text, the named goddess is *Astarte*, a well-known Phoenician deity found in Phoenician sanctuaries across the Mediterranean. The inscription tells us two things: first, much like other sanctuaries at coastal harbours, *Pyrgi* spoke to a multicultural community of worshippers although it is important to note that no Phoenician finds of this period have been so far recovered there. Second, as ruler of *Caere* at the moment of the dedication, *Thefarie Velianas* used the temple in order to convey the most powerful political message that the deities were on his side. Herakles' mythical ascension to divinity may have been part and parcel of that message: did *Thefarie* identify himself with Herakles? Whoever approached the temple would have been able to see the entire architectural decoration crowned by the statue group on top of the roof (Figure 4.10).

Pyrgi was linked to *Caere* by a monumental 10-metre-wide road, which, in the sixth century BCE, upon reaching the sanctuary, bent steeply northwards to a settlement area, currently under excavation by the University of Rome, that was established before the monumentalization of the sanctuary (Baglione et al., 2017). Along this road and roughly 4 kilometres outside *Caere*, another sanctuary was built a few years earlier than *Thefarie*'s temple (*circa* 530 BCE), not far from one of the largest Orientalizing *tumuli* outside the city, the Montetosto Tumulus mentioned in the previous chapter, and other smaller *tumulus* burials (Belelli Marchesini, Biella, and Michetti, 2015). Towards the end of the

Figure 4.10 Golden plaques with *Thefarie Velianas*' dedication, *Pyrgi* (Villa Giulia Museum), photograph by Sailko (CC BY-SA 4.0), from Wikimedia Commons.

sixth century BCE, we are, in other words, in front of a remarkable building programme, sponsored by the ruler of *Caere*, that transformed the landscape on the coast and between it and the city into a veritable landscape of power and control by the city. This was accentuated roughly fifty years later when a larger temple was built nearer the coast as the embankment established for the earlier temple was enlarged to the north. The sanctuary doubled in size, but its monumentality was achieved not simply by the larger dimensions of the new building and the installation of a square in front of it. Its floor plan also made a difference: unlike the first temple that had a single *cella*, the inner temple room, and a columnade running along its perimeter, the new temple sat on a high *podium*, had a series of three *cellae*, adjacent to one another, facing a deep porch which hosted the only columns of the temple set in three lines. The plan followed what the Roman architect Vitruvius, writing centuries later, would call the Tuscanic temple, a local tradition of temple building documented at several other Etruscan sanctuaries (Colonna, 2000, pp. 309–36).

The sanctuary, as it stood in the mid-fifth century BCE, thus created an imposing sacred maritime façade, comparable to the similar, though much more grandiose, façade at *Selinus*, the Greek city in south-west Sicily that built several temples visible from the sea. Indeed, this comparison aptly makes us realize that *Pyrgi* was not simply a harbour sanctuary like Gravisca. Rather, it was a major cult centre where myth and politics were indissolubly intertwined. The myth chosen to decorate the new temple was the Greek Seven Against Thebes, well known from literary sources, as well as later figurative representations in Etruria, to which we will return in Chapter 6. It featured Oedipus' two sons, Eteocles and Polynices, going to war with each other in a power struggle for the control of the city of Thebes. Upon approaching the temple from the *Caere-Pyrgi* road, which by now had become a veritable sacred way, worshippers could view an extremely violent scene in the terracotta decoration of the pediment at the rear of the temple that showed the two brothers slaughtering each other. Like the Herakles' myths displayed on the earlier temple, this myth, too, conveyed an unmistakable political message: the tale was a warning, to those threatening to subvert the divine and human order, of the consequences of their action (Baglione, 2013, pp. 210–11). While we are unable to identify who these people might be, the decision to admonish visually of this danger in such a strikingly violent manner indicates that political instability was not a remote reality at *Caere*. Whether it was more or less remote than it had been fifty years earlier, at the height of *Thefarie Velianas*' power, is difficult to say since the audacious propagandistic tone in *Thefarie*'s Phoenician dedication may reveal an equally supreme yet unstable sovereignty. Indeed, the suggestion that the new temple signalled a change of political rule at *Caere* is not far-fetched (Figure 4.11).

Be that as it may, while *Pyrgi* may be unique, our knowledge of other sanctuaries within and outside cities gives us an indication of their sheer number across Etruria and the remarkable variety in construction, location and refurbishment through time (De Grummond, Edlund-Berry, and Bagnasco Gianni, 2011). At *Caere*, not only do we have monumental temples developing from earlier seventh-century BCE cult areas as at Vigna Marini Vitalini in the vicinity of the *forum* of the later Roman city, and the recently excavated Sant'Antonio area (Thomson de Grummond, 2016), but here, near the gate on the eastern side of the city, two monumental temples on a *podium* were built in a radical renovation at the end of the sixth century BCE, which was followed by other phases of change up to the second century BCE (Maggiani, 2013). From Vigna Marini Vitalini we also have a rich dossier of architectural terracottas that have allowed us to reconstruct the roofs of sacred structures (Lulof, 2008; Fiorini and Winter, 2013). Lastly, near the theatre of the later Roman city, at Vigna

Figure 4.11 Pediment illustrating the myth Seven against Thebes, Temple A, *Pyrgi* (Villa Giulia Museum), photograph by Giuseppe Savo (CC BY-SA 4.0), from Wikimedia Commons.

Parrocchiale, another temple, also Tuscanic in plan, was built upon an earlier residential and manufacturing neighbourhood that was destroyed to make space for the sanctuary in the early fifth century BCE; a large *tufa* quarry dug nearby provided the building material for this monumental building project (Cristofani, 1992, 2003; Bellelli, 2013).

At Tarquinia, continuity of cult is even more remarkable. At Pian di Civita, at the centre of the urban plateau, the beginnings of ritual activities date to the tenth century BCE, as we saw in Chapter 2. In the course of the eighth century BCE, the deposition of offerings, ritual structures and human burials, of an infant and an adult, made the area into a sanctuary that was given a new layout in the early seventh century. At that point, a cultic building with its bench altar in the inner room was erected, and later surrounded by a precinct. Inaugurating the erection of this building were two votive pits in front of it, one of which contained three bronze artefacts, a shield, a trumpet or *lituus* and an axe (Figure 4.12): the first two had been intentionally bent, hence rendered unusable, while the lack of wooden remains on the axe suggests that it had never been used

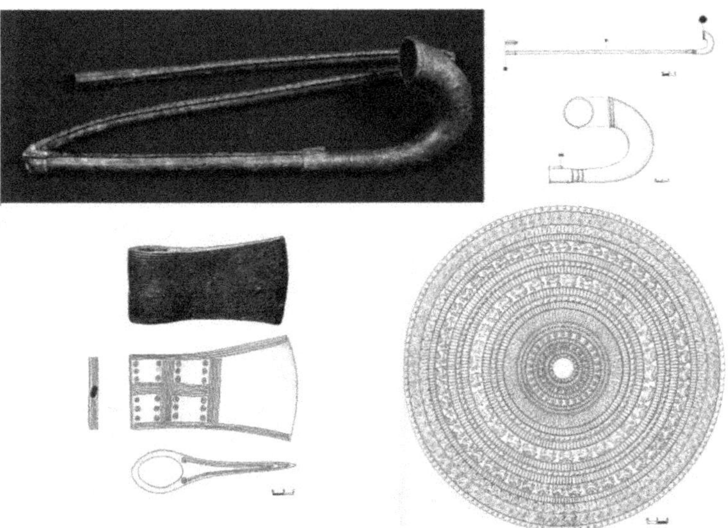

Figure 4.12 Dedication of bronze artefacts, Civita sacred complex, La Civita di Tarquinia, Tarquinia, from Bonghi Jovino, M. 1987 Gli scavi nell'abitato di Tarquinia e la scoperta dei bronzi in un preliminare inquadramento, in M. Bonghi Jovino, C. Chiaramonte Treré (eds), *Tarquinia. Ricerche, scavi e prospettive*, 59–77. Milano.

before deposition (Bonghi Jovino, 2010; Bagnasco Gianni et al., 2018). We are, in other words, dealing with symbols rather than functional objects, which evoked some form of political authority linked to the most powerful elites who, as we saw in the previous chapter, displayed their social power at the tomb through similar symbols. Here, too, and a couple of centuries earlier than *Pyrgi*, we witness the indissoluble link between the political and the sacred at a sanctuary whose cult, according to epigraphic evidence, was to a chthonic deity, perhaps *Uni*. Cultic activities continued in the early sixth century BCE with the refurbishment of the sacred area as well as the placing of more offerings in votive pits and more infant burials. At the same time, *circa* 570 BCE, the earliest temple building of a monumental sanctuary was built west of Civita at Ara della Regina, a site that would become one of the largest temples in pre-Roman Italy, first discovered at the beginning of the twentieth century (Bonghi Jovino and Bagnasco Gianni, 2012). That the ground was levelled and a base of stone blocks created for the earliest building there shows the intention, from the very beginning, to monumentalize. The archaic temple and its related structures, from altars to precinct walls, went through different phases of change until a major phase of refurbishment at the beginning of the fourth century BCE; by then, the sacred complex at Civita had gone out of its original use.

Perhaps the one large south Etruscan city where we have the richest archaeological evidence of sanctuaries is *Veii* thanks to the intense interest and attention that the city has received from Italian and foreign archaeologists alike for a very long time (Edlund-Berry, 2019). Several of the ritual sites attested are, in fact, known from the ploughsoil and thus not easy to characterize. Others are known from votive deposits, architectural features such as roof terracotta decoration and structures suggesting the presence of a sanctuary. This is the case, for instance, of a sacred area near the so-called *Caere* Gate north of the city that included a basin, a cistern, a votive deposit and architectural terracottas (Edlund-Berry, 2019, pp. 130–1). In yet other cases, we can trace phases of refurbishment and change, similar to what can be seen elsewhere, lasting for the whole second half of the first millennium BCE. At the locality of Campetti South-West, for example, on the western limits of the city and just north of the Portonaccio sanctuary, a late seventh-century BCE sacred area, perhaps to do with water cults to judge from the presence of wells, a cistern and votive material, was refurbished in the sixth century BCE, as a roof was added to what was a large open-air precinct.

But it is the Portonaccio sanctuary that has given us the most extraordinary evidence of the long life of an Etruscan sanctuary (Colonna, 2002, 2019; Ambrosini, 2009). Located just outside the city walls on a terrace, the site was first excavated in 1914 by E. Gabrici, followed by the campaigns directed by Giglioli to whom we owe the discovery of the famous walking Apollo (*Apollo che cammina*). Excavations continued to the end of the last century when, in the early 1990s, the most remarkable feat was achieved with the addition of a light non-invasive structure, which recreated the temple; this gives the visitor to the site a clear understanding of the prominence of the temple building around the remains of other structures. Here, too, we have continuity of worship since the first half of the seventh century BCE; the earliest structures, which show that earlier worshippers' activities took place in the open air, date to the second half of the century. The number of votive offerings from then onwards, besides the buildings and the monumentalization of these, makes the Portonaccio record a veritable laboratory for the study of religious behaviour over half a millennium (Michetti, 2002) (Figure 4.13).

Figure 4.13 Portonaccio sanctuary, *Veii*, photograph by Livioandronico2013 (CC BY-SA 3.0), from Wikimedia Commons.

For the early phase, dedications consist mainly of vessels of *bucchero* and Etrusco-Corinthian ceramics, several inscribed, as well as more distinctive offerings such as bronze, ivory and terracotta figurines, smaller objects including textile-making tools such as loom weights, and personal ornaments. That these latter objects point to a cult of a female divinity is confirmed by inscriptions from the first phases of religious activities, which dedicated the offerings to *Menrva*, although other deities worshipped from these early phases included *Herkle*, Etruscan Herakles, and *Rath* connected to *Aplu* (Greek Apollo) (Colonna, 2019, pp. 118–19). The similarity of these early dedicated objects to those of the same date found at Sant' Omobono in Rome, from which comes the ivory *tessera hospitalis* described above, and at other Latial sites such as *Satricum*, attests further to the lively mobility of people, whether worshippers or craftsmen, across Tyrrhenian central Italy. This is confirmed by the inscriptions that give us the elite gentilicial names of the givers of offerings to the deity at Portonaccio (Maras, 2002, 2013): we find both local people and worshippers coming from other cities, Chiusi, *Caere* and Vulci. Among them is a certain *Avle Vipinas*, inscribed on the foot of a *bucchero* chalice or incense burner (Maras, 2002, p. 262): the name is the same as that of *Aulus Vibenna*, known not only from the literary sources but also from other inscriptions. One of these comes from the François Tomb at Vulci where he is represented with his brother *Caile*, whom we will encounter in the final chapter.

At Portonaccio from the middle of the sixth century BCE we see changes in the organization of the sanctuary that would culminate with its monumentalization and the erection of a Tuscanic temple, contemporary with the first temple at *Pyrgi*. An extraordinary repertoire of terracotta sculpture also dates to the end of the sixth century, ranging from figurines to larger pieces, including the *Herkle* and *Menrva* group and even larger, life-size pieces, the *acroteria*, which decorated the ridge pole of the temple roof. Among these *acroteria* were *Herkle* and *Aplu* (walking Apollo), twice represented and illustrating different mythical episodes that saw the two deities in conflict with one another. This echoes the struggle between them for the tripod, which is represented at the Apollo sanctuary at Greek Delphi. Although there are ongoing questions as to how these episodes fit together on the roof, it seems most plausible to associate the main cult at the temple with *Herkle* and *Aplu* even though fragments of a large sculpture possibly representing *Tinia* (Greek Zeus) may also point to another related cult (Colonna, 2019, pp. 120–3) (Figure 4.14).

Figure 4.14 Large-scale terracotta *acroteria*, Portonaccio sanctuary, *Veii* (Villa Giulia Museum), photograph by Sailko (CC BY-SA 4.0), from Wikimedia Commons.

Having thus returned to *Veii* where this chapter began at Piazza d'Armi, we can fully appreciate the enormous growth that Etruscan cities went through in little less than this remarkable century. It is not for nothing that Etruscologists see the sixth century BCE as the apogee of Etruscan civilization. If there is no consensus yet on the dating and function of the so-called *oikos* temple which Stefani dug at Piazza d'Armi, this is not due to our lack of knowledge. It is rather the outcome of a historical trajectory: it is often difficult to distinguish, prior to the second half of the sixth century BCE, religious from other types of structures. It is only after the middle of the century that we see the emergence of temple buildings, clearly differentiated from other, non-religious structures, and a focused investment upon these buildings through architectural decoration as well as monumentalization, as discussed earlier. It is therefore plausible to see such buildings as veritable testimony not only to the wealth and growth of Etruscan cities but also to the astonishing sophistication reached by religion and its related aspects, from ritualization to the adoption and adaptation of Greek-derived myths and the development of an indigenous pantheon. The sociopolitical exploitation of such aspects is part and parcel of urbanism, as exemplified by *Pyrgi*'s sanctuary at the time of *Thefarie Velianas*.

That all of this went hand in hand with the dilation of trade contacts outside the core of Tyrrhenian Etruria is borne out once we begin to look further afield and towards the north: the site that has received equal if not more attention than *Veii* for its sacred areas within the city is that of Marzabotto, located in the middle Reno river valley, an Appennine valley south of the Po river. Here, as noted before, *Tinia*, the head of the Etruscan pantheon, was worshipped at a monumental peripteral temple that was built in the first quarter of the fifth century BCE, fully integrated in the layout of the city. Both the placing of the temple and the layout of the city were established through complex religious practices that set the contours of the relationship between the sky and its deities and the human world on earth. Marzabotto is not known for its sanctuaries only, however: its growth from the last decades of the sixth century BCE along with that of several other settlements in Etruria Padana discussed here attest to a flourishing of this region. This occurred as trade contacts broadened to the north as well as to the south of the core of Etruria in a phase, from the end of the sixth and early fifth century BCE, of increasing mobility and later instability, as we are about to see.

5

BEYOND TYRRHENIAN ETRURIA

HUMAN MOBILITY IN A CHANGING SOCIETY

A 'NEW *POMPEII*'

The phrase 'city of Misano', deriving from Pian di Misano, the low-level river terrace of the ancient settlement between the modern city of Marzabotto and the Reno river, was how sixteenth- and seventeenth-century antiquarians referred to the ancient site. It was only in the late eighteenth century, however, that the Abbot Serafino Calindri, in his studies, recognized the antiquity of the remains found, many of which were then sold on the antiquarian market. Once the site and its surrounding land was acquired by Giuseppe Aria, a wealthy landowner from Bologna in 1831, agricultural and renovation works around his villa not far from the ancient remains brought to light many more, including several bronze statuettes, which came to the attention of Giuseppe Micali and George Dennis and readers of the *Bullettino dell'Instituto di Corrispondenza Archeologica* in 1841. In 1856, Giovanni Gozzadini, who had excavated Villanova, came to Marzabotto after the first walls of temple buildings came to light on high ground at Poggio Misanello, what was soon known to be the religious *acropolis* of the ancient city (Vitali, Brizzolara, and Lippolis, 2001, pp. 11–22). The structures were left in situ, but Gozzadini deplored the lack of written records and plans of the finds discovered up until then. Aria himself had gathered a significant collection of finds and entrusted Gozzadini with the first official excavation campaigns in the early 1860s, which Gozzadini published in 1865, wrongly interpreting the site as a *necropolis*. Further excavations under his direction both in the funerary and urban areas brought to light new finds and led to a further publication in 1870. Meanwhile, a dispute emerged between him and palaeoethnologist Gaetano Chierici, who interpreted the site correctly as a city that had grown out of a village of huts. This view was to win the day, with the support of fellow palaeoethnologist Antonio Zannoni who had seen in Marzabotto a 'large settlement', and called it 'a new *Pompeii* of Etruria Padana' (Zannoni, 1876, pp. 7, 13), a fortunate phrase that was to catch on in the writings of Edoardo Brizio. In the late 1880s, as Soprintendente of the regions of Emilia and Marche, Brizio began a systematic field campaign aimed at realizing a full cartographic documentation of the site and all of its structures; he also coordinated the establishment of a first museum at Villa Aria and wrote the first guide book to the site (1886).

The result was the first scientific publication of ancient Marzabotto in the *Monumenti Antichi* of the Accademia dei Lincei (1890) that was to become the basis for all subsequent research there (Brizio, 1890). Besides giving a full account of all the previous excavations and publishing Gozzadini's excavation reports, Brizio's publication dealt systematically with the different sectors and elements of the city, from the residential quarters or isole/*insulae*, of which Brizio identified eleven, and the urban layout, with the houses, the roads and the sewerage system, to the *necropoleis* and the sacred area on the *acropolis*. In doing so, he raised some historical problems that are still fundamental today: the orientation of temple buildings in relation to Etruscan religious beliefs, and their construction according to the Tuscanic plan, as new finds elsewhere were coming to light such as the temple *podium* at Ara della Regina at Tarquinia, first discovered in 1876; the presence of Gallic Celts in Etruscan settlements following the discovery, in 1871, of a small Gallic *necropolis* south of the *acropolis*; the foundation of the urban layout of the settlement and its main roads, the *cardo* and *decumanus*, according to the *disciplina etrusca*, the body of religious knowledge that included the rites to be carried out for founding cities, as known from literary sources (Figure 5.1).

The extraordinary regularity of the urban plan, never seen before in pre-Roman Etruria, comparable only to other Greek and Roman colonial cities, and primarily *Pompeii*, raised the principal issue that remains at the centre of debate till today, first noted by Gozzadini, namely, the Etruscan presence north of the core of Etruria between the Tiber and the Arno rivers and the reasons for it. Was Marzabotto an Etruscan colony akin to the twelve to which Livy (Lib. V, 33) made reference in tracing Etruscan

Figure 5.1 Marzabotto, photograph from Govi, E. 2019 L'Etruria padana, in *Etruschi. Viaggio nella terra dei Rasna*, Catalogo della mostra, Bologna 2019, 357–61.

dominion between the Po Valley and the Alps? Marzabotto's regular urban layout suggested to Brizio that it had been founded from scratch and this supported a positive answer to the question. The comparison to *Pompeii* also helped: the urban plan in *insulae* of the famous city in Campania, in fact, had been first published in 1858 by Giuseppe Fiorelli, a key figure in Neapolitan and Italian archaeology, under whom Brizio had worked at *Pompeii*, and to whom Brizio dedicated the Marzabotto volume. Roman and Late Antique literary sources on the *disciplina etrusca* helped with the understanding of Marzabotto, but the question remained as to the likely influence upon, and origin of, the orientation and urban layout at Marzabotto (Brizio, 1890, pp. 47–8). At any rate, for Brizio, the Etruscans' ingenuity gave the Romans the idea of a regular city plan, the construction of the urban sewerage and perhaps even the layout of houses, which were again comparable to those excavated at *Pompeii* (Brizio, 1890, pp. 51, 82). Let us then turn our attention to Marzabotto as we know it today and its wider context in order to understand how the questions already arising in the late nineteenth century have been subsequently investigated and advancement made to answer these and other new questions. My intention is furthermore to examine the archaeological evidence that illustrates an unprecedented level of intensification of contacts between the Tyrrhenian and Adriatic side of the Italic peninsula; this will ultimately lead me to explore questions about the societies that lived through this intensification across different parts of Etruria.

MARZABOTTO AND ITS BROADER CONTEXT

After the entire site of Marzabotto came into state ownership in 1933, the Soprintendenza oversaw the restoration of excavated structures and the beginning, once again, of field campaigns which became systematic under Guido Achille Mansuelli from the late 1950s to the mid-1970s, and then again, from the 1980s under the Soprintendenza in collaboration with Italian universities, primarily the University of Bologna. The result is an extraordinary documentation of an Etruscan city at the middle of the first millennium BCE that has allowed the reconstruction of houses and buildings using 3D computer graphics (Garagnani, Gaucci, and Gruška, 2016). Today we know that the urban layout, probably first established *circa* 540 BCE after an earlier settlement of huts no longer survived, came to consist of four main orthogonal roads (*plateiai*) with minor ones; the *acropolis* hosted five sacred structures and the northernmost area of the town other sanctuaries, including a temple dedicated to *Tinia*, mentioned in the previous chapter. This layout divided the settlements into neighbourhoods or *regiones*; the earliest houses may have been built within *insulae* or city blocks *circa* 520–510 BCE.[1] The urban plan bears striking similarities to that of Greek colonial cities *circa* 550–540 BCE in southern Italy such as *Metapontum*, *Paestum*/Poseidonia and Locri Epizifiri (Lippolis, 2005). That the new plan of the late sixth century BCE at Marzabotto may have been perceived as a new settlement reconfiguration by its inhabitants with all the political and institutional implications that it entails is suggested by the Etruscan name of the town, *Kainua*, found on an inscribed bowl at the *Tinia* sanctuary, that may derive from the Greek *kainòn* used to refer to new towns (Sassatelli and Govi, 2010, p. 34). While all of this indicates some level of interaction with the Greek urban world, further corroborated by the use of the Greek Attic foot in Marzabotto's urban reconfiguration, specific local needs led to this development (Govi, 2017, p. 27) (Figure 5.2).

Indeed, the geometry of the city, as suspected by Brizio, followed ritual practices underlying Etruscan cosmological beliefs: the orientation according to cardinal points has been confirmed by the discovery of four *cippi* (stone markers) that were placed at the main road junctions, of which one, placed at the centre of the city, was inscribed with a cross following the cardinal point orientation. This *cippus*' location and the subsequent orientation of the road system, it has been suggested, were determined by the sun's movements that were observed on top of the *acropolis* (Sassatelli and Govi, 2010, p. 27). Here one of the structures

Figure 5.2 Marzabotto, town plan, from Garagnani, S., A. Gaucci and B. Gruška 2016. From the archaeological record to Archaeobim: the case study of the Etruscan temple of Uni in Marzabotto, *Virtual Archaeology Review* 7.15, 77–86.

has been interpreted as an *auguraculum*, namely the structure from which priests (*augurs*), entrusted with the performance of rituals for urban foundations, carried out these rituals (van der Meer, 2011, pp. 82–104). The layout thus projected, on the ground, the sky and its divine order or *templum*, which we know from much later literary sources and from the so-called liver of Piacenza. Found in 1877 and dated to *circa* the first century BCE, this is a small cast bronze model of an animal's liver, divided into sections, each of which is marked by an inscribed deity's name (van der Meer, 1987); it was probably an instrument used for divination and, in particular, the oracular method of extispicy, which involved the inspection of the entrails of sacrificed animals in order to discern divine will. In displaying different spaces with named deities, the Piacenza liver has given us an absolutely fundamental insight into Etruscan religious beliefs that saw the sky divided into sections, each of which was controlled by a specific god, as reconstructed by scholars (Jannot, 2005, pp. 3–33).

At Marzabotto, the northernmost area of the town, *Regio* I, hosted two temples: one, recently excavated, is the already mentioned monumental peripteral temple for the worship of *Tinia*, the deity whose name was found inscribed on a local *bucchero olla* which was probably a cultic instrument used at the sanctuary there; the temple matched the space attributed to *Tinia* in the heavenly *templum*. Further confirmation of this spatial attribution is given by a later, third-century BCE inscribed stone marker named as the 'space of *Tinia*' from a sacred building at Castelsecco near Arezzo (Maras, 2009, pp. 226–7). To the east of the *Tinia* temple is the second newly excavated temple, built in the last decades of the sixth century BCE, this time with a Tuscanic plan and dedicated to *Uni*; it, too, matched the divine space held by *Uni* in the *templum*. Located at the junction of the two main roads at one of the city's entrances, and occupying an entire *insula* or city block, the temple to *Tinia* with its temple to *Uni* commanded the view over the entire Reno river valley, especially for those coming into the town from the north and Bologna (Govi, 2017, pp. 89–92) (Figure 5.3).

Figure 5.3 The temples of *Uni and Tinia*, virtual reconstruction, from Garagnani, S., A. Gaucci and B. Gruška 2016. From the archaeological record to Archaeobim: the case study of the Etruscan temple of Uni in Marzabotto, *Virtual Archaeology Review* 7.15, 77–86.

Beside the sanctuaries, the excavated houses at Marzabotto have also provided profound insight into the functioning of the city. While the houses all share a basic architectural plan of rooms built around large courtyards, the variation in size and other features of this plan among these houses gives us a picture of a socially diverse community. Larger houses of up to 800 square metres, and characterized by a plan that is not dissimilar to that of the famous *atrium* houses at *Pompeii*, belonged to the elite (Govi and Sassatelli, 2010a; Govi, 2017, pp. 94–5). While some dwellings seem to follow a unified plan, others seem to result from the merging of buildings into a single unit; the latter – called *casa-officina* (house-workshop) by the excavators – were devoted to crafts activities, whether pottery making or metallurgy, as well as being residential dwellings (Nijboer, 1998, pp. 171–82, 281–90; Govi and Sassatelli, 2010a, p. 304). This is the case of the recently published House 1 (*Regio* IV, *insula* 2), that uniquely shows the change of function of the building through time (Govi and Sassatelli, 2010b): this unit of exceptionally large size (over 1,000 square metres) began as an elite house and went through four different phases of renovation. By the first half of the fifth century BCE it held four pottery kilns; towards the end of the fifth or first half of the fourth century BCE, it was restructured to become a highly specialized pottery workshop that held all the necessary installations and spaces for the whole process of ceramic production. Interestingly, findings of objects inscribed with gentilicial names indicate that this workshop was run by one or more families of high social status.

Another unit, partially excavated in the 1960s in *Regio* V, *insula* 5, held what has been interpreted as a foundry, from the remains found there of tools, moulds, crucibles, bronze and iron fragments, slags and ingots, as well as bronze statuettes and a furnace for the preliminary refinery of raw metals. Here, again, it seems that the full *chaîne opératoire* or chain of production, from refining raw metals to manufacturing objects, took place under a single roof. Moreover, the likely provenance of the raw material from the Campigliese district, the richest mineral area in Tyrrhenian Etruria, and the similarity of the foundry's furnace with one found at Campiglia Marittima, a key site of this metal district, importantly demonstrate that not only was Marzabotto a key production centre in its wider region (Locatelli, 2005), but it was also a centre for the sorting and redistribution of raw material, able to attract labour and technological know-how from far away, and strategically located as it was at a key cross-roads between the Po Valley and Tyrrhenian Etruria. Fragments of shaped metal ingots known as *aes rude* at the foundry, but also known from other settlements in Etruria Padana, and evidence at Marzabotto for the manufacture of *aes signatum*, a metal ingot with a mark, as well as a series of over sixty stone weights, many of which were incised with numeral marks, are all pieces of evidence underlying a regional pre-monetary exchange system. This shows that standard metrological systems (or systems of measure) were adopted for commercial exchange that was probably based on the weighting of metals. That these stone weights are found at other towns and smaller settlements across Etruria Padana, from Bologna to Forcello di Bagnolo San Vito near Mantova, further demonstrates the key role that Marzabotto played in the economy and trade links of this region (Maggiani, 2002, 2012). Marzabotto, however, did not and could not grow without the expanding trade links that flourished in Etruria Padana and further afield. We therefore need to look at the wider context of this growth.

ETRURIA PADANA AND BEYOND: THE ADRIATIC, THE TYRRHENIAN AND CONTINENTAL EUROPE

As Marzabotto first grew, in the mid to late sixth century BCE, so did other towns in the region such as Bologna; new settlements were established as veritable trade hubs such as Adria, Spina and Forcello, another flourishing trading hub sited on the confluence of the Po and the Mincio, a key tributary of the Po river, attesting to the dynamism of these northern Adriatic regions from the middle to late sixth century, as we saw in the previous chapter.

At Bologna, the poor archaeological record of the settlement, which sits under the modern town, prevents us from assessing its boundaries and its internal organization; however, the few excavated sites do give us a picture of a prosperous community from the end of the sixth century BCE. This picture includes the adoption of new architectural rectilinear plans for residential buildings, possibly indicating the beginning of a different internal organization and urban plan, the development of new forms of commemorating its dead through the use of richly decorated funerary *stelai*, to which I shall return later, and the establishment of a major urban sanctuary. Located at Villa Cassarini at the southern edge of the settlement, the sanctuary, first explored by Brizio at the beginning of the twentieth century, is largely known by the votive material, rather than actual remains of buildings other than small drystone walls and a furnace. The latter was probably established for the manufacture of ritual instruments and vessels: the votive offerings include thirty or so bronze votive statuettes, among which *Herkle* and *Aplu* are represented, travertine *cippi* or altars that supported the offerings, as well as local and imported Attic ceramic vessels, some of which carried votive inscriptions. Its location on high ground overlooking the settlement reminds us of Marzabotto's sacred *acropolis* (Romagnoli, Calastri, Cremonini, and Desantis, 2014).

The similarities with Marzabotto, however, do not end here: we know that the Greek Attic foot, a unit of measure used for the city plan at Marzabotto, was also adopted at Spina, Forcello and at San Cassiano di Crespino, a small settlement in the hinterland of Adria, that included an elite residence later transformed into a manufacturing compound (Govi, 2017). Although partially excavated, Adria itself was planned with a regular layout from the middle to the late sixth century BCE, a change that is contemporary with the planning of San Cassiano. This, together with the geographical distribution of other small settlements in Adria's hinterland along an east–west axis gravitating towards Forcello, reveals a transformation of Adria itself, from *emporion* or trading post to a sizeable centre that controlled its agricultural hinterland and key westward trade links along the Po Valley, as well as northwards towards Veneto. We can judge this from the Venetic provenance of trachyte (*trachite euganea*) used as building material at San Cassiano, and the presence of ceramic imports from Etruria Padana at Este, an important Venetic centre north-west of Adria (Robino, Paltineri, and Smoquina, 2009; Paltineri and Robino, 2016).

Similarly, Spina, located in the Valli di Comacchio, a wetland environment of brackish lagoons on the southern branches of the Po river delta, was laid out according to an orthogonal plan of regular *insulae* on an east–west orientation. Discovered during land reclamation in the early twentieth century, Spina was largely known for its cemeteries, excavated throughout the last century, and amounting to over 4,000 tombs; from these comes a breathtaking number of Attic Greek figured vessels, attesting to an extremely busy trading centre (Berti and Guzzo, 1993). While the settlement was discovered in the middle of the last century from the excavation of wooden pile structures that were well preserved thanks to the wet environment, it was not until recently that new fieldwork projects, including a geophysics prospection, have brought to light the extent of the settlement of houses built on stilts and its internal organization (Cornelio Cassai, Giannini, and Malnati, 2013; Zamboni, 2016; Reusser, 2017) (Figure 5.4).

A north–south axis, probably a large artificial water canal, ran across the settlement; a network of smaller canals defined the space for the house blocks, while minor canals within and between houses provided the sewerage system (Cremaschi, 2017). All of this gives us a remarkable picture of a centralized sophisticated programme of hydraulic engineering, which we see, on a smaller scale, at Adria itself and Forcello. Wooden palisades infilled with clay and perishable material like straw and reeds provided the walls for houses, and wooden planks their roofs (Zamboni, 2017a). As at Marzabotto, dwellings also included

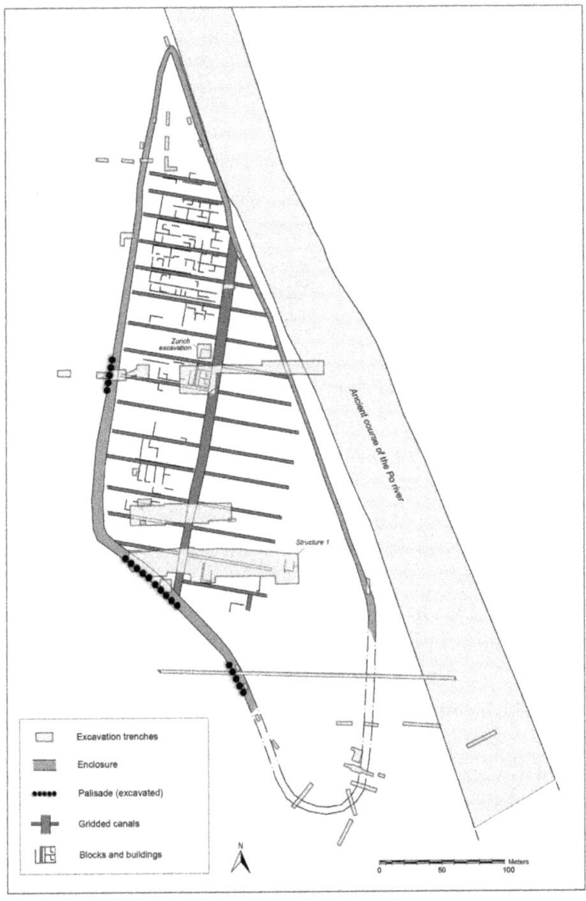

Figure 5.4 Spina, town plan, courtesy Lorenzo Zamboni.

areas for manufacture and craftmanship. The architectural plan of some excavated houses, moreover, matches that of houses at Forcello (Quirino, 2012). We have, in other words, an extraordinary example of wetland city planning where the ingenuity of the settlers helped manage the wet environment, from hydraulic engineering to the exploitation of wood and other organic materials for residential architecture, together with all the resources that the wetland offered. The most recent palaeobotanical evidence of cereal, fruit and hemp crops has shown that the land had already been reclaimed for cultivation before the town was laid out (Marchesini and Marvelli, 2017) (Figure 5.5).

All of these settlements and their archaeological record, from their shared contemporary urban planning to artefacts, both imported and locally made, ultimately reveal a thriving trade network that spanned considerable distances, within and beyond the Italic peninsula. It is clear now that while Bologna stood at a key junction of commercial routes and Marzabotto controlled the southern route into Tyrrhenian Etruria, Adria and Spina stood at the maritime end of the Adriatic network. Moreover, the river port of Forcello acted as a bridgehead between north-west Italy and the Celtic world beyond the Alps. It is, in fact, this world, particularly the so-called West Hallstatt zone (modern central France and south-west Germany), that was the ultimate beneficiary of imported goods, from both Etruria and the Aegean. But not the only

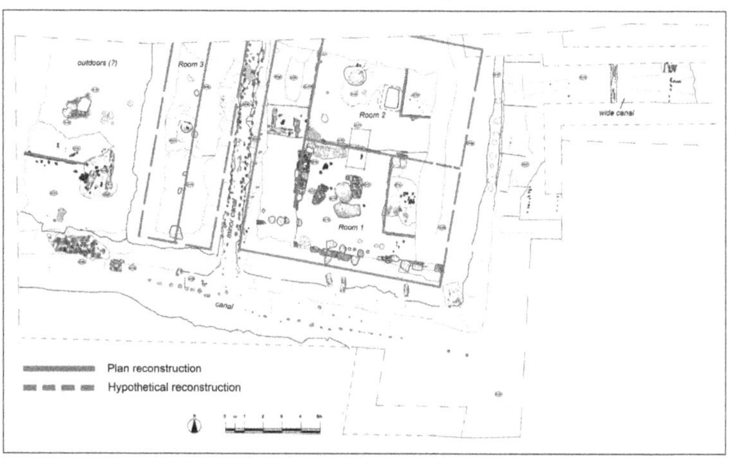

Figure 5.5 House unit, Spina, courtesy Lorenzo Zamboni.

one: indeed, if Attic figured pottery – black, red figure and black gloss – at these northern Adriatic trade hubs and further afield across the Alps attests to lively exchange of fine ware with the Aegean, as noted in the previous chapter, the record of Greek transport *amphorae* in the northern Adriatic widens our perspective on the substantial commodities, namely agricultural produce, being traded and consumed from Spina all the way to continental Europe from the middle of the sixth through to the fifth century BCE. This record, recently examined in a systematic way (Sacchetti, 2012, 2016), shows a fairly widespread distribution of imported Greek *amphorae* in the northern Adriatic, mostly in settlements; this distribution can be aptly matched to that of Greek painted fineware, which consists mostly of drinking vessels. These, together with the *amphorae*, attest to the adaptation of Greek ways of drinking among local communities (Tsingarida, 2009; Bundrick, 2019).

While this record includes most types of *amphorae* known from the Greek world, its presence at Marzabotto shows an unusual pattern for Etruria Padana, namely a predominance of Corinthian *amphorae* and fewer quantities of Western Greek *amphorae*. This pattern resembles more closely the record we have on the northern Tyrrhenian seaboard at sites such as Pisa, and thus confirms Marzabotto's key role in linking Etruria Padana with Tyrrhenian Etruria (Sacchetti, 2012, pp. 265–73). It also shows us how closely interconnected the two regions were by the fifth century BCE as a result of the intensification of commercial networks throughout the central Mediterranean. The northern Tyrrhenian seaboard, with Pisa at its centre, is, in fact, a key witness to this intensification. Pisa, the northernmost sizeable urban centre in Etruria at the confluence of two rivers, the Auser and Arno, grew into a town controlling an extensive maritime–riverine harbour system that developed from the fifth century BCE along the northern Tuscan coast; this system consisted of multiple riverine docks and maritime landing points such as San Rocchino (Pasquinucci, 2003; Pasquinucci and Menchelli, 2010). The excavation of quays and wooden boats at Pisa-San Rossore, a railway station to the north of the modern city, has brought to light the earliest evidence dated from the fifth century (Camilli, 2004). Furthermore, two recently investigated sites, Prato Gonfienti and Poggio Colla, lying between Pisa and Marzabotto, enrich this picture of interconnectivity between the Tyrrhenian and Adriatic seas (Figure 5.6).

To the north of the Arno and at the margins of the plain of Florence and Prato lies the 17-hectare settlement of Prato Gonfienti whose urban layout is similar and contemporary with that of Marzabotto (Perazzi

Figure 5.6 Prato Gonfienti. Su concessione della Soprintendenza Archeologia, Belle Arti e Paesaggio per la Città Metropolitana di Firenze e per le Province di Pistoia e Prato.

and Poggesi, 2011, pp. 309–34). The excavation of the site has largely uncovered courtyard houses whose characteristics indicate inhabitants of high status, clearly benefitting from the northern Adriatic–Tyrrhenian commercial network, but also with access to the inland Chiana Valley to the south. This is seen in the houses' plan, size (in one case over 1,400 square metres), and the documented artefacts found there that included imported Attic figured ceramics. The finding of wells and open-air drainage channels that followed the orientation of the houses' urban layout indicates yet another highly organized community that designed a system of hydraulic engineering for coping with the hydrological instability of the Prato plain (Figure 5.7).

Poggio Colla, on the other hand, high up in the Mugello valley north-east of Florence, was positioned on a strategic route on the upper course of the Sieve river, controlling traffic between the Arno and the Po valley across the Appennines. The presence of fifth-century BCE votive deposits along the transappennine route between Bologna and the Mugello valley, of which the best known is at Monte Bibele, further confirms the strategic location of Poggio Colla (Vitali, Guidi, and Minarini, 1997). Its *acropolis* and centre of the settlement was a fortified hilltop and focus of religious

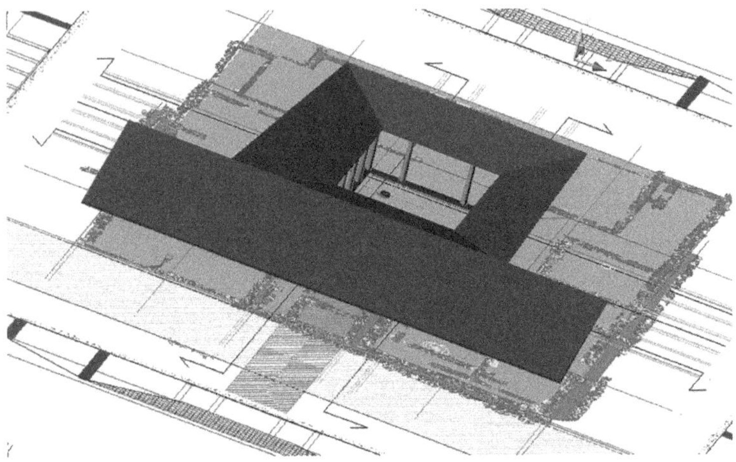

Figure 5.7 Porticoed house unit (lotto 14), hypothetical reconstruction, Prato Gonfienti. Su concessione della Soprintendenza Archeologia, Belle Arti e Paesaggio per la Città Metropolitana di Firenze e per le Province di Pistoia e Prato. New hypotheses on these structures are taking shape and a virtual reconstruction of this house will be published by the end of 2020.

Figure 5.8 Vicchio Stele, photograph by Massimo Legni.

activity for the mountain communities in the nearby valleys: it hosted a sanctuary and a monumental temple built towards the end of the sixth century BCE, then destroyed and replaced by another temple about a century later (Warden, Thomas, Steiner, and Meyers, 2005). Placed in the foundation of the first temple was a richly and carefully inscribed *stele*, probably a dedication, in which the goddess *Uni* and possibly *Tinia* are mentioned (Warden, 2016). This so-called Vicchio *stele* is the longest stone inscription so far discovered and is still under study (Maggiani, 2016); however, similar inscribed *stelai* from the hilly area around Fiesole at the foothills of the Appennines provide a link with this latter as well as further evidence of the communication along routes through the mountains into the Tyrrhenian side (Figure 5.8).

ETRUSCAN MOBILITY OR COLONIZATION?

The intensification and expansion of these networks between the Adriatic and the Tyrrhenian lead us to tackle a key question, which Gozzadini and Brizio had already identified while excavating Marzabotto: were the northern Adriatic sites established as a result of Etruscan colonization? While this question derived from later ancient, primarily Roman authors such as Livy, who tells us of such a colonization, the debate, still lively today, does not solely concern the northern Adriatic. On the contrary, literary, epigraphic and archaeological evidence on Etruscan mobility outside the core of Etruria has often led archaeologists to speak of a so-called Etruscanization or colonization of neighbouring regions since the Iron Age (Torelli, 2014, pp. 352–3). The legacy of the concept of cultural *facies* or archaeological culture, seen in Chapter 2, which, in its earlier and uncritical version, attributed a people to a style and type of such a culture, has a lot to answer for the long-running and continued existence of this debate. Exemplary of this debate are two settlements lying in the middle Adriatic region: Verucchio, inland from modern Rimini, already encountered in Chapter 2, and Fermo, south of Ancona in today's Marche region, were both established in the early Iron Age; this is largely detected from their cemeteries and their Villanovan burial ritual and related material culture. While some believe Verucchio was settled by an Etruscan community that prospered in the eighth and seventh centuries BCE (von Eles, 2013), others find the similarities in material culture inadequate to justify this view (Zamboni, 2017b). The same applies to Fermo, our knowledge of which, however, is scanty (Drago Troccoli, 2003). What is in any case intriguing is that after the middle of the seventh century BCE the occupation of Verucchio ceased, and at Fermo occupation ceased certainly by the fifth century BCE. Several reasons explain the relatively short existence of these settlements: the evidence at Verucchio, however, speaks loudly of a town that was strategically located for the control of the trade of precious commodities from central and northern Europe, such as amber, in which its cemeteries were rich; however, this trade declined once settlements grew across Etruria Padana and Emilia Romagna (Zamboni, 2017b, p. 390).

In southern Campania, the area known as the Picentine region, facing the Salerno Gulf, was known to ancient authors such as Pliny the Elder as having been inhabited by the Etruscans; Capua, a Campanian city in the Volturno river valley to the north, was, according to Strabo, the chief Etruscan city of Campania (Bellelli, 2017). Here, too, the presence of the Villanovan funerary rite at the cemeteries of Iron Age Capua and Pontecagnano, an important Picentine settlement, has influenced scholars to speak of an Etruscanization of the area (Cuozzo, 2007; Cinquantaquattro and Pellegrino, 2017). The presence of Etruscan inscriptions, which date from the seventh century BCE at Pontecagnano and include the famous Capua tile, a fifth-century BCE calendar of religious festivities inscribed in Etruscan, do suggest, however, some Etruscan presence there. The tantalizing new discovery of a corpus of Etruscan inscriptions containing the gentilicial names of Etruscan individuals at Fondo Iozzino, an important extra-urban sanctuary of archaic *Pompeii*, further confirms not only Etruscan mobility and settlement outside of Etruria but also the remarkable openness of archaic Campanian society (Osanna and Pellegrino, 2017).

Further to the north and inland, another porous boundary of Etruria is the one with Umbria, marked by the Tiber in its upper inland valley (Sisani, 2009; Fontaine, 2010; Stoddart, 2012; Paoletti, 2014). Notwithstanding the long-running debate on the role of the Tiber as an ethnic or cultural frontier between Tyrrhenian coastal and inland regions (Cifani, 2003), scholars nowadays tend to recognize that in Umbria, too, communities along the Tiber, a key communication route inland, were open societies where ethnicity was a transient and dynamic form of individual or collective identity that only crystallized with the Roman conquest much later (Bradley, 2000). Along this fluvial artery, we see, in the late sixth and fifth century BCE, the flourishing of inland centres such as Perugia, *Volsinii* and Todi, similar to the situation further north in Etruria Padana. An example of this openness is the so-called Mars of Todi, a fifth century BCE bronze life-size statue dedicated to the extra-urban sanctuary of Montesanto of Todi, an Umbrian settlement sited along the Tiber north-east of *Volsinii* (Bergamini, 2001, pp. 79–87). Found in 1835 in a votive deposit, the statue was probably made in *Volsinii* itself. It represents a warrior in the act of making a libation to the god, probably Mars himself, and probably stood upon a stone base at the sanctuary; its inscription in Umbrian language but using an Etruscan alphabet states that the dedication was by a certain *Ahal Trutitis*, probably an Umbrian name. This Mars tells us not only of *Volsinii*'s and Todi's own prosperity but also more generally that of the middle Tiber Valley, which was itself a response to the multiple and diverse inland commercial networks between the northern Adriatic and the Tyrrhenian (Figure 5.9).

Figure 5.9 Mars of Todi (Musei Vaticani), photograph by Jean-Pol Grandmont (CC BY-SA 3.0), from Wikimedia Commons.

While the end of the sixth century BCE marks the beginning of that prosperity, it is in the fifth century BCE that we see its acceleration. At *Volsinii*, sited on a dramatic *tufa* outcrop overlooking the Tiber to the south as its course turns abruptly eastwards towards Todi, an urban plan, hidden under the modern town, is probably contemporary with the urban-like layout and reorganization of the suburban *necropoleis* of Crocifisso del Tufo, located just below the northern cliff edge of the town's *tufa* outcrop, and of Cannicella, on the other side of the outcrop (Feruglio, 2003). At Crocifisso del Tufo, from the middle of the sixth century BCE, chamber tombs with a rectangular plan were built of *tufa* blocks and arranged according to *insulae*. The gentilicial name of the deceased was engraved on the architrave of the tomb entrance, while later tombs, called *a cassetta* (or box tombs), were surmounted by a stone marker (*cippus*) also engraved with the deceased's name (Bruschetti, 2012). We see a similar organization at Cannicella, where, from the second half of the sixth century BCE, a sanctuary was also established, probably connected with a chthonic cult given its location and the hydraulic infrastructure that included water channels and a large pool (Bonamici, Stopponi, and Tamburini, 1994). Other sanctuaries within the town, built from the early fifth century BCE, and largely known from

Figure 5.10 The *tufa* outcrop of Orvieto (ancient *Volsinii*) emerging from the clouds, author's photograph.

architectural terracottas, further confirm a prosperous community: the terracottas from the pediment of the Belvedere temple at the north-east end of the town show phases of redecoration and refurbishment from the fifth to the fourth century BCE (Stopponi, 2003) (Figures 5.10, 5.11 and 5.12).

At Perugia, the settlement underneath the modern town has similarly given us fifth- to fourth-century BCE evidence of temple building, again in the form of architectural terracottas. To the sixth century BCE dates the establishment of burial grounds in and outside the settlement, either just outside it or a few kilometres away from it; unfortunately, the poor record of these sites, particularly within the town, prevents us from assessing accurately its internal organization and society (Della Fina, 2002; Bratti, 2007, pp. 27–34). Some of the burials, lavishly equipped with bronze banqueting sets as well as parade armour, clearly belonged to the social elites of Perugia and its environs. One characteristic shared by particularly wealthy elite tombs around Perugia and, indeed further afield in Umbria, is their siting along communication routes, not unlike the seventh-century BCE elite monumental burials we see outside the cities of southern Etruria, as examined in Chapter 3. In a mountainous region

Figure 5.11 Crocifisso del Tufo *necropolis*, *Volsinii*, photograph by Paolo Binaco.

Figure 5.12 Crocifisso del Tufo *necropolis*, aerial view, *Volsinii*, photograph by Paolo Nannini.

such as Umbria, the control of inland east–west and north–south routes was, not unexpectedly, a crucial asset for local socially prominent groups and the wider community alike; this is seen in the choice of location of extra-urban sanctuaries that allowed these to be visible to each other and to the settlements (Bruschetti and Trombetta, 2013, pp. 15–19).

But the similarities with the earlier monumental burials of southern Etruria do not end here: the most prominent ones, at Castel San Mariano near Corciano, a few kilometres east of Perugia on the way to Lake Trasimeno and Cortona in Valdichiana, perhaps a tomb at San Valentino di Marsciano on the route to *Volsinii* and another tomb near Todi, all contained parade chariots. Fragments of these chariots were dispersed among various museums around the world after their discovery in the nineteenth century. The three or four chariots from Castel San Mariano, dated to the second half of the sixth century, are particularly notable:[2] they were covered with embossed laminated bronze sheets, decorated with Greek mythological narratives, including an Amazonomachy and a Gigantomachy with Zeus and Herakles (Bruschetti and Trombetta, 2013). The decoration is stylistically and iconographically close to that of the fragments from San Valentino and of the bronze sheets that covered another chariot from a slightly earlier elite tomb at Monteleone di Spoleto in the mountain behind modern Spoleto, south-east of Perugia (Emiliozzi, 2011). The decoration on all of this material was thus likely the product of the same workshop of craftsmen, well versed in the production of images that recall the style and iconography of contemporary Greek Attic and Ionic painted fineware that circulated throughout Etruria. At this point, we must ask ourselves about the very societies that lived at these settlements and produced this material culture: this will force us to widen our vista upon fifth-century BCE Etruria.

URBAN SOCIETIES: PUBLIC AND PRIVATE

This pattern of lavish elite burials across the hinterland of a main settlement such as Perugia is also found at nearby Cortona in the Valdichiana where two monumental *tumulus* burials, the so-called Sodo I and II *tumuli*, built at around 580 BCE, were located on a major route towards Arezzo (Zamarchi Grassi, 2006; Fedeli, 2012, pp. 49–56). It suggests a divergence between these inland areas and coastal southern Etruria or Etruria Padana; there, as we have seen before and in the last chapter, public investment in monumental sanctuaries and the decision by the ruling elites to redirect wealth display, and hence social power, from a private context, such as a funerary monument, to a public communal religious space speaks eloquently of sociopolitical change that went hand in hand with urban growth. Is this divergence a symptom of a disparity in socio-economic development, as has been argued before (Torelli, 2014, pp. 353–5)? Or, in sustaining this view, do we not run the risk of approaching the question through an evolutionistic lens and a Graeco-

Roman frame of reference, where the monumentalization of sanctuaries and other public spaces was the hallmark of a fully urban world?

To be sure, the archaeological record of cities in southern Tyrrhenian Etruria would allow such a frame of reference. Indeed, the sanctuaries examined in the previous chapter went through phases of refurbishment and, in some cases, enlargement in the fifth century BCE. At Gravisca, we have seen, a radical refurbishment took place at the sanctuary from the end of the sixth through to the fifth century BCE. At Tarquinia, the main sanctuary of Ara della Regina saw the construction of an enormous terrace at the beginning of the fourth century BCE as the temple pediment featured the famous pair of terracotta winged horses, now at the Museum of Tarquinia, which was probably part of a representation of the apotheosis of Herakles (Bagnasco Gianni, 2009) (Figure 5.13). At *Caere*, contemporary with the construction of the Vigna Parrocchiale Tuscanic temple discussed in the previous chapter, was the erection of a horse-shoe-shaped, almost elliptical open-air structure south-east of the temple, in the early fifth century BCE. Despite the difficulty in interpreting such a peculiar structure, its purpose, certainly public, was probably not religious, although its closeness to the temple may hint at some functional relationship. Whatever the case, public structures

Figure 5.13 Ara della Regina, Tarquinia, photograph by Robin Iversen Rönnlund (CC BY-SA 3.0), from Wikimedia Commons.

built around the same time near the *agora* of Greek cities for hosting assemblies such as the *ekklesiasterion* of *Metapontum* in southern Italy, provide a useful parallel for this elliptical structure, which, too, may have held public assemblies or religious festivals (Bellelli, 2011b, 2016). Finally, the urban infrastructure, from roads to the building of defensive monumental city walls, mostly dating to the sixth century BCE but replacing earlier fortifications, add to this picture of significant public investment.

One way of explaining the differences between settlements and their urban form across Etruria at the middle of the first millennium BCE is to examine the relationship between public and private within these settlements in relation to the physical definition of spaces as such and the wealth invested in them.[3] First, as to the investment of resources, the monumentalization of public spaces did not wholly take over from private investment and display of wealth. Expenditure on houses, for instance, was not constrained where cities invested in sanctuaries, as Marzabotto shows. In the large south Etruscan cities the lack of evidence on contemporary houses is unfortunate; however, the finding of an earlier, sixth-century BCE 330-square-metre *atrium* house, the so-called *Casa dell'Impluvium*, at Roselle, a town on the plain of Grosseto overlooking the coast in southern Tuscany, gives us a glimpse of the character of elite houses elsewhere (Donati, 1994). Houses from the same period excavated on the Palatine in Rome can be equally helpful for the Tyrrhenian region (Cifani, 2008).

An analogous argument can be made for burials: that sanctuaries were monumentalized as large *tumuli* ceased to be built in southern Etruria is indicative of a sociopolitical change that drove, in turn, changing modes of display expressing social distinction, and perhaps different beliefs about death, rather than a lower investment in the funerary sphere. One exception to this is *Veii*, where some form of austerity is detected from the middle of the sixth century BCE in the contraction of grave goods and the diffusion of a tomb type, a chamber-like trench accessible via an open-air staircase, that held cremation urns in niches carved into the walls of the trench (Drago Troccoli, 1997; Bartoloni and Michetti, 2019, pp. 111–12). Scholars have attributed this austerity to *Veii*'s proximity to Rome and Rome's growing influence on neighbouring Latin towns such as *Crustumerium*, which lies only 14 kilometres away from *Veii* on the other side of the Tiber. Here, too, as in Rome, we see similar changes in funerary rituals, which have been attributed to the implementation of sumptuary legislation, the so-called Twelve Tables, known from ancient Roman writers, which restricted the display and lavishness at funerals. Although appealing, this explanation fails to take into account the role of changing beliefs in the afterlife and in the treatment of the dead (Willemsen, 2013). But the archaeological record at *Veii* for this period is unfortunately wanting, a result of the little attention given to poorer burials in the history of excavation.[4] This lack of attention applies equally elsewhere, although, where we do have better documentation, it seems that changing beliefs were reflected in different rituals.

Beside the continuity, at some cities, of the use of inhumation rites in chamber tombs, the adoption of cremation and other tomb types such as pit (*tomba a buca/pozzetto*) or *cassetta*/box-type tombs is seen at *Caere*, *Volsinii*, Chianciano and its environs near Chiusi, Vulci and Tarquinia, which holds a particularly rich record of Attic figured vessels used as cinerary urns (Paleothodoros, 2002; Masseria, 2009). At *Volsinii*, *impasto* and *bucchero* non-figured vessels were more popular urns; at the well-documented *necropolis* of Tolle near Chianciano, on the other hand, Etruscan black figure vessels fulfilled this role (Paolucci, 2007). At *Caere*, conversely, the deposition of *sarcophagi* and small urns surmounted by terracotta sculptures representing the deceased, among which are the famous *sarcophagi* of the married couple at Villa Giulia and the Louvre museums, offers yet another funerary tradition (Buranelli, 1985; Gaultier, 2013). These customs, either in the choice of urn or tomb type, varied across Etruria and within a single cemetery: while at a single cemetery this probably signalled the deceased's different social status and individual identity, diversity across the broader region is notable. But the overall picture reflects anything but a lack of investment since these changes coexisted with a continuity and evolution in local funerary traditions, which indicate shifts in the private and public nature of funerary space.

Hence, at *Caere*, for example, as the chamber tomb was no longer built under a *tumulus* after the middle of the sixth century BCE, a new architectural type, the so-called *tomba a dado*, was adopted; soon after, this new type was built in the cemeteries of the Tolfa Hills and at San Giuliano further inland, where it evolved into rock-cut tombs at sites such as Blera and Tuscania and this style continued to be in use until the third century BCE (Brocato, 2012). Built with stone blocks or partly dug from *tufa*, the *dado* tomb had a square plan that allowed for the setting of tombs along rectilinear roads inside the cemetery, not unlike the orthogonal plan at Crocifisso del Tufo at *Volsinii* where, in fact, the new type may have been adopted from *Caere*. This new arrangement reflected a new mode of conceptualizing funerary space; moving in and out of a tomb and along the orthogonal roads, onto which the tomb entrances faced, meant a different, arguably higher, degree of visibility than had been possible at the earlier round *tumulus* structures, whose earliest tomb entrances were oriented to the north-west according to Etruscan beliefs on the location of the underworld (Izzet, 2007, pp. 115–21). *Dado* tombs, furthermore, occupied a much smaller interior space than even the smaller *tumuli* that preceded them; the interior space was simpler than the earlier chamber tombs under *tumulus*; in these earlier tombs, the soft *tufa* was carefully carved to re-create furniture such as seats and tables and architectural features such as gabled roofs, or, in one word, a domestic interior, as we saw in Chapter 2 (Figure 5.14).

However, the outside and interior decoration of *dado* tombs were no less carefully thought out and realized: the moulding of the outside blocks, and architectural features of the tomb entrances; the presence of staircases either dug into the rock or built with blocks hinting at the use of the tomb's roof for rituals; the interior plan, which in some cases included several chambers, not unlike the plan of tombs under *tumulus*, even though the standardized plan of two chambers built along the same

Figure 5.14 *Dado* tombs, Banditaccia *necropolis*, *Caere*, author's photograph.

axis later prevailed; the presence of stone furnishings which consisted mostly of the funerary couches (Brocato and Novelli, 2012). All of these features bear witness to the high degree of investment in death, as does the wealth of grave goods, which, when preserved from later looting, suggests the high status of the tomb's owner. What remains unclear are the reasons behind this new manner of funerary display, visibility and organization of the cemeterial space. Whether it indicates a central authority imposing the new organization and/or new emerging social groups exploiting these changes is difficult to ascertain, but these are certainly not far-fetched explanations.

Some form of standardization of tomb architecture also prevailed at Tarquinia where the best documented urban cemetery of this phase, at Monterozzi, has nevertheless only been partially excavated, and many tombs have been heavily plundered over time. Be that as it may, and as far as we can see, no such radical changes as those seen at *Caere* occurred here in the sixth century BCE; we see rather a reduction in the size of the *tumuli* and chamber tombs underneath as the cemetery grew organically with trench and pit graves holding cremations placed between the *tumuli* (Leighton, 2002, pp. 86–106). Investment in the tomb, however, is notable not only in the actual construction of the *tumulus* and of the chamber dug into the rock underneath but also in the tomb's interior and exterior decoration: a series of slabs in *nenfro*, the local stone, or limestone, richly carved with figured decoration, dated from the late seventh until the later sixth century BCE, probably stood outside the tomb's entrance; the carved architectural features inside the chamber, which first mostly consisted of the ridge of the sloping ceiling and of benches, was enriched, in the first half of the fifth century BCE, with other carved relief decoration such as door jambs and beams as well as niches into the walls, indicating the presence of more than one burial (Marzullo, 2017, pp. 80–8); the tradition of wall painting in the tomb's interior, begun in the late seventh century, continued and noticeably increased in the course of the sixth century BCE and throughout the first half of the fifth century (Marzullo, 2017, pp. 143–8).

From the late sixth century BCE, this painted decoration culminated in complex figurative imagery that covered all the walls of the tomb and attests to the practice of banqueting and later *symposia* and Dionysiac rites. From that period on, several painted tombs exhibited extraordinary scenes of banquets, wine drinking, dances, hunting, games and other scenes (d'Agostino and Cerchiai, 1999; Roncalli, 2001; Steingräber, 2006; Cerchiai, 2008); the meaning of these scenes, allegorical and otherwise, is often challenging to capture, although it was certainly governed by religious beliefs about life and death, in which Dionysiac cults played an important role (see below). The extant number of painted tombs overall, *circa* 500, while staggering to the modern observer, is small in comparison with the total number of known tombs at Monterozzi (roughly 6,400), and thus indicates a small percentage of burying groups whose tombs were decorated in this way. However, the use of wall paintings clearly peaked from the late sixth to the first half of the fifth century BCE and hints at a definitive investment in funerary rites during this period (Marzullo, 2017, pp. 143–4) (Figure 5.15).

In Etruria Padana, funerary investment is unquestionable, but there, too, we see variations across the region and urban *necropoleis*. The well-documented cemeteries at Bologna, for example, reveal important transformations detected from the late sixth century BCE, including the internal organization of burials according to the regular spacing of graves among which single plots have been identified, either belonging to family groups or determined by other, possibly ideological and sociopolitical reasons. These reasons may have also determined the choice of burial ritual, either cremation, reserved for the most powerful dead linked to heroic military values, or the less common inhumation, although here,

Figure 5.15 Tomb of the Lionesses, Monterozzi *necropolis*, Tarquinia, photograph by Jean-Pierre Dalbéra (CC BY-SA 2.0), from Wikimedia Commons.

too, namely at Certosa cemetery, we see the presence of cremations in Attic imported vessels, particularly kraters, from the second quarter of the fifth century BCE (Govi, 2009). Another key change beginning at *circa* 500 BCE until the early fourth century BCE is the use of richly decorated stone *stelai* to mark graves. Their figured decoration, which was clearly borrowed from the imagery of Attic vessels buried with the deceased, varied across time, but was mostly centred upon the underworld and the deceased. The latter was either represented in their social role – for example, warriors, horse-riders, veiled men and women in various stances – or later accompanied by mythical figures such as Hermes and winged underworld demons or on their journey to the underworld on a chariot (Govi, 2015b). We will see, in the next chapter, the intriguing parallels between these images and the contemporary ones painted on tomb walls at Tarquinia. Importantly, these *stelai* signalled a shift in the modes of expressing social distinction, which now occurred outside the tomb, and along the main road of the cemetery as seen at the Certosa *necropolis*. Confirmation of this shift is seen after the middle of the fifth century BCE when more imposing and hence visible funerary monuments facing the main road were built, again detected at Certosa, coinciding with a contraction of imported grave goods and Attic fineware. Although at other cemeteries, for instance the Arnoaldi *necropolis*, some tombs still held exceptionally wealthy grave goods, the monumental size of some of the *stelai*, reaching up to 2 metres in height in the second half of the fifth century, and the inscriptions sometimes carved on them further highlight the exploitation of the cemetery's public space for asserting the sociopolitical power of the ruling elite (Govi, 2009).

THE CULTS OF DIONYSOS: A CHANGING SOCIETY

What all the aforementioned evidence demonstrates is the occurrence of shifts, between the sixth and fifth century BCE, in the private and public nature of the space devoted to the performance of funerary rituals. These shifts varied greatly across time and space both within a settlement's cemeteries and among settlements; the evidence discussed earlier, in fact, is merely a snapshot of this vast variation. However, it is enough to show two things. First, the distinction between the public space of, and investment upon, sanctuaries and the private space of, and investment upon, burials takes us only so far. While this is self-evidently correct, to presuppose too rigid a distinction nevertheless conceals the blurred line between the two, and the likelihood that public investment most probably shared in the shaping of the cemetery. Some of the evidence examined before does indeed emphasize this blurring: the *nenfro* slab at Tarquinia, the staircases abutting the *dado* tombs at *Caere*, and the open-air staircase at the trench tombs at *Veii* all suggest the performance of some rituals outside and around the tomb entrance and its visibility beyond the burying family group. This is certainly the case at Cortona with *tumulus* II of the Sodo *tumuli*, where a finely sculpted majestic staircase abutting the *tumulus* drum led to a platform, probably used as an altar or for cultic purposes (Figure 5.16); the finding of architectural terracottas near the drum and on top of the *tumulus* also points to the presence of a structure built for such purposes. The placing of burials near the staircase, some dated before the collapse of the structure and others to the late first millennium BCE, finally hints at the importance of this sacred area (Zamarchi Grassi, 2006). The placement of a sanctuary within the Cannicella cemetery at *Volsinii* is perhaps the most unmistakable clue to the encroachment of communal cults into a cemetery. Equally eloquent is the placing of a sanctuary at Montetosto, along the *Caere-Pyrgi* road, examined in the previous chapter, on the other side from the seventh-century BCE monumental *tumulus*.

Figure 5.16 Monumental staircase, Sodo Tumulus II, Cortona © Alamy.

The second aspect to note, as these examples demonstrate, is the dynamic relationship between built space and ritual practices, and the role of those practices in shaping that space and modifying its private or public function. It may not be fortuitous that these shifts between public and private occurred as Dionysiac cults became more intensively practised, eroding the boundary between religious and funerary cult. These cults at sanctuaries are well documented throughout Etruria, from wine-drinking vessels, cups and kraters, locally made and imported, which were used for libation and then deposited as votives, to the architectural decoration of sacred buildings. The few fifth-century BCE inscriptions we have referring to *Fufluns*, the Etruscan deity that was merged with Greek Dionysos, virtually all come from Vulci: they were engraved on four Attic drinking vessels, mostly found in tombs, among which were two cups and a *rhyton*, a conical drinking vessel, in the shape of the head of a mule. On imported Attic pottery the *rhyton* is often depicted as held by Dionysos, who is often shown with a mule or riding on one. The identical inscription on these vessels reads '*Fufluns Pachie* at Vulci' (Maras, 2009, pp. 395–7): *Pachie* derives from the Greek Βακχειος and refers to the ecstatic invocation of the wine god by his worshippers during Bacchic mystery cults. These cults, about which we know a great deal from Greek literary sources, developed in the Greek world and spread across the Mediterranean from the Black Sea to Spain. The reference to Vulci in these inscriptions, furthermore, squarely puts Bacchic cults in the context of the city, perhaps indicating a cult place dedicated to the god. It is likely that the Vulcian vessels were the possessions of the deceased while alive, who used them for their initiation into Dionysiac mystery cults in order to ensure their life after death. This eschatological dimension of mystery cults is, in fact, attested in southern Italy, where, in the fifth century BCE, Pythagoreanism, a popular religious and philosophical movement, also developed an interest in the survival of the soul after death (Riedweg, 2005).

In Etruria, the earliest images of the wine god on imported black figure Attic vessels date to the sixth century BCE, although Dionysiac drinking rituals may have arguably originated even earlier when drinking and libation practices had already become part and parcel of the funerary ceremony, as examined in Chapter 3. Undoubtedly, however, the overwhelming occurrence, from the late sixth century, of images of the god and his related attributes such as masks and the *thyrsus*, of drinkers and banqueters, revellers and dancing women, some of whom hold a snake, a chthonic attribute particularly visible on Etruscan black figure vessels, signals the increasing popularity of the cults (Werner, 2005; Paleothodoros, 2007). That these images mostly come from tombs, from vase painting to tomb figured decoration, is certainly a result of the excavation history of Etruria; it also suggests, however, the close link between Dionysiac cults and funerary rituals (Colonna, 1991, 1996). Thus, we see Dionysiac motifs and themes such as the ivy leaf and the silen, companion to the wine god, on the Bologna *stelai* (Govi, 2015a). The thousands of Attic painted vessels deposited in the cemeteries across Etruria, particularly those from the cemeteries of Etruria Padana, from Bologna to Spina, allow us to trace not only the popularity of these cults but also the several different forms and configurations which they took for different individuals, their social role and status in Etruria as much as in the Greek world and beyond. Particularly salient is the use of black figure pottery, both Etruscan and Attic, displaying Dionysiac imagery as cremation urns in southern Etruria; similarly notable is the use of the Attic krater to hold cremations at Bologna Certosa and Spina (Pizzirani, 2009, 2010). Indeed, starting from being socially restricted, Dionysiac cults broadened out across different social levels, particularly after the middle of the fifth century BCE and later once eschatological and mystery beliefs came to be at the centre of these rites (Roth, 2004).

Finally, the close link between Dionysiac cult and death may be compared with the chthonic nature of religious cults that is evident in sanctuaries, as already pointed out in the previous chapter, and clearly apparent at the Cannicella sanctuary–*necropolis*. The only fifth-century BCE *Fufluns* inscription from a sanctuary underlines this close link: found in a deposit in the southern sanctuary at *Pyrgi* is the renowned but poorly preserved Attic red figure column krater, depicting Herakles lying on a couch and about to drink from an oversize *kantharos*, another attribute of Dionysos, while attended to by a satyr (Baglione, 1997; Maras, 2009, p. 334). Its inscription contains the epithet *fuflunusra*, translated as 'belonging to the entourage of *Fufluns*' and most probably referring to *Śuri*, an Etruscan chthonic deity, as noted in the previous chapter.

Understanding fifth-century BCE Etruscan society by drawing out the social and ritual practices occurring within the private and public spaces of settlements and cities, from *Veii* to Forcello, from Pisa to Perugia, as I have attempted to do thus far, helps us trace the continuity and transformations of all these settlements without needing to invoke any divergence between them or their river valleys, whether inland, along the coast or in the Appennines. Indeed, the sheer diversity among them, of which this chapter has only been able to give the reader a mere glance, as well as the multidirectional and multi-pronged networks linking them together is what made the Etruscan world such a dynamic region across the central Mediterranean. Such a dynamism, however, went hand in hand with greater instability in this broader region, which became the theatre of increasingly frequent wars and battles fought on land and sea: of these, the Battle of the Sardinian Sea, previously mentioned, was the first one recounted by ancient writers. Another historically recorded war saw the Greek city of *Cumae* in Campania asking for the help of *Hieron* I, tyrant and ruler of Syracuse, against Etruscan incursions; this ended into a naval battle in 474 BCE, in which Greek allies came out victorious, and which Greek sources, notably the poet Pindar (Pyth. 1.71.81), celebrated as a Greek victory not unlike that of the Athenians against the Persian fleet at Salamis (Prag, 2010, pp. 55–7). Some scholars have argued that these wars were accompanied by mobility over greater distances than previously across the peninsula, as evidenced by the increasing presence and distribution of so-called La Téne or Celtic material culture in Etruria Padana from the end of the fifth century BCE (Lejars, 2006). Brizio had already encountered such material during his field research at Marzabotto, when a small *necropolis* was excavated south of the *acropolis*. This inaugurates a new phase in Etruscan Italy, the fourth century BCE, when that instability came to be heavily defined by Rome's imperial expansion, which saw the falling of *Veii* to the power of Rome in 396 BCE. We turn to this new phase in the next chapter.

6

ETRURIA AND ROME

THE TOMB OF THE INFERNAL CHARIOT, SARTEANO

On 11 October 2003, archaeologists from the Museum of Sarteano excavating the Pianacce *necropolis*, located south-west of Chiusi and overlooking the Valdichiana, found a painted chamber tomb with a 19-metre-long *dromos*, the corridor leading to the main chamber, along which were four niches. The plan of the main chamber included other smaller spaces, probably side chambers used at different phases of use of the burial. The tomb as a whole may have been conceived, along with three other similar chamber tombs adjacent to it, in the eastern area of the *necropolis* which holds the best documented fourth-century BCE tomb groups of the hinterland of Chiusi. A large travertine *cippus* found inside the *dromos* probably stood at the entrance to the chamber, which was closed by a stone door, still in situ. The tomb had been sadly plundered; however, the alabaster *sarcophagus*, surmounted by the sculpted representation of the deceased lying on a *kline*, or banqueting bed, and left in the main chamber, held the only burial inside, but it had been smashed and only a few bone remains of the deceased were recovered (Minetti, 2006). Despite this and the medieval occupation of the tomb, the careful excavation and rigorous application of conservation techniques and scientific analyses of all the material left have given us an exceptional record of a late fourth-century BCE painted tomb that is unlike other contemporary painted ones known so far because they have not benefitted from such analyses.[1]

Hence, osteological analyses on the human remains identified a single male adult inhumation (Minetti, 2006, pp. 89–91); the scientific dating of wooden remains, which probably belonged to tomb furnishings, also confirmed the date of the tomb, its decoration and of the *sarcophagus*, the earliest in a series of Hellenistic alabaster *sarcophagi* known at Chiusi (Minetti, 2006, pp. 96–100). This series succeeded the Chiusine tradition of stone life-size statue-urns that lasted until the beginning of the fourth century BCE, and culminated with the terracotta *sarcophagus* of *Seianti Hanunia Tlesnasa* now on display at the British Museum (Swaddling, 2002). Furthermore, the painting technique – it was found – was particularly accurate and involved three distinct layers of paint, of which one was the preparatory stage when the figures were first incised onto the fresh paint. We also know that the tomb was left unfinished since the right-hand-side wall of the tomb chamber was never painted, prompting questions as to whether the tomb had been intended for more than one deposition (Minetti, 2006, pp. 87–8). Though plundered, the grave goods included drinking and banqueting equipment, and a series of terracotta plates decorated with small sculpted birds and belonging to footed censers, of which we have examples in bronze, notably from the Settecamini *necropolis* outside *Volsinii* (Ambrosini, 2013).

The wall paintings of this new tomb, which have given the tomb its name, the Tomb of the Infernal Chariot (*Quadriga Infernale*), are at once unique and in line with other images from contemporary and later tombs: they depict scenes of the underworld, which became common in the visual culture of this period across Etruria, from figured painted vessels to scenes sculpted on *sarcophagi* and urns from Tarquinia to Bologna. Scenes depicting the underworld were populated by underworld demons, creatures and deities such as *Phersiphnai* (Greek *Persephone*) and her husband *Aita* (Greek Hades), and by the deceased on his/her way to the underworld, often on a chariot, as visible on funerary *stelai* at Bologna noted in the previous chapter. These scenes replaced earlier ones centred, as we have seen, on banquets, dances and drinking underlying Dionysiac rites. To be sure, the banquet does not disappear in the funerary iconography from the fourth century BCE, but it is squarely located in the underworld (Cerchiai, 2011). This is exemplified by the paintings, dated to the middle of the fourth century, where *Phersiphnai* and *Aita* are shown seated at a banquet in Tomb Golini I at the Settecamini *necropolis*, and in the Tomb of Orco II at Tarquinia. In the Tomb of the Infernal Chariot, two men, most probably the deceased, reclining on a *kline* facing each other and in conversation, were painted on the walls of the corridor, attended to by a young male servant holding a metal strainer used to filter the wine (Minetti, 2006, pp. 25–44). That the men, one younger than the other, may have been relatives or lovers is difficult to ascertain, but in the Golini I Tomb at *Volsinii* the brother relation between the painted pair of male banqueters is confirmed by the inscriptions accompanying them.

This banquet scene was preceded by a chariot, the infernal chariot, painted on the same wall, pulled by fantastic animals, two lions and two griffins, towards the exit of the tomb, and led by a demonic figure with wind-blown hair and enveloped by a black cloud (Figure 6.1). Below these scenes, a strip of black waves into which small dolphins plunge also signals the world of the dead, where the banquet is taking place. Further reference to this world is the enormous three-headed serpent painted on the side wall of the main chamber, and adjacent to a large hippocampus filling the space of the gable of the back wall of the chamber. What is unusual about this painting is that the chariot is not led by the deceased, but by a demon or a mythological figure, either the demon *Charun* (Greek Charon ferrying the dead to the underworld) or *Aitia* himself (Harari, 2011). This is unusual although images of chariots pulled by winged dragons and led by *Phersiphnai* are found in two renowned red figure Etruscan *amphorae* of the so-called Vanth Group painters' workshop from *Volsinii*. Indeed, the stylistic and iconographic analogies with the visual culture of *Volsinii* cannot be fortuitous: the painters'

Figure 6.1 Tomb of the Infernal Chariot, Pianacce *necropolis*, Sarteano © Bridgeman.

traditions we see there in vase painting and in the painted tombs of the Settecamini *necropolis* must have influenced the painter of this tomb, if not indeed the Volsinian workshop itself, which may have been involved in the painting of the tomb at Sarteano (Minetti, 2006, pp. 39–44).

FROM DIONYSIAC CULTS TO ESCHATOLOGICAL BELIEFS AND BEYOND: THE TOMB BECOMES POLITICAL

Like other contemporary tombs, principally at Tarquinia and *Volsinii*, the Tomb of the Infernal Chariot thus conveyed a very different mood from that of the images in the wall and vase paintings of the previous two centuries, and yet the eschatological themes of the paintings find their origins in the mystery Dionysiac cults that grew in the fifth century BCE, as noted in the last chapter. Indeed, it is to these cults we must look, and the transfer of the Dionysiac rites to a funerary dimension. We can accurately trace this transfer in some earlier tomb paintings at Tarquinia, namely in the tombs of the Ship and of the Blue Demons, both dated to the third quarter of the fifth century BCE. In the former, the *symposium*, painted on the back wall of the tomb chamber, as had become customary in the tomb paintings of this century, is next to a scene, painted on the left-hand-side wall, of servants attending to a *kylikeion*, the table on which stood the wine mixing vessels for the *symposium*. Behind the *kylikeion*, ships at sea between large cliffs occupy the rest of the wall: although variously interpreted, this scene seems to be most convincingly read as a metaphor for the perilous journey to the underworld (Colonna, 2003) (Figure 6.2).

This reading is supported by the painting of the Tomb of the Blue Demons that also shows a *symposium* of reclining men with the deceased couple on the back wall of the chamber, while the side walls depict scenes oriented towards this back wall. On the left hand side is a procession with dancers and other attendants, and the chariot of a man, most probably the male deceased; on the other side, the female deceased is being led by winged demons, together with a wingless one brandishing serpents, to the ship with a dark-skin *Charun* at the helm and ready to ferry her to the other side. The direction of both paintings towards the back wall leads us to believe that the *symposium* is, in fact, taking place among the ancestors of the family, among whom was the deceased couple; it even suggests, in fact, an analogous reading for other similar *symposium* scenes in Tarquinian tomb paintings before any explicit reference to the

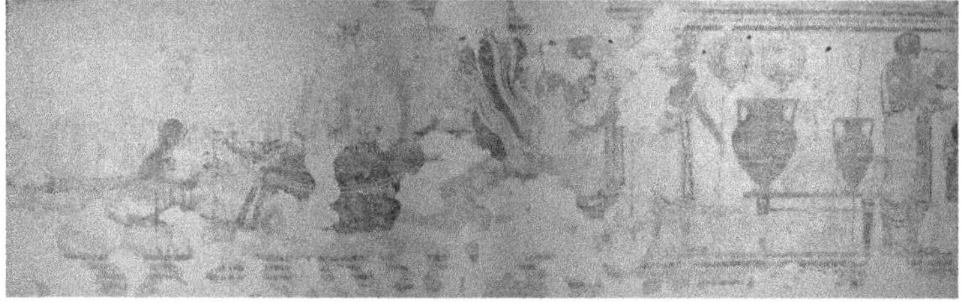

Figure 6.2 Tomb of the Ships, Monterozzi *necropolis*, Tarquinia, from Marzullo, M. 2016 *Grotte Cornetane. Materiali e apparato critico per lo studio delle tombe dipinte di Tarquinia*, Tarchna suppl. 6, Milano, pg. 247.

underworld was made. The Greek character of *Charun*, identified by his pointed cap who also appears on contemporary images of Attic white-ground funerary unguent containers or *lekythoi*, is unique in Etruria, and attests to the adoption and adaptation of a Greek funerary register. This can also be detected in the material recovered in the tomb and in the burial ritual. The ritual included a male incineration, a separate funeral pyre for the offerings, and probably a female inhumation on a *kline*. The grave goods included Attic black and red figure fineware, of which one was a krater, two Panathenaic *amphorae*, weapons, horse bits and, exceptionally for this period, a chariot associated with the remains of two horses: all of this material together with the 13-metre-long monumental *dromos* made this a notable tomb group on Monterozzi, belonging to a family that was clearly at the forefront of remarkably innovative funerary imagery (Adinolfi, Carmagnola, and Cataldi, 2005).

However, underworld demons were not new in Etruscan beliefs of the underworld: among them, *Vanth*, who becomes the companion of *Charun* in Hellenistic images of the underworld, was first mentioned in an inscription that reads 'I am the beautiful Vanth', painted on an Etrusco-Corinthian *aryballos*, an unguent container, from Marsiliana d'Albegna, dated to the end of the seventh century BCE. The name *Charun* itself was incised on the foot of a late sixth-century BCE Greek *kylix*, signed by Athenian ceramic painter Oltos, attesting to the dedication of this drinking cup to the ferryman of Hades (Colonna, 1996). More generally, symbolic references to the underworld such as marine waves and dolphins also date back to the archaic period, most famously seen in the Tomb of Hunting and Fishing at Tarquinia (Figure 6.3). Like the dolphins, the hippocampus, too, symbolized the underworld and was depicted in the gable of late sixth-century BCE painted tomb chambers, most famously the Tomb of the Bulls at Tarquinia, and in other fourth-century BCE tomb paintings there, namely the Tomb of the Pygmies, and at *Caere*, in the Tomb of the Sarcophagi and the Tomb of the Triclinium. Lastly, the motif of the false door, another symbolic figurative reference to the world beyond that was painted on the wall of archaic tombs, continued through to the third century BCE at Tarquinia (Marzullo, 2017, pp. 23–7).

If the continuity of these motifs and emphasis upon them thus shows the growth in eschatological beliefs in the fourth century BCE, this growth was not limited to Etruria: as noted in the previous chapter, such beliefs were widespread in southern Italy and the Greek world. This continuity, however, goes hand in hand with a key change in fourth-century representations of the underworld, namely the glorification of

Figure 6.3 Tomb of Hunting and Fishing, Monterozzi *necropolis*, Tarquinia © Getty.

the deceased and his/her family: this was effected by the depiction of themes and motifs that intersected the paradigm of the final journey with the paradigm of the social and political standing of the deceased and his/her family. This practice became increasingly explicit: these themes and motifs included the chariot, the procession with or without chariot, and the banquet itself. This is not surprising: not only were the use of chariots and lavish banqueting elite practices, but both had also been employed as focal components of funerary rites for expressing social distinction and, in the case of the chariot, political authority, since the early first millennium BCE, as examined previously. From the fourth century BCE, however, the family group and the *gens* became overtly exalted in the material and visual culture of the tomb: not only were different members of the family depicted, often among demons, or mythical figures and deities as at Tarquinia; their names, their family relations, and the political roles of some of the family members were also deliberately flaunted through inscriptions and overt symbols of political power. Hence, in the painting of the Golini I Tomb at *Volsinii*, which we know to belong to the *Leinies* family thanks to those inscriptions, the seated banquet of *Phersiphnai* and *Aita* is adjacent to the banquet of the family ancestors, reclining and dressed in white robes or *togae*. On the other side of this scene and moving towards it is the deceased driving the chariot accompanied by a winged female demon (Feruglio, 1995). Among the reclining family members were two brothers, suitably accompanied by inscriptions giving details of their political career: of these, *Vel Leinies*, we learn from the inscription, had been a *zilaθ meχl rasneas clevsinsl*, that is, the top magistrate at Chiusi, a political office to which I return below.[2]

Even more remarkable for the abundance of inscriptions, over twenty, which allows us to trace the genealogy of the family owning the tomb, is the Tomb of the Shields (*Tomba degli Scudi*) at Tarquinia. This is a monumental chamber tomb with three chambers surrounding a central *vestibulum* (a vestibule), dated to the second half of the fourth century BCE. Beside the fourteen shields painted on the walls of the back chamber, which gave the name to the tomb discovered in 1870, all the other wall paintings, representing eleven members of the *Velcha* family and attendants, many of them *toga*-clad, decorated this central *vestibulum* along with accompanying inscriptions. Here, the tomb founder *Larth Velcha* and his father *Velthur Velcha* are represented twice, first with the other family members, and second at a banquet in the afterlife. On the rear wall, in a solemn seated position that reminds the viewer of seated *Phersiphnai* and *Aita* in the Golini I Tomb at *Volsinii*, the deceased father and head of the family is enthroned next to his wife who is pointing at him and perhaps also to his hero status. Upon this enthroned couple converges the procession of the family, including *Larth* himself, the tomb founder. To the right of the tomb entrance, where the painting is sadly poorly preserved, *Larth* appears as a magistrate in a highly solemn moment of the procession; he is preceded by attendants or lictors carrying the hallmarks of his political role, perhaps *fasces* and a *sella curulis*, a bundle of metal rods and a folding seat respectively. These were the *insignia* of a magistrate's power in republican Rome; I will return to these below. The two underworld banquet scenes emphasize the married couple: the founder and deceased father are both banqueting with their respective wives in the company of the two winged demons painted on each side of the door to the back chamber, which confirmed the funerary setting of these scenes. Above *Larth*'s banquet, the long inscription confirms the political office or magistracy that *Larth* held in life, that of *zilχ ceχaneri* (Maggiani, 2005) (Figure 6.4).

This political office, which combined the name *zilath*, already found a couple of centuries earlier in the word *zilac* from the inscribed golden plaques at *Pyrgi* (see Chapter 4), and *ceχaneri*, which refers to something 'superior', occurs two other times at Tarquinia (Maggiani, 1996, p. 100). The second is found on a contemporary *sarcophagus* discovered in a tomb in 1876: decorated with mythological battles around the side of the casket, the top of the *sarcophagus* shows the recumbent deceased on a *kline*, as customary on *sarcophagi* of this period and seen in the *sarcophagus* at Sarteano; below him, the inscription tells us his identity, *Velϑur Partunus*,

Figure 6.4 Right-hand wall of back chamber, Tomb of the Shields, Monterozzi *necropolis*, Tarquinia, from Marzullo, M. 2016 *Grotte Cornetane. Materiali e apparato critico per lo studio delle tombe dipinte di Tarquinia*, Tarchna suppl. 6, Milano, p. 340.

who died at age 82 and held *zilχ ceχaneri*. The third occurrence comes from the Tomb of the Meeting (*Tomba del Convegno*), a later tomb, dated to the first half of the third century BCE and discovered in 1970: its poorly preserved wall painting shows a procession of male *togati*, carrying symbols of political power, including the *fasces*, among whom are men identified as magistrates. One of these, older and holding some unidentifiable object, is named *Larth* by the inscription over his head, his gentilicial name no longer preserved, and is given the role *zilχ ceχaneri*. The nature of this superior magistracy is suggested by the iron *fasces* with a two-headed axe and spears carried by attendants walking in front of him. Each of these, according to the ancient author Dionysius of Halicarnassus, represented each city when handed to a federal commander in chief during military campaigns that involved allied city states (Maggiani, 1996). The military function of *zilχ ceχaneri* may have been further celebrated by the shields painted in the back room of the Tomb of the Shields although military virtue, in fact, was part and parcel of the social and political standing of all the ruling families across Etruscan cities and hence duly exalted here as elsewhere. In this respect, the contemporary friezes of weapons dated to the end of the fourth century BCE and painted in the Giglioli Tomb at Tarquinia are also notable (Harari, 2007, p. 45).

From the end of the fourth century BCE, processions of male attendants carrying these symbols of political rule also decorated the caskets of *sarcophagi* from Tarquinia and its hinterland, Tuscania and Vulci, and, from the third century BCE, on *tufa*, limestone and alabaster cinerary urns at Volterra. The procession was accompanied by the magistrate either in a chariot or on foot (Maggiani, 1996, pp. 127–32; Tassi Scandone, 2001). The Tomb of the Shields marked a watershed in Etruscan funerary imagery, whereby the procession depicted was no longer entirely funerary (Maggiani, 2005, pp. 125–6); any demon or underworld reference was an add-on, so to speak. Aimed at commemorating the political standing of the deceased, the procession decorating the tomb and the receptacle holding the dead had, in other words, become a fully political, even public, statement. All of this raises some key points, to which I now turn: first, the political system in Etruria underlying the political offices or magistracies that become visible in the epigraphic and visual record, and their Roman counterparts; second, the context in which this transformation took place and the reasons behind it, namely Rome's imperial expansion and the ensuing political instability and warfare; and third and concurrently, the relationship between the archaeological and the literary evidence. This third point is fundamental for it informs so much of our interpretations of the archaeology that tackling it first will be helpful for addressing the first two points.

ROME AND ETRURIA: LITERARY SOURCES VIS-À-VIS ARCHAEOLOGY

It is not, by any means, far-fetched to suggest, as has been done (Naso, 2001, p. 24), that the *zilχ ceχaneri*, if it indeed referred to a federal military commander in chief, held by *Larth* of the Tomb of the Shields and by *Larth* of the Tomb of the Meeting respectively, was linked to military campaigns. These saw the city pitted against Rome in the fourth century BCE, and ended up with its fall to Roman power in the third century. Livy (Livy 7.17.2–9), after all, mentions a multi-city alliance against Rome and led by Tarquinia in the fourth century. Indeed, we are very luckily extremely well informed about Rome's takeover in Etruria and across Italy from later literary sources. The information we have of the time of the fall of *Veii* in 396 BCE, for instance, gives us the calibre of military might to which Rome subjected its conquered cities, but also more generally of the violence prevailing then: *Veii* fell after a ten-year siege, recounted in mythical terms by later sources, not unlike the siege of Troy. Its final destruction went hand in hand with its moral one: the statue of Juno (Etruscan *Uni*) housed in a temple dedicated to her on the citadel of the city was taken away to Rome and placed in a temple on the Aventine (Livy 5.22.3–7), an act of imperial power, which the Romans named *evocatio* (Orlin, 2010, pp. 36–40). The word referred to the summoning, by the Romans, of the divinity that was then transferred and incorporated into Rome's urban religious geography; it ensured the easy capture by force of cities that in this way no longer had divine protection. Soon after, in 390 BCE, Rome suffered a sack by the Gauls. In fact, the historical information we have of all this, as with much else for this period, is a result of layers of historical material transmitted by later ancient authors. Importantly, the treatment by these authors of this material was ideological, deeply bound up with a process of self-fashioning by Rome's growing imperial power, and therefore difficult for the modern historian to disentangle. Hence, the fall of *Veii* and the Gallic Sack together became part and parcel of a narrative, constructed by later authors such as Livy, in which Rome conquered, was sacked and was finally vindicated; the narrative was centred upon the Roman general *Camillus* who had taken *Veii* and was involved in the fight during the

Sack; he thus became central in the political discourses of late republican Rome, and was later exploited by Augustus when Livy was writing (Gaertner, 2008; Smith, 2019).

While historians of Roman history today recognize its deeply ideological and one-sided agenda, we can nevertheless still use that history in order to have a context in which to place and understand the archaeological record and its patterns of change. In the case of *Veii*, that understanding is not as detailed as one would like: there is no actual evidence of destruction on the sites of the city, other than the levelling of earlier structures upon which Roman republican villas and houses were built. On the other hand, the archaeological material recovered from field surveys on the urban plateau shows a shrinkage of the town and an occupation restricted to the centre from the middle of the fourth century BCE (Di Giuseppe, 2012). The temple of *Uni*/Juno has not yet been found, although the votive deposit at the site of Piano di Comunità on the urban plateau may be evidence of that temple (Smith, 2019, p. 223); indeed, here, the votive material shows the performance of cult practices from the fifth to the second century BCE, with a hiatus in the fourth century, and the deposition of different types of votive offerings from the end of the fourth century, that are in line with those found at sanctuaries elsewhere, some of which had been founded by Roman colonists *ex novo* (Bartoloni and Benedettini, 2011).

Yet, despite the regrettable lack of details in the material record, it is reasonably clear that Rome gained enormously from conquering *Veii* and its hinterland; its long-standing relationship with its closest Etruscan neighbour must have had an impact on the motivations behind the conquest and its consequences (Terrenato, 2019).[3] It was not simply a question of a substantial land grab, which was then distributed to Roman citizens as was to become customary in Rome's conquest of the rest of the peninsula; conquering *Veii*'s 50,000-hectare land meant for Rome a threefold increase of its territory. Just as importantly, the confiscated land was along the Tiber Valley, a key communication route, as we saw in the last chapter, and, in the eyes of Rome, a critical frontier. It is no accident that soon after *Veii*, Rome captured Capena, Sutri and Nepi, towns to the north of *Veii*, and transformed the latter two into colonies (Marcone, 2017); indeed, the fate of these communities was deeply entangled with that of their neighbours. The evidence from archaeological field survey, furthermore, does point to a reorganization of the agricultural landscape, which followed a decrease in the number of rural sites in the second half of the fifth century BCE throughout the middle Tiber Valley (Di Giuseppe, 2008). I will return to these data later.

Elsewhere, we have an epigraphic record, as we have seen earlier, that can be particularly helpful in allowing us to trace in a little greater depth the historical context in which the conflicts with Rome grew. There, too, however, the difficulty of combining literary with other sources remains. At Vulci, one of the most monumental chamber tombs of the period, the renowned François Tomb, named after Alessandro François, the Florentine archaeologist who discovered it in 1857 at the Ponte Rotto *necropolis*, is a highly cited source for our knowledge of early Roman history. At the same time, its political and historical wall painting, with the forty or so inscriptions that accompany it, has been the object of an extraordinarily enduring debate that exemplifies the tricky business of disentangling the palimpsest of our literary sources in order to assess these and their value for our interpretations (Steingräber, 1986, pp. 377–81; Rathje, 2014).[4] The paintings that concern us occupied the walls of the two main spaces of the tomb, as one entered it from the very long corridor. Placed on the same axis and forming a T-shaped large room, these two spaces, known as *atrium* and the smaller *tablinum* (terms borrowed from Roman domestic interior architecture) provided access to several funerary chambers. The painted images on the long walls facing each other in the *tablinum* featured violent scenes of battle and killing, and were organized in a symmetrical fashion. Their fulcrum for the viewer was the end wall that led to the very back chamber: here, each side of the door was painted with half a shield, and a naked prisoner next to it, providing a reference point to the larger scenes of men fighting depicted on the long walls (Figure 6.5).

The men are identified by their inscriptions, which allow us to recognize a mythical and a historical fight facing one another: on one side, the mythical scene represents Achilles' (Etruscan *Achle*) killing of Trojan prisoners by the shadow of his friend Patroclus (Etruscan *Patrucle*) and accompanied by a winged Vanth and *Charun*; the prisoner next to the door of the back chamber and the shield is identified as a Trojan. This mythical episode, recounted by the Iliupersis, an epic cycle on the capture of Troy that influenced the Homeric epic, was popular at Vulci and elsewhere in Etruria, and was illustrated on figured painted vases, including Faliscan and Apulian vessels, urns and *sarcophagi*. Facing this scene is the historical fight representing a group of men who are identified in the inscriptions by their names and, in some cases, by their own city. Among them were brothers *Caile* and *Avle Vipinas*, *Macstrna* and a certain *Cneve Tarchunies Rumach*; this latter was represented on the side wall of the *atrium* that saw the continuation of the painted scene;

Figure 6.5 François Tomb, reconstruction of the painting of the *tablinum*, Ponte Rotto *necropolis*, Vulci, courtesy Parco Archeologico di Vulci (Fondazione Vulci).

the naked man next to the half shield at the door of the back chamber is *Caile* being freed by *Macstrna* (Rathje, 2014, pp. 57–60). While *Cneve Tarchunies*, a Tarquin coming from Rome, is not known through literary sources, the Vibenna brothers and *Macstrna* are.

Among these sources, the most famous mention of these characters comes from a speech by the Roman emperor Claudius, recorded by Roman historian Tacitus (*Ann.* 11.24) and a Latin inscription found in Lyon (di Fazio, 2018, p. 324). In the speech, Claudius, famous for his knowledge of Etruscan history, described the deeds of the Vibenna brothers and their faithful companion (*sodalis fidelissimus*) Mastarna, featuring Mastarna's departure from Etruria due to a change of fortune and, with the aid of *Caile*'s private army, his arrival in Rome. Here, he changed his name to none other than *Servius Tullius*, one of the Roman kings. This story, along with the information from other written sources, places the activities of these companions or *sodales* (Paltineri, 2012), whom some scholars have recognized as warlords or *condottieri*, squarely in the political instability of archaic Tyrrhenian city states, including Rome (Rich, 2017). It is no accident that this context also includes the legendary figure of another *condottiere*, Porsenna of Chiusi who, according to literary sources, seized Rome and then fought unsuccessfully at the Battle of *Aricia*, a Latin town, at the end of the sixth century BCE (Colonna, 2001; di Fazio, 2007). Although the Roman and Greek tradition calls him a *rex* or king, Porsenna's deeds place him closer to powerful individuals such as *Thefarie* at *Pyrgi*, whom we have already encountered jostling for power at *Caere*. It is not difficult to imagine, at this time, the use of military force by aristocrats such as the Vibennas who could lend a hand to their friends engaged in their own power struggles. That there is some historical truth, furthermore, to the existence – rather than the specific deeds transmitted by the sources – of these archaic figures is confirmed by one sixth-century BCE dedicatory inscription on a *bucchero* vessel by a certain *Avile Vipiiennas* at the Portonaccio sanctuary, which we encountered in Chapter 5.

The question, however, is why these characters were remembered at Vulci a couple of centuries later in an aristocratic tomb owned by *Vel Saties*, who was also represented in the tomb painting, and his family. The Vibenna brothers, incidentally, are also found depicted on other contemporary artefacts, from urns to an engraved mirror from Bolsena where their name is inscribed (di Fazio, 2018, p. 324). That their characters were painted at Vulci a few decades before Rome took over this city at 280 BCE cannot have been fortuitous. Indeed, scholars have suggested that the historical struggle in the presence of legendary local heroes may have represented, for the ancient viewer, a conflict either among neighbouring cities in Etruria or among these cities and Rome (Coarelli, 1983; Musti, 2005).[5] Whichever the case, what is far more critical and revealing for our understanding of a powerful city state on the eve of its conquest by Rome is the very representation of past deeds that gave meaning to, and perhaps relieved the strain from, the very unstable political present. This would have affected not just the *Saties* family, but the city as a whole, at least insofar as the fate of the family would have depended upon the fate of the city. Notably, that representation fully integrated myth, history and local legends without any distinction between them. Not only, as scholars have suggested (Harari, 2007; di Fazio, 2018), does this indicate a different conception of time, very much unlike our own linear one. These integrated images also highlighted the intention, by the *Saties* family, to memorialize the family and its history through the burials of its members inside the tomb, customary among Etruscan elite families, vis-à-vis the political and hence public and collective past; in doing so, the wall paintings enhanced the memory of both. Just as in the tombs and on funerary receptacles decorated with solemn processions of magistrates, the public and private spheres, once again, shifted: the one merged into, and reinforced the other.

ETRUSCAN MAGISTRATES AND HELLENISTIC POLITICAL INSTITUTIONS

The François Tomb furthermore exemplifies what some scholars have compellingly argued, namely that the Roman takeover of Etruria forced the political and social structure of its cities to become visible to the modern observer (Smith, 2014, p. 104; di Fazio, 2018). Indeed, as the tombs examined earlier make clear, it is thanks to their inscriptions that we have the names of specific political roles or magistracies, which in turn help us understand the political and institutional structure underlying these magistracies with the help of other epigraphic and archaeological evidence. This is useful, particularly because the literary sources are fairly silent on this structure, although the reporting by them of social strife within conquered cities, most famously *Volsinii* (see below), gives us a glimpse into the abrasive relationships between different social groups or classes. However, it remains challenging to disentangle from these sources what may have been typical of the nature of those social relations from the pressures generated by the Roman aggression.

In other instances, the literary sources are investigated to try and understand institutional change, particularly the transition from monarchical to what we may call republican forms of power, not unlike the transition we see in Rome. These attempts are unfortunately also fraught with difficulty, not least because of the ambiguity surrounding the term when those sources employ the word king – *rex* in Latin, *basileus* in Greek and the Etruscan *Lucumo*, according to Servius, a fifth-century CE commentator of Virgil's *Aeneid*. One has to peel back and untangle the very complex palimpsest of the literary tradition in order to assess what was meant by this term centuries before the time that the ancient authors were writing. Indeed, the word *Lucumo* for king may simply be the result of this late tradition that transformed what was a personal Etruscan name, *lauχume*, into a Latin name for an institution (Maggiani, 2001, p. 39); not coincidentally, *Lucumo* was also the name of one of the Roman kings, Lucius Tarquinius. The case of King Porsenna is also instructive: his military power may suggest that an archaic king was a ruler able to secure power by force. Yet, at the same time, *Thefarie* at *Pyrgi* refers to his 'reign' in the Phoenician text (*mlk.j*), but this is translated as *zilac selaita* in the Etruscan text, a compound which may refer to a supreme magistracy that had a time limit (Maggiani, 1996, pp. 102–5; 2001, p. 39).

The epigraphic record for our later period, on the other hand, is reasonably rich: it is made up of *circa* eighty attestations of magistracies or political offices, although the majority of them, almost fifty, comes from Tarquinia and its hinterland, while none, for this period, from Etruria Padana. It is rich enough to allow us to trace, as has been done (Maggiani, 2001), at least for Tarquinia, a veritable *cursus honorum*, to use a Latin phrase that referred to the sequence of political offices pinpointing a politician's career to the highest of magistracies. In fact, we have earlier evidence showing the existence of different types of political office: *zilath* itself, the name of the magistrate holding *zilac*, is recorded at Rubiera, east of Bologna, on a funerary *cippus* or marker dated to the end of the seventh or early sixth century BCE, where it is inscribed referring to a town called *Misala* (or *Sala*). This indicates that *zilath* was a political office specifically attached to the city. Another type of office, known as *marunuχ*, is known from another *cippus*, possibly a boundary stone completely covered by the sixth-century BCE monumental inscription from Tragliatella, not far from *Caere*. The later epigraphic dossier, from the fourth to the second century BCE, indicates that *marunuχ* was, in fact, the first step in a politician's career, and that there were different specializations held by a *maru* in office, identified in compounds of the word and that pertained to civic matters such as tracing the boundaries of landholdings, or, conversely, to a sacred function that had to do with Bacchic rites (Maggiani, 2001, pp. 40–1). Higher offices beyond *marunuχ*, too, had some priestly function: this is the case with *cepen*, which appears in ritual texts from a fifth-century BCE engraved lead plaque from Magliano near Vulci, and from the renowned so-called Zagreb mummy (Maggiani, 1996, pp. 116–17). The mummy is, in fact, a fragmented linen cloth inscribed with a religious calendar of an unknown inland Etruscan town dating to the second century BCE that ended up as a wrapping of an Egyptian mummy (van der Meer, 2007).

In fact, this religious calendar is useful for another reason: it contains terms that Etruscologists have identified as pertaining to socio-institutional entities and that occur elsewhere such as *spura*, which refers to an autonomous urban community and its territory and thus corresponds to the Latin *civitas*. Another term mentioned only once in the text of the mummy is *rasna*, which Etruscologists have identified, at least originally, with the citizenry bearing arms and thus fit for defending the territory of such a community, and which therefore corresponds to the Latin *populus* (Colonna, 1988). The occurrence of the term on a boundary *cippus* found outside Cortona and inscribed with *tular rasnal* (the boundaries of the *rasna*) lends support to this interpretation (Becker, 2013). *Rasna* on its own, however, also carries a lot of baggage, again as a result of the literary tradition, since it occurs in Dionysius of Halicarnassus (Dion. Hal. *Ant. Rom.* 1.30): according to him, *rasna* is how the Etruscans together called themselves. We need not go there, however, since our epigraphic record is rich enough to confirm the above interpretation: in it is included the inscription *zilaθ meχl rasneas clevsinsl*, which we found earlier in the Golini I Tomb, related to *Vel Leinies*, and which can be translated as the supreme magistrate of the city state of Chiusi. It is interesting that a Volsinian could hold such a high office of another city, suggesting, as has been argued (Maggiani, 2001, p. 46), that *Volsinii* and Chiusi may have been at this stage united under the authority of a Volsinian. That other inscriptions mention different attributes of *zilath* also suggests that in any one city state there were different types of *zilath*, some holding office in smaller towns, and who were under this supreme magistrate. This is further corroborated by the so-called *Tabula Cortonensis*, an engraved bronze tablet dated to the late third–early second century BCE, that mentions a supreme *zilath* together with other *ziliaths* (Becker, 2013, pp. 363–4).

At this point it is worth reflecting upon the correspondence and thus the relationship between these political institutions in Etruria and in Rome. Evidence of the interaction between Tyrrhenian city states, of which Rome was one, throughout the first millennium BCE is enough to justify our expectation that that relationship was close; indeed, the depiction of magistrates' processions and all the *insignia* of power which we also find in republican Rome, as examined above, suggests the exchange of these symbols between Etruria and Rome. Ancient writers pointed out that Rome borrowed them from Etruria or Tarquinia (Strabo 5.2.2; Verg. *Aen.* 8.505) in earlier times (Livy 1.8.3; Dion. Hal. *Ant. Rom.* 3.61.3, 3.61.1). Earlier archaeological evidence further corroborates this borrowing, from the two-headed axes represented in various forms and used as *insignia*, to the isolated iron two-headed axe attached to the bundle of rods from the seventh-century BCE Tomb of the Lictor (*Tomba del Littore*) at Vetulonia, which scholars deem to be the earliest lictor's *fasces* ever recorded. From Vetulonia also comes a contemporary *stele* bearing a dedicatory inscription and depicting a warrior brandishing a two-headed axe (Tassi Scandone, 2001, pp. 201–21); I have already discussed in Chapter 4 the deposition of an axe, together with a bronze shield and *lituus*, all symbols of political authority, at the Civita sacred complex of Tarquinia.

Similarly, official garb worn by successful public figures such as triumphant commanders in Rome, namely the *toga picta*, a purple toga with gold thread decoration, has been identified in the purple mantle worn by *Vel Saties*, the owner of the François Tomb, as represented in the wall paintings (Rathje, 2014, p. 61); the *toga picta* belongs, too, to the series of symbols that the Etruscans gave the Romans, according to some sources (Dion. Hal. *Ant. Rom.* 3.61.1) (Tagliamonte, 2017, p. 126). If all of this is enough to place the origins of these symbols in Etruria, the question of when they came to be used as civic symbols, that is, symbols of coexisting political institutions of the *spura*, is still debatable because the evidence so far discussed only gives us the point at which they become visible rather than when they were in existence. And although the epigraphic record is most useful, as seen above, in tracing the range of Etruscan magistracies from the seventh century BCE, we are still in the dark when it comes to the details of the overall political set-up of the *spura* and its evolution. It is nevertheless reasonable to conjecture that oligarchic systems underlay these institutions, not unlike the broadly oligarchic nature of political power in republican Rome (Cerchiai, 2001). But it is also worth reminding the reader that even for early republican Rome our knowledge is limited (North, 2006).

When it comes to these symbols featuring in Etruscan representations of magistrates' processions, the evolution of these representations can show us the extent to which Roman institutions affected them. A case for this has been argued, for instance, for Volterra's cinerary urns where behind the changing iconography of the procession from the third century BCE may lie changes in the institutions of the city once it was under Rome. For a group of three cinerary urns, in particular, all dated to the first century BCE and showing a procession of a magistrate on foot, the suggestion that the represented lictors carry *bacula*, rather than *fasces*, namely staffs that accompanied magistrates of Roman *municipia*, means, if correct, that these urns probably belonged to the magistrates of the Roman *municipium* of Volterra (Tassi Scandone, 2001, pp. 142–6, 170–5); I will return to Volterra and its relationship with Rome below. Ultimately, this demonstrates the documentary value of these political images for our understanding of the institutional evolution of Etruria before and after Rome. It also raises the theme, the second key point referred to above, to which I now turn, namely Rome's expansion and takeover in Etruria and all that this entailed. What it primarily entailed, as exemplified by these first-century BCE urns, is Etruria's transformation under Rome and what, for want of a better term, scholars have called Romanization.

ROME IN ETRURIA: FROM CONQUEST TO TRANSFORMATION

After the conquest of *Veii*, Rome's confrontation with other Etruscan cities occupied most of the fourth and the first half of the third century BCE. As we learn from literary sources, that confrontation involved Rome in conflict with single cities or alliances of two or more cities, the most famous of which was the League of the *Duodecim Populi* or twelve *populi*, mostly mentioned for the meetings that the League held at the *Fanum Voltumnae*. This was a federal sanctuary dedicated to *Vortumnus-Voltumna*, which Roman sources considered to be the main god of Etruria (Varro *Ling.* 5.46). I shall return to this in the epilogue. The history of these conflicts includes truces and treaties that Rome agreed upon with the cities involved, as well as the quashing of rebellions and outright destructions of entire communities (Marcone, 2017). Well known, both historically and archaeologically, is the destruction of the Faliscan town of *Falerii* in the middle Tiber Valley in 241 BCE and the displacement of its inhabitants to a new site, *Falerii Novi* (Keay et al., 2000). An earlier turning point for Etruria had come in 295 BCE with the Battle of *Sentinum*, a site located in the Appennines on the Adriatic side of central Italy, in which Rome defeated an alliance of Etruscans, Umbrians, Samnites and Gauls who, by then, were settled in the Po Valley. This battle reminds us that Rome had foes well beyond Etruria and the Faliscan territory. Indeed, the fourth century BCE saw Rome fighting the Samnites, either as single communities or as a coalition, in the central and southern Appennines of Italy. The Umbrians were taken over in 290 BCE after Rome's victory at *Sentinum*, and, to the south, Rome's advance did not spare the communities of Lucania, Apulia and *Magna Graecia*: *Tarentum* (modern Taranto), a principal Greek city in the region, fell to Rome in 272 BCE, after a series of battles that saw the Greek king Pyrrhus of Epirus, allied with *Tarentum*, come to the rescue of the Greek city and succeeding against Rome twice before being finally defeated at *Beneventum* in 275 BCE.

These battles also saw the conflict go beyond the borders of Italy as military interventions came from the Aegean and the east Mediterranean, but, with the fall of *Tarentum*, the whole of the peninsula came under Rome's control (Raaflaub, 2006). By then, all Tyrrhenian Etruscan cities had entered into the political orbit of Rome. After *Sentinum*, Rome's aggression towards them led to their annexation one after the other: as noted earlier, Vulci fell in 280 BCE along with *Volsinii*, which rebelled in 265 BCE and was destroyed, forcing its inhabitants to move to a new site near Lake Bolsena. A year later, the Volsinian deity *Vertumnus* made its entry into the sacred geography of Rome, just as Veian Juno had done, along with the celebration of the triumph of *M. Fulvius Flaccus* over the victory at *Volsinii*.[6] *Caere*, the last city to be annexed in 273 BCE, had a substantial portion of its territory confiscated; soon afterwards, as early as a decade later, maritime colonies were established in the coastal hinterland, first at *Castrum Novum*, then *Alsium*, *Fregenae* and *Pyrgi*, which was destroyed (Torelli, 2016). The fate of Etruscan cities in Etruria Padana was different: here, the scenario is complicated by the presence – rather than invasion, as literary sources claim – of Gallic settlers among Etruscan communities from the fourth century BCE, which progressively changed the urban landscape of the main cities in the region (Lejars, 2006; Bourdin, 2012, pp. 592–604). Along with that also came a redirection of trade routes, which expanded along the Adriatic region and led to the decline of Bologna and Marzabotto. In fact, Rome's conquest in Etruria Padana, by then identified by the literary sources as Gallic territory, belongs to the story of the annexation of the Adriatic region more broadly, marked by the colonial foundations of *Hadria* (modern Atri) and *Sena Gallica* (modern Senigallia) in the 280s BCE, and *Ariminum* (modern Rimini) in 268 BCE.

Beyond the very detailed historical narrative of the conquest, of which the above is but a brief overview, the archaeological record provides another, much richer angle through which one can understand what is meant by Roman takeover and the likely stimuli behind it, from inscriptions and iconography examined above, to the changing agricultural landscape and settlement distribution. Settlement and landscape archaeology in southern Etruria, in fact, is particularly valuable for setting the scene of the conquest: the increasing number of small rural sites and farms across the southern Etruscan landscape in the fourth and third century BCE, detected by field surveys, indicates a level of agricultural intensification, which must be considered vis-à-vis the elite families seen in the funerary and epigraphic record above (Sewell, 2016; Terrenato, 2019, pp. 97–108). While oligarchic systems ensured the political control of city states by these families, their land-based economic wealth was also maintained, if not enhanced. At Tarquinia, for instance, where our evidence is particularly plentiful, the flourishing of smaller settlements in its hinterland such as Musarna, Tuscania, Norchia and Castel d'Asso speaks highly of buoyant elite groups holding political offices locally and controlling the agricultural wealth of that hinterland (Andreau, Broise, and Jolivet, 2002).

These politically and economically dominant elites coexisted with lower social groups, at times visible in the funerary record through modest burials, and smaller land owners who may also explain this growth of farm sites. The later *Tabula Cortonensis* mentioned above was, in fact, a legal document giving details of the sale of land, in which Etruscans of different social backgrounds were involved; although this document only refers to Cortona, it is not far-fetched to imagine similar situations occurring elsewhere. The power of a few wealthy elite families can also be assessed by the social strife within single city states recorded by the literary sources: the rebellion of *Volsinii* mentioned above was a result of social tension, but we are unable to say anything more, other than to presume that it was not an isolated incident. Livy's report of one such rebellion in *Arretium* (modern Arezzo) against the powerful *Cilnia* family (Livy 10.3.2) suggests that these rebellions originated in the excessive power of local elite families. Who participated in them, however, is impossible to say, partly because of our scanty knowledge of lower social groups, from small landowners to slaves. Once again, inscriptions come to the rescue: we know, for instance, of the existence of slaves by inscriptions that record their status as freedmen, known in Etruscan as *lautni*; drawing parallels with the Roman *liberti*, however, as tempting as it might be, does not provide much further insight (Amann, 2017).

Be that as it may, this social and economic background of Etruria is the setting for Rome's imperial expansion. Some most recent scholarly views highlight this background as an opportunity for Rome that can also be seen at a broader level, in the central Mediterranean (Sewell, 2016; Terrenato, 2019). Etruscan land-owning elites, old and new, had power, interests and investments to defend locally, which could be preserved despite, or arguably even thanks to, Rome's expansion. Personal contacts between them and Roman ruling families could not but help in preserving them; conversely, Rome could benefit from local support for its expansionist agenda by maintaining local power structures. The *Cilnia* family's fortunes in *Arretium* ended positively thanks to Roman troops sent for help to quash the rebellion; the family's favourable connections to the Roman corridors of power endured until the early imperial period when a *Cilnius* by the name of *Maecenas* came to be part of Augustus' inner circle (Marcone, 2017, p. 677).

The network of alliances and reciprocity relations among ruling elites from *Latium* to Etruria since the early first millennium BCE had, after all, a long genealogy, as we saw in previous chapters. Its evolution into the later centuries of the millennium is largely detected in the epigraphic sources, from which we learn of marriages, military aid provided between families of different cities, and personal links between Roman ruling families and Etruscan elites. Particularly insightful is the epigraphic record at Tarquinia, from the *Elogia Tarquiniensia* to a recently published set of inscriptions from tombs dated from the middle of the fourth to the middle of the first century BCE. The *Elogia Tarquiniensia* is a series of first-century Latin inscriptions set up by the powerful *Spurinna* family at Tarquinia recounting earlier fifth- and fourth-century events and actions by the family ancestors, which included helping elites in *Arretium* fight social unrest: perhaps the same event that Livy reported, as seen before (Torelli, 1975, 2019). The recently published material comes from the urban *necropoleis* at Calvario and Fondo Scataglini as well as from cemeteries of the Tarquinian hinterland: the remarkable amount of inscriptions gives us more than a 100 family names and allows us to trace family lineages and relations established through marriages between different families (Chiesa, 2005).

At *Caere*, we know of personal links between Rome's ruling class and local families from literary and epigraphic sources; powerful Caeretan families with Roman connections are also visible in the urban cemeteries (Ciuccarelli, 2015). This may in fact explain the reasons behind *Caere*'s ambiguous position, known from the literary sources, vis-à-vis the fate of its neighbour *Veii* and its own favourable treatment by Rome, which included a treaty and the granting of *civitas sine suffragio*, that is, Roman citizenship with no voting rights (Torelli, 2016, pp. 264–5). Although this approach changed in the third century BCE as Rome embarked on a series of military campaigns resulting in the confiscation of land, as seen above, new fieldwork and recent studies are modifying our views of the effects of the Roman conquest at *Caere*, highlighting the third century as a period of building activity and refurbishment of extant structures in the city, from the Vigna Parrocchiale to the Sant'Antonio sites. New investigations of a hypogeum building, known since the 1970s, and its surrounding structures at Vigna Marini Vitalini have revealed the complexity of this structure and the phases of building renovation there too, which continued through to the early second century BCE (Colivicchi, 2015). The hypogeum itself, a sacred space decorated with wall paintings, bears the inscription of C. *Genucius Clepsina*, who was consul in Rome twice in the 270s BCE and may have sponsored some of the refurbishment of the urban sanctuaries as the city came to be a *praefectura* under him, that is, juridically incorporated into the Roman state. *Clepsina* is, in fact, the Latin transliteration of Etruscan *Clevsinas*, a powerful family from Tarquinia in the fourth century BCE: originating from Tarquinia, *Clepsina* then built his political career in Rome once he joined the *Genucii*, a powerful Roman family (Torelli, 2016, pp. 263–70).

Emphasizing these elite connections between Etruscan cities and Rome advances our understanding of the Roman conquest and its effects in two interconnected directions: first, the monolithic view of Rome as the conqueror breaks down, as does the dichotomy, largely deriving from the literary sources, between Rome the conqueror and Etruria the conquered. Second, the power struggles between families, which intersected cities and states, meant that there were losers and those who resisted as well as the winners who took advantage of Rome's agenda and elbowed themselves into Rome's power structures. The archaeological record gives us some insight into the losing side and resistance both at a small and large scale. On a small scale, the popularity, from the fourth century BCE, of mythological scenes that decorated the caskets of *sarcophagi* and cinerary urns and focused on murder, combat and violence may reflect power struggles within local communities and families. While not specifically reflecting the losers or winners in Rome's power games, this gives us some indirect clues to the losing side in factional conflicts.

In particular, the portrayal of mythological family feuds and their tragic outcomes, exemplified by the myth of the Seven Against Thebes and the story of Oedipus' family, served as a stark reminder to those left alive of the consequences of fratricidal wars and the breaking down of family bonds for political interests to those burying their dead (De Angelis, 1999). We see this myth depicted in various ways and featuring different mythological characters on artefacts such as gems and bronze mirrors, on the chests of funerary receptacles, urns and *sarcophagi* and the François Tomb. Here, before arriving at the paintings of the historical and mythological battles examined earlier, upon entering the tomb the viewer could see wall paintings of the figures belonging to the myth, including the brothers Eteokles and Polyneikes (*Aizucle* and *Phulnice* in Etruscan) in the act of killing one another in a particularly bloody scene: the contrast with the Etruscan *sodales* depicted further into the tomb is striking. The scene of the fratricide became particularly common in the decoration of mould-made terracotta urns at Chiusi in the second and first century BCE (De Angelis, 2015).

This myth was also represented in the terracotta pedimental sculpture of a coastal temple dated to the first half of the second century BCE on the Talamonaccio hill, west of the Talamone bay, between Vulci and Roselle, near ancient *Telamon*, the site of a definitive military defeat of the Gauls by Rome in 225 BCE. With a blind and visibly woeful Oedipus on his knees at the centre of the pediment between his two dying sons, the temple, remodelled on an earlier one, carried a message against the subversion of civic and divine order and an admonition against civic chaos (Vacano, 1985, pp. 97–127; 1988; Pairault-Massa, 1992, pp. 240–3; De Angelis, 2015, pp. 65–79). However, unlike the pedimental sculpture of the fifth-century BCE temple at *Pyrgi* encountered in Chapter 4, the sculpture at Talamone was characterized more by tragic pathos and poignancy than violence. It was speaking to a community subjected to Rome, where fragile power balances may have rested on real or potential conflicts between and within leading local families. That a colony, *Heba*, near modern Magliano, was founded inland from Talamone sometime in the second century BCE further adds to this scenario (Marcone, 2017, pp. 673–5). The message transmitted through the myth, in other words, had radically changed with the different times (Figure 6.6).

On a larger scale, we must look to the landscape. The establishment of small, hilltop fortified settlements known as *oppida* along strategic routes and interstate boundaries in some Etruscan city states at the time of the growing military threat of Rome is evidence of a centralized strategy by these states to safeguard their territories and resist outside threats: known sites of this type are found, for instance, between the territories of Tarquinia and *Caere*, and in northern Etruria, in the territory of Populonia. The short life of many of these sites indicates their

Figure 6.6 The temple pediment, Talamone, photograph by Mariagrazia Celuzza.

specific function to protect resources and control routes in the context of general instability and Rome's expansion (Cambi, 2012; Cambi and Di Paola, 2013). Well-known and excavated *oppida* clearly point to the fortifications as their principal feature and raison d'être, so to speak. At the sites of Poggio Civitella di Montalcino near Siena and Rofalco, in the hinterland of Vulci, the deployment of sophisticated military architecture, which, in the case of Civitella, included three concentric levels of fortifications, is particularly notable (Cerasuolo, Pulcinelli, and Rubat Borel, 2008; Cappuccini, 2012) (Figures 6.7 and 6.8).

If these *oppida* are any evidence of some form of resistance to Rome's expansion, the confiscation of land by Rome through its colonial foundations unquestionably demonstrates that, for some, Rome's agenda imposed harsh losses. Importantly, many of these colonies were of Latin type, that is, colonies that were juridically autonomous, but which were occupied by thousands of colonists, and had the obligation of providing a military contingent to Rome when needed. Recent research on Roman republican colonies has highlighted the role of the colonies in providing loyalty to Rome not out of an act of imperial aggression, but rather out of a reorganization of local social hierarchies and power structures that ensured this loyalty via local networks (Terrenato, 2019, pp. 219–26). While many lost land and fortunes to the colonial foundation, the mixed make-up of colonial communities, which included local and Roman citizens, many of whom also had local origins, shows that some fared better than others.

All of this should not make us lose sight of the fact that Rome's expansion into Etruria and its consequences was anything but a uniform phenomenon. This was not only due to the timeline of the events, among

Figure 6.7 Fortification, Rofalco, Selva del Lamone nature reserve (VT), photograph by Antonio Baragliu.

Figure 6.8 View from the site, Rofalco, Selva del Lamone nature reserve (VT), photograph by Antonio Baragliu.

which were Rome's wars with other powers such as the Punic Wars, that made the period of Roman expansion extremely dynamic and volatile, but also a result of Rome's broader strategy of conquest and annexation involving the maintenance or realignment of local privileges and social networks. The colonies themselves differed from one another depending upon the local circumstances and the new relationships being forged. Smaller colonies such as the maritime ones on *Caere*'s coastal hinterland coexisted with others, whose history and development were influenced by a combination of both local and global circumstances. An example of this is *Cosa* (modern Ansedonia), a Latin colony founded at the aftermath of the fall of Vulci on the coast north-west of the city (Dyson, 2013). Well excavated since the 1940s and not built over by a modern town, *Cosa*'s internal organization with its urban grid of roads, houses, forum and temples is well known, as are its port and hinterland divided by the Roman grid of land plots known as centuriation. As the only Latin colony to hold a temple of Capitoline Jupiter on the sacred hilltop, modelled on the temple devoted to this deity, Juno and Minerva in Rome, it used to be known as a mini-Rome. Further investigations, however, found that this temple was preceded by an earlier one, and was, in fact, built in the aftermath of the Second Punic War, some time in the first half of the second century BCE, perhaps as a testimony to the colony's loyalty to Rome at this time (Dyson, 2013, pp. 473–6). While only the circuit wall of polygonal limestone blocks was built at the time of foundation, the residential quarters, forum and public buildings were developed over time from the third to the first century BCE when *Cosa* was destroyed possibly as a result of coastal attacks, and subsequently abandoned until the Augustan age. Its hinterland, too, was not immediately fully occupied: survey evidence and the excavation of two Roman *villae* at Settefinestre and Le Colonne show a progressive infill of the landscape with small farms and agricultural activity, especially from the second century BCE (Dyson, 2013, pp. 481–2) (Figures 6.9 and 6.10).

Further north, Volterra and its territory provide an exemplary illustration of how different life could be under Rome for an Etruscan city from the republican period to the early empire. We are very lucky to have for Volterra a complete range of evidence from which to draw: literary, epigraphic and archaeological sources, from excavation of the city and rural sites to field surveys. Beyond a war recorded in the last years of the third century BCE (Livy 10.12), the city helped Rome during the Second Punic War by contributing to *Scipio Africanus*' campaign, and thus became an allied city or *civitas foederata*. After receiving

Figure 6.9 The *Arx* or sacred hilltop, *Cosa*, photograph by Mariagrazia Celuzza.

Figure 6.10 Circuit wall, *Cosa*, photograph by Mariagrazia Celuzza.

citizenship rights in 90 BCE, it suffered a sack in 80 BCE under *Sulla*, the Roman politician and military leader who invaded Rome, became dictator during a power struggle with *Marius* and confiscated land, reducing Volterra's citizenship rights. Against this historical background, the archaeological record gives a picture of little change and overall social and economic stability: the results of the Cecina Valley Survey project show slight variations in the agricultural landscape, with just a few *villae* dotting the coastal plain, which was peripheral to the centre of Volterra, indicating continuity of rural life into the Roman period. This continuity and the lack of large land estates or *latifundia* also suggest less agricultural intensification and its social consequences, namely, the growth of a large slave population. The evidence also indicates that the *villae* themselves may have been owned by individuals of Etruscan origin (Terrenato, 1998b).

The behaviour of the local elites, on the other hand, does not appear to be as straightforward. As we saw earlier with the cinerary urns elaborately carved with magistrates' processions, Etruscan funerary rites continued well into the early imperial period (Cristofani, 1978): cremations in these urns were deposited in rock-cut chamber tombs that hosted several generations of deceased family members, as exemplified by the so-called Inghirami Tomb, discovered in 1861. The tomb was owned by the *Ati* family and hosted up to sixty urns starting from the third century BCE. While this tomb holds few Etruscan inscriptions, the epigraphic record of other elite tombs also included Latin inscriptions, which were the norm by the end of the first century BCE: this is the case with the later of the two tombs of the *Ceicna/Caecina* family (Nielsen, 2013). Indeed, the epigraphic record shows plenty of Etruscan names that had been Latinized. If the funerary face of Volterran elites was thus sticking to local traditions, their civic and more public face was enthusiastically Roman: in the Augustan period, a phase of renovation in building activity in the city included the erection of a monumental theatre that was dedicated and paid for by the *Caecinae* themselves, and decorated with portraits of the imperial Julian family, following an impressive work of levelling the land at the southern periphery of the city (Munzi and Terrenato, 2000). The imperial favour enjoyed by Volterra then is confirmed by an inscription that gave the city the title of *Colonia Augusta*, an inheritance from an earlier decision by Caesar to turn the city into a colony in order to accommodate veterans' settlements. The lack of archaeological evidence, however, of any change to the agricultural landscape either at this point or earlier under *Sulla's* alleged land confiscation can only be explained by the political intercession in Rome by *Cicero*, a friend and patron of the *Caecinae* in defence of such a stable *municipium*: these are, in fact, the very words of *Cicero* in his written correspondence aimed at averting disruption for his clients, the *Caecinae* themselves (Terrenato, 1998b, pp. 106–08) (Figure 6.11).

Beside the personal connections with influential figures at the very centre of power, what we see at work here are the differences in the effects of these connections and other local circumstances, and therefore in the ultimate fate of Etruscan city states. Another case that can be compared to that of Volterra's aristocratic families can be found at Perugia where perhaps the most renowned of local families to the interested visitor of this city are the *Volumni*, buried in the famous hypogeum of the Palazzone *necropolis*. In another funerary area north-west of Perugia, a tomb group belonging to a hypogeum of the *Cacni*, another local family, was recently salvaged from the illicit antiquities trade: the decorated and inscribed cinerary urns and a *sarcophagus* displayed mostly the genealogy of the male line of the *Cacni*, a custom found among other local families, at the time of the Roman takeover (Benelli, 2015; Cifani, 2015a). This reasonably suggests that, along with others, the *Cacni*,

Figure 6.11 The Roman theatre, Volterra, photograph by Spike (CC BY-SA 4.0), from Wikimedia Commons.

too, benefitted from this takeover. However, the last burial, dated by the middle of the first century BCE, indicates the last generation of the family and the end of its fortune; this is further corroborated by the lack of any Latin epigraphic evidence related to it, and was probably the outcome of the events surroundings the civil wars before Octavian became Augustus. What can finally be seen in great detail at Volterra as elsewhere is a long process whereby Etruscan cities not only were incorporated into the Roman state but their cultural traditions, institutions and social relations were also progressively and fundamentally transformed; in other words, they became Roman. This becoming Roman, however, a process otherwise known as Romanization, was anything but straightforward, linear or homogeneous, nor did it lead to the end of Etruria, so to speak. Recent scholarship in Roman history and archaeology has been at pains to underline continuity and change between the late first millennium BCE and the early first millennium CE, and the legacy of Etruscan cities and their relationship with Rome in Rome, from political discourses and imperial ideology to institutions made manifest in visual and material culture, and other spheres of public life such as religion (see next chapter) (Bradley, 2007; Smith, 2014).

This becoming Roman for Etruria was slow and complex as it was elsewhere in the expanding empire (Woolf, 2000).[7] It was not arguably even an outcome, but rather a kaleidoscope of responses to what Rome itself was becoming: the phrase 'cultural bricolage' suitably describes and explains the different ways in which local traditions and existing cultural forms were given new local functions and meanings serving new purposes in a changing (Roman) era. Importantly, 'local' worked at different scales: the larger scale went from regions across the Italic peninsula, for instance, Etruria versus Samnium in the south-eastern Appennines, to city states across Etruria; the smaller scale refers to cultural forms adopted by specific social groups within a community, down to the individual, whether defined by gender, social affiliation or other. The outcome was a veritable 'collage' of changing cultural forms not just within the Italic peninsula but throughout the Roman empire that was expanding beyond it (Terrenato, 1998a).

In this varied scenario, no small part was played by the cultural construction of Rome itself and its own becoming Roman (or the making of Romanness) as the borders of the empire expanded. Some time ago, scholars recognized that this process took shape under a phase of intense emulation and imitation of Greek culture not just in Rome but across Italy in the so-called Hellenistic period (Wallace-Hadrill, 2008). More recently, archaeologists of the Roman empire have underlined that in this process the ancient empire put in motion a polycentric mechanism of cultural borrowings, re-formulation and change that had no centre or single points of departure, but was Mediterranean-wide and circular in action. The most fitting way, it has been argued, to understand this process is to align it with a very contemporary concept, that is, globalization and all that it entails such as the shifting of identities (Versluys, 2014; Pitts and Versluys, 2015). This, in fact, brings us to a whole new level of understanding the history of the Etruscans, and not just for its later periods, namely through a contemporary lens. Does it work?

EPILOGUE

FROM GLOBALIZATION TO NEW QUESTIONS

CAMPO DELLA FIERA (ORVIETO) AND THE *FANUM VOLTUMNAE*

At Campo della Fiera, a site of market fairs located on the plain west of the *tufa* spur that hosted *Volsinii*, now the site of modern Orvieto, isolated finds, among which were architectural terracottas now in Berlin, were recovered in the second half of the nineteenth century. Preliminary excavations began in the early 1990s, but it was not until the turn of the twenty-first century that systematic excavations began at what was then known to be a sanctuary under the direction of Simonetta Stopponi. Since then, the sanctuary has proven to be one of the longest-living cult places in the whole of Etruria: the earliest structures date to the mid-sixth century BCE, while the latest ones belong to the thirteenth-century CE Church of San Pietro in Vetere, later abandoned in the middle of the Europe-wide epidemic known as the Black Death. Given the longevity of the site and the over 30,000 square metres of excavated areas, its plan, archaeological stratigraphy and assemblages are complex, and undoubtedly will require a major effort for the final and complete publication of the site. However, today, even with the excavation and study of the finds ongoing, there is an overall picture one can build of it (Stopponi, 2012, 2013)[1] (Figures 7.1, 7.2).

The importance of the sanctuary is indicated by two paved ways leading to it: one was the Sacred Way (*Via Sacra*) closely connected to the sanctuary, along which statues and altars were placed, and first built in the mid-sixth century BCE with three phases of renovation down to the mid-fourth century BCE. The other, built in the mid-third century BCE, linked *Volsinii* to Bolsena, narrowing into the centre of the sanctuary where we have the earliest archaic evidence of cult. A boundary wall

Figure 7.1 Aerial view of the site, Campo della Fiera, Orvieto (ancient *Volsinii*), courtesy Simonetta Stopponi.

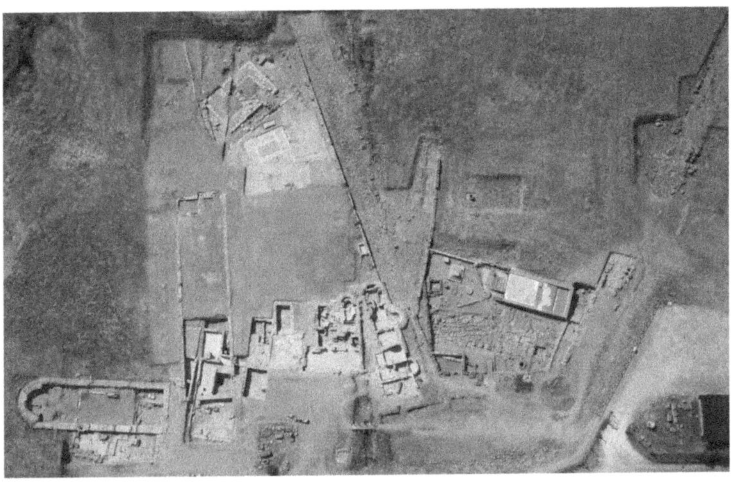

Figure 7.2 The excavation, Campo della Fiera, Orvieto (ancient *Volsinii*), courtesy Simonetta Stopponi.

defining this area and rebuilt over several centuries confirms this to be the centre of the sanctuary. Some of the earliest structures in this central bounded area were refurbished over time, while others were obliterated in the Roman period: one of these, Temple A, in existence in the fourth century BCE, was repaved some time in the first half of the first century BCE. In front of it and following the same orientation was a trachyte stone offering table that would have hosted bronze statuettes; nearby was a treasure of over 200 bronze and silver coins, with the latest, dated to 7 BCE, providing the latest date of this assemblage, and a sacrificial altar. The altar was associated with a *bucchero* cup inscribed with *apas*, translated as 'of the father', an epithet referring to a chthonian deity, and found elsewhere, including *Volsinii*, at the urban sanctuary of Belvedere. In this central area was also a quadrangular structure. Inside it was a trachyte stone base for a statue, a votive gift given by a woman named *Kanuta*, about whom we know, thanks to the inscription on the base that reads as follows: *Kanuta*, freedwoman (*Lauteniθa*) of the *gens Larecena*, wife of *Aranθ Pinie*, gave to the *Tlusχva* (group of gods) of the *Marveθ* (of the seat/residence) in the *Faliaθere/Faliaθera* (in the celestial [place]) (Stopponi, 2011, p. 42). Aside from the religious terminology of the inscription, for which some uncertainty remains (van der Meer, 2013), we learn here that a freedwoman, who was an Oscan speaker, was proudly showing off what must have been a notable gift, perhaps a bronze statue to the deities worshipped at the sanctuary (Figure 7.3).

The amount of contemporary and subsequent votive gifts, from fine decorated ceramic vessels, personal ornaments in precious metal, amber and glass paste, bronze statuettes, terracotta and bronze votive female and male heads and statues, is remarkable. This material has been linked to the practice of cults by women and related to Demeter and chthonic deities such as *Vei* or *Cavatha*, already encountered in previous chapters, as well as Dionysiac rites. Later refurbishments of the boundary wall, which included the building of two further walls and of the centre of the sanctuary, lasted down to the Roman imperial period: whether there is continuity of the same cults and the worship to the same deities, however, is another matter and difficult to ascertain.

The excavation at Campo della Fiera has also included a southern area where another archaic sacred building (Temple B) in use until the Roman republican period has been found, and the southern end of the Sacred Way where another temple (Temple C) was in use from the sixth to the first half of the third century BCE. The stratigraphy of Temple C is complex and includes pits and a few burials that may be related to the

Figure 7.3 Trachyte stone base with inscription of *Kanuta*, Campo della Fiera, Orvieto (ancient *Volsinii*), courtesy Simonetta Stopponi.

end of its religious function and its abandonment: this phase is dated between the end of the fourth and the beginning of the third century BCE. Beyond these phases of abandonment for both this temple and building B, Temple A continued to be used with the rebuilding of the boundary wall. Lastly, at the northern end of the Sacred Way, a bath building was established some time in the first century CE; it was replaced by a

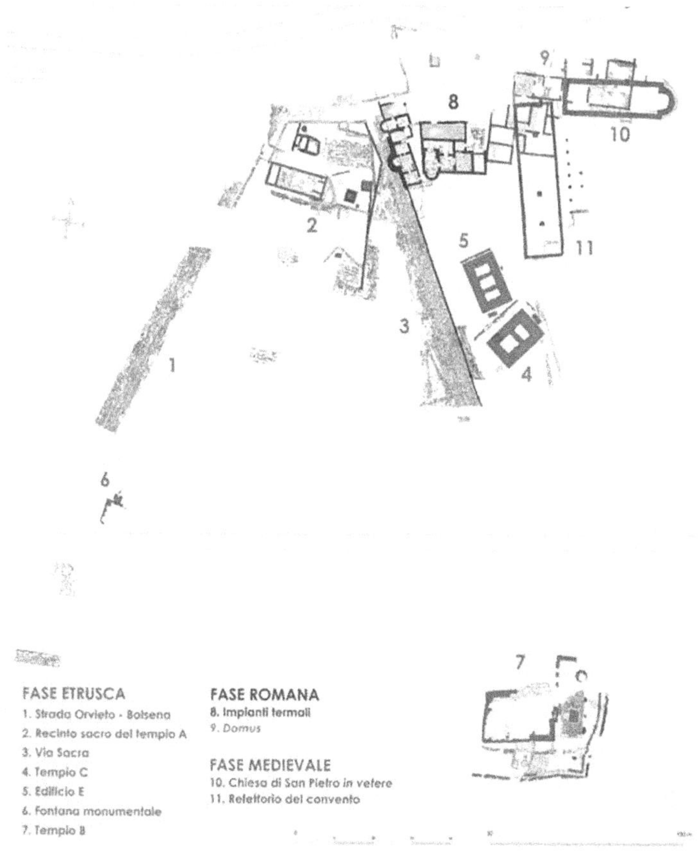

Figure 7.4 Site plan, Campo della Fiera, Orvieto (ancient *Volsinii*), courtesy Simonetta Stopponi.

domus (house) in the fifth century CE. We seem to have, in other words, overlapping phases of construction and use, which, here too, leave the question of continuity of belief and practice open (Figure 7.4).

FROM CULTURAL BRICOLAGE TO A RESEARCH AGENDA FOR THE FUTURE

This brief overview of the most significant discoveries at Campo della Fiera is enough to convey to the reader the excitement that this excavation provoked among Etruscologists since the preliminary results were communicated. In fact, the excitement mostly derives from the initial hypothesis, now become a near-certainty for several scholars,[2] that the sanctuary was the *Fanum Voltumnae*, the federal sanctuary dedicated to *Vortumnus-Voltumna*, and where, according to the literary tradition (cf. Livy 4.23.5, 25.7–8, 61.2; 5.17.6–10; 6.2.2), the League of the *Duodecim Populi* or twelve Etruscan *populi* met and organized annual assemblies from the fifth century BCE (Bourdin, 2012, pp. 299–314). This self-confidence in matching the site to the *Fanum Voltumnae* of the literary tradition is based on a wide range of sources, harnessed and brought together, starting with the archaeology of the site itself, its location and the various interpretations brought to bear on the chthonian deities worshipped there; in particular, on the basis of other epigraphic sources, some scholars assume that the Latin god *Voltumna* was, in fact, an epithet of *Tinia*. We have also seen, in the previous chapter, that Varro (*Ling.* 5.46) considered *Vortumnus*, assumed to correspond to *Vultumna*, to be the principal deity of the Etruscan pantheon. Different views, however, exist on the Etruscan name of Latin *Voltumna*, perhaps *Veltumne* or *Veltune* as locative of *Veltuna*, which occurs on a famous bronze mirror from Tuscania (van der Meer, 2013). Ultimately, there are a few discordant voices (Bourdin, 2012, pp. 309–13; van der Meer, 2013, p. 105)[3] on the interpretation of the sanctuary as the *Fanum Voltumnae*, mostly because the incontrovertible evidence for the existence of such a federal sanctuary here comes from the literary tradition only. However we wish to interpret the site, it is clear that the question and the evidence from this tradition have dominated, perhaps excessively, the debate. At present, for instance, evidence of destruction and discontinuity at the site date to before the date of *Volsinii*'s destruction in 264 BCE, as reported by the literary sources.

Campo della Fiera, on the other hand, raises other issues and provides evidence of interesting aspects related to the Roman period of Etruria: the most significant of these is the continuity of cult, on current knowledge limited to Temple A only, and the reuse of the site in the Roman period, a phenomenon known elsewhere in Roman Italy, most notably at the Lucanian sanctuary of Rossano di Vaglio in southern Italy (Battiloro and Osanna, 2015). At Campo della Fiera, this continuity and reuse can be intriguingly related to what scholars have called an Etruscan revival, promoted under Emperor Augustus by his entourage (Bradley, 2007; Torelli, 2017). The revival emerged out of the 'antiquarian climate' of the second century BCE, to borrow a phrase from Mario Torelli (Torelli,

2017, p. 695), as a result of a growing interest in Etruscan local histories, myths and *etrusca disciplina*. This interest was, in turn, fostered by a wish to promote the past of Etruscan cities and their families in an attempt to gain local political favours in conjunction with the commemoration of the imperial family as the cult to Emperor Augustus was developing across Italy and the empire. It is in this context that the Latin inscriptions known as *Elogia Tarquiniensia*, recounting the past deeds of the *Spurinna* family at Tarquinia and encountered in the previous chapter, must be placed. The past of single cities and their families, furthermore, was not only materialized in celebratory inscriptions, and the great religious monuments still standing, but also fabricated and enhanced through mythological stories and figures attached to the history of these cities. Thus, among the eulogizing inscriptions at Tarquinia is one referring to *Tarchon*, the legendary founder of the city, who may have been remembered by a cenotaph at the sanctuary of Ara della Regina (Torelli, 2017, p. 714). A marble relief fragment, probably belonging to an altar for the imperial cult, was found in a dump together with various imperial statues in 1840 near the Roman theatre at *Caere*. It depicts three Etruscan *populi* personified by figures who are named after the *populi* themselves, namely the Vetulonians, the Vulcians and the Tarquinians; the figure for the latter may be representing *Tarchon* (Liverani, 1989). From Tarquinia again, not far from Ara della Regina, come some fragmentary inscriptions listing the names of the masters of the religious order of the *haruspices*, the priests practising divination, which – the literary sources tell us (Tacitus, *Ann.* 11.5) – had been restored by Emperor Claudius in 47 CE, evidence of a renewed Roman interest in this Etruscan religious practice (Torelli, 2017, pp. 711–13).

All of this evidence gives us a glimpse at how intricate and multilayered the relationship between Rome and Etruria was once the region was fully incorporated into the Roman state. It confirms what was stated at the end of the previous chapter, namely that Romanization, for want of a better word, was not straightforward or unidirectional, nor can it be fully appreciated by breaking it down according to a certain set of criteria such as the adoption of Latin inscriptions, the end of use of Etruscan, the use of Roman architecture or institutional change. It finally prompts us towards asking questions on the role of memory, the historical imagination and the uses of the past in Etruscan communities becoming 'Roman', and the extent to which these were deployed by these communities and different social groups within them to reinvent their relationship with Rome and their self-perception vis-à-vis Rome or, in one word, their own local identity. Indeed, identities, modes of self-perception and the expression of both in visual and material culture have been a prominent theme in archaeological research more generally since the late 1990s, and particularly in Anglo and Francophone scholarship, that is, scholarship in European countries that have been undergoing processes of decolonization (Haack, 2008). This theme stems from recent concerns, developed in the social and historical sciences, over the effects of people's diasporas and long-distance mobility from the end of European colonial empires to the forces of globalization today. One of the key effects has been the transformation of self-positioning of those involved in these recent historical and contemporary phenomena at all levels, from the collective to the individual. Scholarship on the Roman empire has been particularly influenced by these concerns, and debates on the global reach of the empire have, as a result, produced an enormous body of scientific literature.[4] Some of this literature has even discarded Romanization itself, deeming it to be a concept with colonialist undertones that overemphasizes, through a top-down perspective, the homogenizing and unifying forces of empire, and thus obscures local realities and transformations (Versluys, 2014, p. 4).

Etruscology, on the other hand, has remained largely immune from these debates: in fact, while only recently has 'cultural bricolage' (see previous chapter) entered the literature,[5] there has been circumspection, if not resistance and outright rejection, of the use of concepts deriving from our own contemporary world upon Etruscan antiquity (Cecconi, 2006; Haack, 2008). The theme of identities, aside from ethnicity, has not been extensively pursued for earlier periods either, despite the significant role this has played in the archaeology of the Mediterranean of the first millennium BCE over the last twenty years or so.[6] Insofar as Romanization is concerned, the explanation for this may be twofold: on the one hand, disciplinary boundaries count, as the Roman period belongs to Roman archaeology that reaches out to all regions of the empire from Syria to Britain; on the other hand, Etruscology's long-term interest in the study of local traditions and differences among city states and their continuity under Roman rule has effectively fostered a bottom-up view of Romanization. This view is, in fact, one of the key aims of those most critical of this term, although the match between this specific aim and this interest of Etruscology has not been widely recognized. More generally, the explanation for this circumspection may, in fact, derive from the historiography of Etruscology and the legacy of classical archaeology in Italy, laid out in the first chapter; this legacy –

it can be argued – has not (yet?) moved the discipline towards the big questions driving the social and historical sciences today.

Nevertheless, as we approach the middle of the twenty-first century, disciplinary boundaries are breaking down; the large volume of finds from field projects and related publications across Etruria is offering scholars the opportunity to employ a whole range of scientific analytical methods, from DNA analysis and organic residue analysis to isotope analysis, that have recently produced a methodological revolution in archaeology more generally. While Etruscology is taking part in this revolution, disciplinary advances also come from asking new questions that can fill the gaps in our knowledge and be the basis for a future research agenda. Indeed, new themes and objectives are already being pursued as recent publications attest. What gaps are they filling? First, our knowledge of the economy in Etruria is still wanting as are also data on technology and production, all themes that new research is addressing (Cifani, 2015b; Sacchetti, 2016; Biella, Cascino, Ferrandes, and Revello Lami, 2017; Riva, 2017; Biella, 2019). The archaeological record is beginning to be investigated for questions on the agricultural economy: farms and manufacturing sites such as kiln sites and related waste materials, coarse wares from transport *amphorae* to *pithoi* and their contents, are all elements of the puzzle that are slowly being filled in. Devoting our attention to this kind of archaeological record, away from the monumental and the permanent at different scales, whether the large urban site or stone architecture, and towards the impermanent and organic materials such as wood and textiles (Gleba and Laurito, 2017; Zamboni, 2017a), will also help towards advancing our knowledge on a second front, namely on social structure and the inner layers of social stratification. Notwithstanding the enormous value of inscriptions, social history is still largely dominated by the epigraphic record. As a result, our picture is very much elite-driven, as is our knowledge on other social aspects touched on in previous chapters, such as public versus private, time and memory.

Last but not least, thinking comparatively across Italy and the central Mediterranean throughout the first millennium BCE, and not only for the Roman period, will promote a fuller understanding of social and historical phenomena that are not culturally specific to Etruria, but belong to the context of this broader region, from the economic processes themselves, trade and exchange, to urbanism, religion and the functioning of the state.[7] A comparative Mediterranean perspective is beneficial for other reasons, too: it prevents us from understanding these phenomena from a Tyrrheno-centric viewpoint, and helps us recognize that the Tyrrhenian core of Etruria is not that unique in that broader context. If it appears so, it is ultimately because of the Roman literary tradition that has pushed antiquarians, historians and archaeologists to pay overwhelming attention to Etruria for a whole range of reasons that have to do with the history of ideas since the Middle Ages. Attention towards this history, which brings us back to the beginning of this book, is also valuable for bringing into question whether and to what extent a contemporary lens can be brought to bear on our understanding of Etruscan antiquity, notwithstanding Etruscology's seeming resistance to this lens noted earlier.

The answer cannot be clear-cut: intellectual history demonstrates that none of us, whether historians or archaeologists, is immune to the influence of our times upon our attempts at understanding the past. On the other hand, awareness of this problem forces us to exercise critical vigilance about the adequacy of contemporary concepts for successful historical analysis; this is especially the case with concepts such as globalization, the meaning of which is constantly shifting at the speed of the twenty-first century. The question of whether and to what extent first-millennium BCE Etruria belonged to a globalizing Mediterranean cannot be exempt from a scrutiny of the history of ideas; this is because that history shaped those European scholarly traditions for which colonialism, whether ancient or modern, has been and continues to be a key research interest. At the same time, we can turn the legacy of classical archaeology in Italy upon Etruscological research to our advantage. In the current research climate that privileges big comparative, global histories, Etruria can provide the detail and the micro-scale of larger processes at play all the way from the Mediterranean to continental Europe, precisely because of that overwhelming attention by antiquarians, historians and archaeologists that has produced so much rich material from the Middle Ages onwards.

Glossary

Acroterion (plural: *acroteria*) — Base to support an ornament (e.g. a statue) or the ornament itself.

Aryballos (plural: *aryballoi*) — Unguent container with a bulbous vessel body.

Amazonomachy — Mythical battle between Greeks and the Amazons.

Bucchero — Black pottery produced in Etruria evolving from *impasto* (see *impasto)* and fired in a reduction atmosphere. The earliest *bucchero*, produced at *Caere*, in the early seventh century, is so fine that the phrase *bucchero sottile* is used to differentiate it to later and other forms of *bucchero*.

Canopic urn — Type of terracotta cinerary urn from Chiusi and its surroundings, that was made by adding anthropomorphic details to the vessel, such as arms attached to the urn's handles or a lid in the form of a human head.

Chronology — Bronze Age: *circa* 2200–975 BCE (Early Bronze Age: *circa* 2200–1700 BCE; Middle Bronze Age: 1700–1300 BCE; Recent Bronze Age: 1300–1150 BCE; Final Bronze Age: 1150–975 BCE).

	Early Iron Age: *circa* 975/950–730 BCE.
	Orientalizing period: *circa* 730–580 BCE.
	Archaic and classical periods: 580–450 BCE.
	Late classical and Hellenistic periods: 450 BCE–first century BCE.
Chthnoic	Of or relating to the world of the dead.
Cinerary	Related to the incineration of the human body, part of the burial ritual of cremation (see **Cremation**).
Cippus (plural: *cippi*)	Marker of tombs or a landmark, either made of stone or terracotta of various shape.
Cremation	The burial ritual involving the burning of the body of the deceased into ashes through intensive burning (cf. **Inhumation** below).
Dromos	Corridor of a chamber tomb leading from the tomb entrance to the main chamber.
Eschatological	Of or relating to beliefs concerning death and life after death.
Gens (adj. gentilicial)	Family clan in which members identified themselves by an individual personal name (*praenomen*) and the name of the family or *gens* (*nomen*).
Gigantomachy	Mythical battle between the Olympian gods and giants.
Guilloche	Ornament of interlaced ribbons.

Impasto	Handmade ceramic ware manufactured from non-purified clay.
Inhumation	The burial of the body of the deceased into a tomb.
Lekythos (plural: *lekythoi*)	Unguent container, to be distinguished from the *aryballos* for being a taller, slimmer vessel.
Lituus	Trumpet or a curved staff.
Kantharos (plural: *kantharoi*)	Drinking stemmed cup with two high handles.
Kyathos (plural: *kyathoi*)	Drinking stemmed cup with a single high handle.
Kline	Bed for reclining at the banquet.
Kylikeion	Table on which banqueting vessels were laid out.
Oinochoe (plural: *oinochoai*)	Pouring jug.
Olla (stamnoid)	Storage vessel with two handles.
Olpe	A type of pouring jug.
Orthogonal	Intersecting at right angles.
Peripteral	Referring to a temple surrounded by a columned portico.
Petrographic analysis	The study of the micro-structural characteristics of materials such as pottery.
Prothesis	The laying out of the body of the deceased before the funeral procession and interment.
Pyxis (plural: *pyxides*)	Small round box vessel.
Rhyton (plural: *rhyta*)	Drinking horn.
Silens	Mythical male members of Dionysiac bands, characterized by animal traits and belonging to the wild, similar to satyrs.

Skyphos (plural: *skyphoi*)	Deep-bowled drinking cup.
Symposium (or *symposion*)	Wine-drinking party.
Thyrsus	Staff covered in vine branches carried by Dionysos and his followers.
Tufa	Type of rock made of volcanic ash.

Notes

PREFACE

1 http://www.centralemontemartini.org/it/mostra-evento/colori-degli-etruschi

ACKNOWLEDGEMENTS

1 C. Riva (2018), 'The Freedom of the Etruscans', *International Journal of the Classical Tradition* 25(2): 101–26.

CHAPTER 1

1 Cipriani (1980) provides a detailed overview of Etruscan antiquity in Tuscany in these centuries.
2 Riva (2018) gives a full account of the relationship between Winckelmann's and Lanzi's ideas about Etruscan art.
3 De Francesco (2013) is a full account on the uses of antiquity in nation-building from the *Risorgimento*.
4 Exemplary in this respect: (Cristofani, 1978; Torelli, 1985). On iconological approaches, see Pairault-Massa (1992) and Cerchiai (2012).
5 D'Agostino and Cerchiai (1999) on structuralist analysis. Marxism featured prominently in the post-war research of Bianchi Bandinelli and that of his pupils, exemplified by the papers published in the scientific journal *Dialoghi di Archeologia* founded by them in the late 1960s (Cella, Gori, and Pintucci, 2016).

CHAPTER 2

1 The chronological framework put in place then has been recently radically revised for the Bronze/Iron Age phase of transition; as a result of a series of dendrochronological and radiocarbon dates, the Final Bronze Age phase has been shortened and the beginning of the Iron Age has been pushed back (Bruins, Nijboer, and Plicht van der, 2011).

CHAPTER 3

1 The attention to Phoenician and Punic Sardinia in a recent companion to Etruscology is notable (D'Oriano and Sanciu, 2013).
2 Etruscan National Museum of Villa Giulia in Rome at https://montemichele.wordpress.com
3 This argument is fully teased out here: Riva, 2010a.
4 Anthony Tuck (2017) provides all the previous bibliography on the site; the excavation also has a digital archive of all the artefacts at http://www.poggiocivitate.org/

CHAPTER 4

1 The masterful Winter (2009) provides the most complete overview on architectural terracotta decoration in Etruria and central Italy.
2 For a Mediterranean view, see Eric Gailledrat, Dietler, and Plana Mallart (2018).
3 For a detailed argument and overview on wine production and trade in this section, see Riva (2017). See Botto and Vives-Ferrándiz (2006) on Etruscan imports in the west Mediterranean from the eighth to the fifth centuries BCE.
4 For a Mediterranean-wide view of sanctuaries, see Kistler, Öhlinger, Mohr, and Hoernes (2015) and Russo Tagliente and Guarneri (2016).
5 On these developments and the urban growth at *Caere*, see: Bellelli (2014); Gaultier, Haumesser, and Santoro (2013).

CHAPTER 5

1 This is the hypothesis of Lippolis, discussed, along with that of others, in Govi and Sassatelli (2010a).
2 The dispersion of the material belonging to the San Mariano chariots has made it difficult for scholars to reconstruct an accurate picture. A. Emiliozzi

has suggested most recently that the chariots were four rather than three as commonly assumed (Bruschetti and Trombetta, 2013, p. 62).

3 A distinction applied, for instance, in sixth-century BCE domestic architecture by V. Izzet (2007, pp. 143–64).

4 However, this is now changing (Arizza, 2019).

CHAPTER 6

1 With the exception of the Tomb of the Blue Demons (see From Dionysiac cults to eschatological beliefs).

2 On the reading of the inscription of *Veil Leinies* and the relationship between Chiusi and *Volsinii* from the fourth century see Maggiani (Maggiani, 2002).

3 In his most recent book (Terrenato, 2019), which contains previous references on *Veii's* relationship with Rome, Terrenato puts forward a bold new interpretation of that relationship following *Veii's* fall to Rome that goes in a different direction from that often invoked.

4 Rathje summarizes the debate and provides the fundamental previous bibliography on it.

5 A good overview of different interpretations on the painting and some new perspective also in relation to the fratricide between Eteokles and Polineikes (see section Rome in Etruria: from conquest to transformation) are given by De Angelis (1999).

6 The only literary source, however, that gives us the suggestion of an *evocatio* is from Festus (Bourdin, 2012, pp. 310–11).

7 The literature on Romanization and the debates that it has engendered since the late twentieth century is immense. Woolf's study is exemplary in forging the path forward at the beginning of those debates.

EPILOGUE

1 What follows is a summary drawn from the publications by Stopponi (Stopponi, 2011, 2012, 2013).

2 This is most clearly seen in the 2012 volume of the journal *Annali della Fondazione per il Museo Claudio Faina* dedicated to Campo della Fiera as the *Fanum Voltumnae*.

3 Circumspection is found elsewhere: (Stek, 2015, p. 20).

4 This literature and some bibliography is summarized by Versluys (Versluys, 2014).

5 Marcone (Marcone, 2017) is the first author in a compendium on Etruscology to discuss Terrenato's seminal concept of bricolage in studies on Romanization; Jolivet (Jolivet, 2013) cites Terrenato's work, but does not engage with it.
6 Some notable examples: Urso (Urso, 2008), Bourdin (Bourdin, 2012).
7 Such comparative thinking is exemplified by Bourdin (Bourdin, 2012).

Select bibliography

As mentioned in the Preface, the last ten years have seen the publication of a series of English companions to the Etruscans of different weights, from the comprehensive two-tome *Etruscology*, edited by A. Naso (Berlin and Boston, 2017), to the brief introduction *The Etruscans. A Very Short Introduction* by C. Smith (Oxford, 2014). While these companions provide the student and interested reader the most up-to-date publication on all sorts of topics and themes, this brief select blibliography offers them further readings on the specific themes touched in the chapters of this book. It must be underlined, however, that the choice is extremely limited when restricting it to publications written in English.

On the history of the discipline, there is no single English publication devoted to the topic, but the Italian *L'archeologia degli italiani: storia, metodi e orientamenti dell'archeologia classica in Italia* by M. Barbanera, (Rome, 1998) is highly recommended. *The scarith of Scornello: a tale of Renaissance forgery* by I. Rowland (Chicago, 2005) is a captivating window into the forgery of Etruscan antiquity in the seventeenth century. The beginnings of Etruscan civilization are usually treated within scholarship on the prehistory of the Italic peninsula and increasingly so, for Anglophone archaeology, in the context of the Mediterranean: *Across Frontiers: Papers in Honour of David Ridgway and Francesca R. Serra Ridgway*, edited by E. Herring, I. Lemos, F. Lo Schiavo, L. Vagnetti, R. Whitehouse and J. Wilkins (London, 2006), and the *Cambridge prehistory of the Bronze and Iron Age Mediterranean*, edited by A. Bernard Knapp and P. van Dommelen (Cambridge, 2014) are recommended.

On the urbanization of Etruria, the role of the Italian scholarly tradition of late prehistory is absolutely central both in the field and in print. While no English book representing this tradition for Etruria exists, the book by Italian scholar M. Pacciarelli *Dal villaggio alla città. La svolta protourbana del 1000 a.C. nell'Italia tirrenica* (Florence, 2000) is essential. *The urbanisation of Etruria: funerary practices and social change, 700-600 BC* by C. Riva (Cambridge, 2010) gives, instead, a perspective that combines the topic with questions on the meaning of Orientalizing. These questions, still open to debate, can be found in *Debating orientalization: multidisciplinary approaches to processes of change in the ancient Mediterranean*, edited by C. Riva and N. Vella (London, 2006). On cities more generally, one conference in the series of regular conferences on Etruria was devoted to the large cities of southern Etruria; the proceedings, edited by A. M. Sgubini Moretti, have been published in 2005 (*Dinamiche di sviluppo delle città nell'Etruria meridionale: Veio, Caere, Tarquinia Vulci.* Pisa).

Archaic Etruria and the social changes associated with it are dealt with in a highly original way by V. Izzet in her *The archaeology of Etruscan society* (Cambridge, 2007). The site of Poggio Civitate near Murlo gives a particularly insightful view of what an archaic elite complex and its underlying social world is about: the exhibition catalogue *Poggio Civitate and the Goddess of Wine, Vinum*, edited by T. Tuck and R. Wallace (Sheridan WY, 2015), centred on wine drinking and the banquet, is a good introduction to the site, as does the website of the field project, which includes a database of the site's artefacts (http://www.poggiocivitate.com). Nancy Winter's *Symbols of wealth and power: architectural terracotta decoration in Etruria and Central Italy, 640-510 B.C.* (Ann Arbour, 2009) is the most authoritative scholarly source on architectural terracottas in archaic Etruria and central Italy. On religion, *The Religion of the Etruscans* edited by N. Thomson de Grummond and E. Simon (Austin, 2006) and J.-R. Jannot's *Religion in Ancient Etruria* (Madison, 2005) both offer some strong groundings. No single publication has dealt with Etruscan economy and trade in English or in Italian: M. Cristofani's *Gli etruschi del mare* (Milan, 1983) and *Il commercio etrusco arcaico*, edited by M. Cristofani, P. Moscati, G. Nardi and M. Pandolfini (Rome, 1985) both set the ground for future research. Although focused on Rome and *Latium*, the forthcoming book *The Origins of the Roman Economy* by G. Cifani (Cambridge, 2020) will no doubt prove useful for anyone interested in the subject for central Tyrrhenian Italy as a whole.

Studies on Etruria Padana are largely published in Italian, but a forthcoming volume on the town of Marzabotto is planned in the series devoted to single Etruscan cities by University of Texas Press (see below). A good and up-to-date summary, however, is provided by the article Kainua-Marzabotto: the archaeological framework by E. Govi, the excavator of the site, in the 28.2 (2017) issue of the journal *Archeologia e Calcolatori*. On Dionysos in Etruria, the book by I. Werner *Dionysos in Etruria: The Ivy Leaf Group* (Stockhom, 2005) deals with the production of Etruscan black figure painted vessels decorated with Dionysiac imagery.

On Etruria and Rome, the most recent full account that includes the wider context is N. Terrenato's *The early Roman expansion into Italy: elite negotiation and family agendas* (Cambridge, 2019). The scientific literature on Romanization in English is truly immense; some of the latest debates can be found in *Globalisation and the Roman world: world history, connectivity and material culture*, edited by M. Pitts and M. J. Versluys (Cambridge, 2015).

The University of Texas Press at Austin has recently begun a series devoted to each of the main Etruscan city states, conceived and coordinated by N. Thomson de Grummond and Lisa Pieraccini: the first two volumes, on *Caere* (2016) and *Veii* (2019) have been published.

Last but not least, the many exhibitions devoted to Etruscan civilization throughout Italy, Europe and beyond have produced lavish catalogues that belong to the scientific literature but are also of interest to the lay reader. One of the most important of these exhibitions took place at the turn of the twenty-first century at Palazzo Grassi in Venice; the English catalogue, *The Etruscans* (ed. M. Torelli) was published in 2001. The most recent exhibition, which opened in late 2019, is on at Bologna (http://www.etruschibologna.it), but due to the Covid-19 emergency it has had to close temporarily.

References

Acanfora, M. O. (1976). *Civiltà del Lazio primitivo, Palazzo delle Esposizioni, Roma, 1976*. Rome: Multigrafica.

Acconcia, V. (2019). Veii, the stratigraphy of an ancient town: a case study of Piazza d'Armi. In J. Tabolli and O. Cerasuolo (Eds.), *Veii* (pp. 9–16). Austin: University of Texas Press.

Acidini, C. (2009). Ferdinando I, il granduca delle città. In M. Bietti & A. Giusti (Eds.), *Ferdinando I de' Medici* (pp. 18–27). Florence: Sillabe.

Ackerman, J. (1983). The Tuscan/Rustic order: a study in the metaphorical language of architecture. *Journal of the Society of Architectural Historians, 42*(1), 15–34.

Adinolfi, G., Carmagnola, R., and Cataldi, M. (2005). La tomba dei demoni azzurri: le pitture. In F. Gilotta (Ed.), *Pittura parietale, pittura vascolare. Ricerche in corso tra Etruria e Campania* (pp. 45–56). Naples: Arte Tipografica.

Allegri, E., and Cecchi, A. (1980). *Palazzo Vecchio e i Medici: guida storica.* Florence: Studio per Edizioni Scelte.

Amann, P. (2017). Society, 450–250 BCE. In A. Naso (Ed.), *Etruscology* (pp. 1101–15). Berlin; Boston: De Gruyter.

Ambrosini, L. (2009). *Il Santuario di Portonaccio a Veio*. Rome: Giorgio Bretschneider Editore.

Ambrosini, L. (2013). Candelabra, Thymiateria and Kottaboi at Banquets: Greece and Etruria in comparison. In *Etruscan Studies*, *16*(1), 1–38. https://doi.org/10.1515/etst-2013-0007

Ampolo, C. (2009). Presenze etrusche, koiné culturale o dominio etrusco? *Annali della Fondazione per il Museo «Claudio Faina»*, *XVI*, 9–41.

Ampolo, C. (2017). Demarato di Corinto 'Bacchiade' tra Grecia, Etruria e Roma: rappresentazione e realtà, fonti, funzione dei racconti, integrazione di genti e culture, mobilità sociale arcaica. *Aristonothos, 13*(2), 25–134.

Andreau, J., Broise, H., and Jolivet, V. (2002). *Musarna*. Rome: École française de Rome.

Anti, C. (1920). L'Apollo che cammina. *Bollettino d'Arte, Maggio-Agosto 1920, 14*, 73–83.

Arancio, M. L., et al. (2014). *Principi immortali: fasti dell'aristocrazia etrusca a Vulci = Immortal princes: the splendour of the Etruscan aristocracy at Vulci*. [S. l.]: Soprintendenza per i Beni Archeologici dell'Etruria Meridionale.

Arizza, M. (2019). Ideologia funeraria a Veio tra età arcaica e classica: architetture, oggetti e ritualità. In M. Arizza (Ed.), *Società e pratiche funerarie a Veio dalle origini alla conquista romana* (pp. 45–66). Rome: Sapienza Università editrice.

Babbi, A., Peltz, U., and Benelli, E. (2013). *La tomba del guerriero di Tarquinia: identità elitaria, concentrazione del potere e networks dinamici nell'avanzato VIII sec. a.C. = Das Kriegergrab von Tarquinia: Eliteidentität, Machtkonzentration und dynamische Netzwerke im späten 8. Jh. v. Chr.* Mainz: Verlag des Römisch-Germanischen Zentralmuseums.

Baglione, M. P. (1997). Cratere a colonnette a figure rosse con Herakles simposiasta. In A. Maggiani (Ed.), *Vasi attici figurati con dediche a divinità etrusche* (pp. 85–93). Rome: Giorgio Bretschneider.

Baglione, M. P. (2013). Pyrgi, un santuario nel cuore del Mediterraneo. In F. Gaultier, L. Haumesser, and P. Santoro (Eds.), *Gli etruschi e il Mediterraneo: la città di Cerveteri* (pp. 204–20). Paris: Somogy.

Baglione, M. P., et al. (2017). Pyrgi, l'area a nord del santuario: nuovi dati dalle recenti campagne di scavo. *Scienze dell'antichità, 23*(1), 149–94.

Baglione, M. P., and Gentili, M. D. (2013). *Riflessioni su Pyrgi: scavi e ricerche nelle aree del santuario*. Rome: L'Erma di Bretschneider.

Bagnasco Gianni, G. (2009). I cavalli alati di Tarquinia. Una proposta di lettura. In M. Bonghi Jovino and F. Chiesa (Eds.), *L'Ara della Regina di Tarquinia, aree sacre, santuari mediterranei.* (pp. 93–139). Milan: Cisalpino Istituto Editoriale Universitario.

Bagnasco Gianni, G. (2012). Origine degli etruschi. In G. Bartoloni (Ed.), *Introduzione all'Etruscologia* (pp. 47–81). Milan: Hoepli.

Bagnasco Gianni, G. (2010). Fenomeni di contatto nelle più antiche iscrizioni etrusche: spunti tarquiniesi. *Annali della Fondazione per il Museo «Claudio Faina», XVII*, 113–27.

Bagnasco Gianni, G. (2016). Fascino etrusco nel primo Novecento. *Aristonothos, 11*, 11–50.

Bagnasco Gianni, G., et al. (2018). Civita Di Tarquinia (Comune Di Tarquinia, Provincia Di Viterbo, Regione Lazio). *Papers of the British School at Rome, 86*, 328–32. doi:10.1017/S0068246218000132

Baldassarra, D. (2013). *Dal Saronico all'Adriatico: iscrizioni greche su ceramica del Museo archeologico nazionale di Adria*. Pisa: Edizioni ETS.

Baldassarri, S. U. (2009). Like fathers like sons: theories on the origins of the city in late medieval Florence. *MLN*, *124*(1), 23–44. doi:10.1353/mln.0.0098

Barbanera, M. (1998). *L'archeologia degli italiani: storia, metodi e orientamenti dell'archeologia classica in Italia*. Rome: Editori riuniti.

Barbanera, M. (2008). The impossible museum: exhibitions of archaeology as reflections of contemporary ideologies. In N. a. J. N. Schlanger (Ed.), *Archives, ancestors, practices: archaeology in the light of its history* (pp. 165–77). New York: Berghahn Books.

Barbanera, M. (2009). 'Lo studio dell'arte etrusca era fermo al volume di Jules Matha'. Le ricerche sugli Etruschi nel primo trenennio del Novecento. In M. Barbanera (Ed.), *L'occhio dell'archeologo. Ranuccio Bianchi Bandinelli nella Siena del primo '900* (pp. 17–31). Cinisello Balsamo: Silvana Editoriale.

Barbanera, M. (2015). *Storia dell'archeologia classica in italia: dal 1764 ai giorni nostri*. Rome: GLF Editori Laterza.

Barbaro, B. (2010). *Insediamenti, aree funerarie ed entità territoriali in Etruria meridionale nel bronzo finale*. Florence: All'Insegna del Giglio.

Barker, G. (1972). The conditions of cultural and economic growth in the Bronze Age of central Italy. *Proceedings of the Prehistoric Society*, *38*, 170–208. doi:10.1017/S0079497X0001210X

Barker, G. (1981). *Landscape and society: prehistoric Central Italy*. London: Academic Press.

Barocchi, P. (1983). La storia della Galleria degli Uffizi e la storiografia artistica. In P. Barocchi and G. Ragionieri (Eds.), *Gli Uffizi. Quattro secoli di una galleria* (pp. 49–150). Florence: Leo S. Olschki.

Bartoloni, G., et al. (2005). Veio-Piazza d'Armi. In A. M. Sgubini Moretti (Ed.), *Dinamiche di sviluppo delle città nell'Etruria meridionale. Veio, Caere, Tarquinia, Vulci* (pp. 73–85). Pisa: Istituti editoriali e poligrafici internazionali.

Bartoloni, G., et al. (2006). Veio: l'abitato di Piazza d'Armi. Le terrecotte architettoniche. In I. Edlund-Berry, G. Greco, and J. Kenfield (Eds.), *Deliciae Fictiles III. Architectural terracottas in ancient Italy: new discoveries and interpretations* (pp. 510–76). Oxford: Oxbow Books.

Bartoloni, G., and Acconcia, V. (2007). La casa del re. In L. Botarelli, M. Coccoluto, and M. C. Mileti (Eds.), *Materiali per Populonia 6* (pp. 11–29). Pisa: Edizioni ETS.

Bartoloni, G., and Benedettini, M. G. (2011). *Veio: Il deposito votivo di comunità (scavi 1889–2005)*. Rome: Giorgio Bretschneider Editore.

Bartoloni, G., and Michetti, L. (2019). Veii during the Archaic period (sixth and fifth centuries BCE). In O. Cerasuolo and J. Tabolli (Eds.), *Veii* (pp. 107–16). Austin: University of Texas Press.

Bartoloni, G., ten Kortenaar, S., and Acconcia, V. (2012). Viticultura e consumo del vino in Etruria: la cultura materiale tra la fine dell'età del Ferro e l'Orientalizzante Antico. In A. Ciacci, P. Rendini, and A. Zifferero (Eds.), *Archeologia della vite e del vino in Toscana e nel Lazio: dalle tecniche dell'indagine archeologica alle prospettive della biologia molecolare* (pp. 201–75). Florence: All'Insegna del Giglio.

Battiloro, I., and Osanna, M. (2015). Continuity and change in Lucanian cult places between the third and first centuries BC: new insights into the 'Romanization' issue. In T. Steck and J.-G. Burgers (Eds.), *The impact of Rome on cult places and religious practices* (pp. 169–98). London: Bulletin of the Institute of Classical Studies.

Becker, H. (2013). Political systems and law. In J. MacIntosh Turfa (Ed.), *The Etruscan World* (pp. 351–71). Abingdon: Routledge.

Belelli Marchesini, B., Biella, M. C., and Michetti, L. M. (2015). *Il santuario di Montetosto sulla via Caere-Pyrgi*. Rome: Officina Edizioni.

Bellelli, V. (2010). L'impatto del mito greco nell'Etruria orientalizzante: la documentazione ceramica. *Bollettino di Archeologia On Line, Volume Speciale. Congresso di Archeologia AIAC 2008*, 27–40.

Bellelli, V. (2011a). *La ceramica a figure nere di tipo attico prodotta in Italia* (Vol. VIII). Pisa: Fabrizio Serra editore.

Bellelli, V. (2011b). Un'iscrizione greca dipinta e i culti della Vigna Parrocchiale a Caere. *Studi Etruschi, 74*, 91–124.

Bellelli, V. (2013). L'area archeologica della Vigna Parrocchiale: dalle origini alla costruzione del tempio tuscanico. In F. Gaultier, L. Haumesser, and P. Santoro (Eds.), *Gli etruschi e il Mediterraneo: la città di Cerveteri* (pp. 170–5). Paris: Somogy.

Bellelli, V. (2014). *Caere. Il territorio, la viabilità e le fortificazioni. Atti della giornata di studio: Roma, Consiglio nazionale delle ricerche, 1 marzo 2012*. Pisa: Fabrizio Serra editore.

Bellelli, V. (2016). The urban area. In N. Thomson de Grummond and L. Pieraccini (Eds.), *Caere* (pp. 49–58). Austin: University of Texas Press.

Bellelli, V. (2017). Northern Campania. In A. Naso (Ed.), *Etruscology* (pp. 1395–434). Berlin; Boston: De Gruyter.

Bellelli, V., and Xella, P. (2016). *Le lamine di Pyrgi: nuovi studi sulle iscrizioni in etrusco e in fenicio nel cinquantenario della scoperta*. Verona: Essedue Edizioni.

Benelli, E. (2015). I Cacni, famiglia perugina. *Römische Mitteilungen* (121), 177–98.

Benelli, E. (2017). Approaches to the study of language. In A. Naso (Ed.), *Etruscology* (pp. 95–108). Boston; Berlin: De Gruyter.

Berardinetti, A., De Santis, A., and Drago, L. (1997). Burials as evidence for proto-urban development in southern Etruria: the case of Veii. In H. Damgaard Andersen, H. W. Horsnaes, S. Houby-Nielsen, and A. Rathje (Eds.), *Urbanization in the Mediterranean in the 9th to 6th centuries BC* (pp. 317–41). Copenhagen: Museum Tusculanum Press.

Beretta, M. (2000). At the source of Western science: the organization of experimentalism at the Accademia del Cimento. *Notes and Records of the Royal Society*, *54*(2), 131–51. doi:10.1098/rsnr.2000.0104

Bergamini, M. (2001). *Todi: antica città degli Umbri*. Assisi (PG): TAU.

Berkin, J. M. (2003). *The Orientalizing bucchero from the lower building at Poggio Civitate (Murlo)*. Boston, MA; Oxford: Archaeological Institute of America Oxbow.

Bertelli, S. (1981). Firenze, la Toscana e le origini 'aramee' dell'etrusco. *Annali della Facoltà di Lettere e Filosofia dell'Università di Siena*, 2, 199–207.

Berti, L. (1967). *Il Principe dello studiolo: Francesco I dei Medici e la fine del Rinascimento fiorentino*. Florence: Edam.

Berti, F., and Guzzo, P. G. (1993). *Spina: storia di una città tra greci ed etruschi. Ferrara, Castello Estense, 26 settembre 1993–15 maggio 1994*. Ferrara: Comitato Ferrara Arte.

Biella, M. C. (2019). Gods of value: preliminary remarks on religion and economy in pre-Roman Italy. In C. Moser and C. Smith (Eds.), *Transformations of value: lived religion and the economy* (pp. 23–45). Tübingen: Mohr Siebeck.

Biella, M. C., Cascino, R., Ferrandes, A. F., and Revello Lami, M. (2017). *Gli artigiani e la città: officine e aree produttive tra VIII e III secolo a.C. nell'Italia centrale tirrenica*. Atti della giornata di studi, British School at Rome, 11 gennaio 2016. Rome: Edizioni Quasar.

Blake McHam, S. (2006). Structuring communal history through repeated metaphors of rule. In R. J. Crum and J. T. Paoletti (Eds.), *Renaissance Florence. A social history* (pp. 104–37). Cambridge: Cambridge University Press.

Blanck, H. (2008). The Instituto di Corrispondenza Archeologica. *Fragmenta. Journal of the Royal Netherlands Institute in Rome*, 2, 63–78.

Blok, J. H. (1984). Quests for a scientific mythology: F. Creuzer and K. O. Müller on history and myth. *History and Theory*, *33*(4), 63–78.

Bocci Pacini, P., and Bartoloni, G. (2003). The importance of Etruscan antiquity in the Tuscan Renaissance. In J. Fejfer, Tobias Fischer-Hansen and Annette Rathje (Eds.), *The rediscovery of antiquity: the role of the artist* (Vol. 10, pp. 449–79). Copenhagen: Museum Tusculanum Press.

Boitani, F. (2001). La tomba principesca n. 5 di Monte Michele. In A. M. Moretti Sgubini (Ed.), *Veio, Cerveteri, Vulci. Città d'Etruria a confronto* (pp. 113–18). Rome: L'Erma di Bretschneider.

Boitani, F. (2004). La tomba di guerriero AA1 dalla necropoli dei Quattro Fontanili di Veio. In A. M. Moretti Sgubini (Ed.), *Scavo nello scavo. Gli Etruschi non visti* (pp. 128–49). Viterbo: Union Printing.

Boitani, F. (2010). Veio, la Tomba dei Leoni Ruggenti: dati preliminari. *Archeologia nella Tuscia, 10*, 23–47.

Bonamici, M., Stopponi, S., and Tamburini, P. (1994). *Orvieto: la necropoli di Cannicella: scavi della Fondazione per il Museo 'C. Faina' e dell'Università di Perugia (1977)*. Rome: L'Erma di Bretschneider.

Bonaudo, R. (2004). *La culla di Hermes: iconografia e immaginario delle hydriai ceretane*. Rome: L'Erma di Bretschneider.

Bonaudo, R. (2008–2009). In rotta per l'Etruria: Aristonothos, l'artigiano e la metis di Ulisse. *AION (Archeologia)*, 15–16, 143–9.

Bonfante, L. (1986). *Etruscan life and afterlife: a handbook of Etruscan studies*. Warminster: Aris & Phillips.

Bonghi Jovino, M. (1997). Considerazioni sulla stratigrafia e ipotesi interpretative dal bronzo finale avanzato all'orientalizzante medio. In A. M. Bonghi Jovino and C. Chiaramonte-Treré (Eds.), *Tarquinia. Testimonianze archeologiche e ricostruzione storica. Scavi sistematici nell'abitato. Campagne 1982–1988. Tarchna I* (pp. 145–81). Rome: L'Erma di Bretschneider.

Bonghi Jovino, A. M. (2001). Il complesso 'sacro-istituzionale' di Tarquinia. In A. Carandini and R. Cappelli (Eds.), *Roma: Romolo, Remo e la fondazione della città* (pp. 265–7). Milan: Electa.

Bonghi Jovino, A. M. (2010). The Tarquinia Project: a summary of 25 years of excavation. *American Journal of Archaeology, 114*(1), 161–80.

Bonghi Jovino, M., and Bagnasco Gianni, G. (2012). *Tarquinia: il santuario dell'Ara della Regina: i templi arcaici*. Rome: L'Erma di Bretschneider.

Borsi, F. (1985). Architettura. In F. Borsi (Ed.), *Fortuna degli etruschi* (pp. 36–43). Milan: Electa.

Botto, M., and Vives-Ferrándiz, J. (2006). Importazioni etrusche tra le Baleari e la Penisola Iberica (VIII - prima metà del V sec. a.c.). *Annali della Fondazione per il Museo «Claudio Faina», 13*, 33–112.

Bourdin, S. p. (2012). *Les peuples de l'Italie préromaine: identités, territoires et relations inter-ethniques en Italie centrale et septentrionale (VIIIe-1er s. av. J.-C.)*. Rome: École française de Rome.

Bradley, G. (2000). *Ancient Umbria: state, culture, and identity in central Italy from the Iron Age to the Augustan era*. Oxford: Oxford University Press.

Bradley, G. (2007). Romanization: the end of the peoples of Italy? In G. Bradley, C. Riva, and E. Isayev (Eds.), *Ancient Italy: regions without boundaries* (pp. 295–322). Exeter: University of Exeter Press.

Brandt, J. R., and Karlsson, L. (2001). *From huts to houses: transformations of ancient societies*. Stockholm Jonsered, Sweden: Svenska institutet i Rom: Norske institutt i Roma Distributor, P. Aströms Förlag.

Bratti, I. (2007). *Forma urbis Perusiae*. Città di Castello (PG): Edimond.

Brizio, E. (1890). Relazione sugli scavi eseguiti a Marzabotto presso Bologna 1888–89, *Monumenti Antichi*, I, columns 249–426.

Brocato, P. (2012). *Origine e primi sviluppi delle tombe a dado etrusche*. Arcavacata di Rende (Cs): Università della Calabria.

Brocato, P., and Novelli, M. (2012). Alcune osservazioni preliminari sui caratteri tipologici. In P. Brocato (Ed.), *Origine e primi sviluppi delle tombe a dado etrusche* (pp. 181–91). Arcavacata di Rende (CS): Università della Calabria.

Bruins, H. J., Nijboer, A. J., and Plicht van der, J. (2011). Iron Age Mediterranean chronology: a reply. *Radiocarbon*, *53*(1), 199–220.

Bruni, S. (2000). L'architettura tombale dell'area costiera dell'estrema Etruria settentrionale. Appunti per l'Orientalizzante antico e medio. In A. Zifferero (Ed.), *L'architettura funeraria a Populonia tra IX e VI secolo a.C.* (pp. 151–72). Florence: All'Insegna del Giglio.

Bruni, L. (2001). *History of the Florentine people. edited and translated by James Hankins* (Vol. 1). Cambridge, MA; London: Harvard University Press.

Bruschetti, P. (2012). *La necropoli di Crocifisso del Tufo a Orvieto: contesti tombali*. Pisa; Rome: Fabrizio Serra.

Bruschetti, P. (2014). *Seduzione etrusca: dai segreti di Holkham Hall alle meraviglie del British Museum*. Milan: Skira.

Bruschetti, P., and Trombetta, A. (2013). *I Principes di Castel San Mariano: due secoli dopo la scoperta dei bronzi etruschi 1812–2012*. Perugia: Effe Fabrizio Fabbri: Comune di Corciano.

Bundrick, S. D. (2019). *Athens, Etruria, and the many lives of Greek figured pottery*. Madison, WI: The University of Wisconsin Press.

Buranelli, F. (1985). *L'urna Calabresi di Cerveteri*. Rome: L'Erma di Bretschneider.

Buranelli, F. (1991). *Gli scavi a Vulci della Società Vincenzo Campanari-Governo Pontificio (1835–1837)*. Rome: L'Erma di Bretschneider.

Burke, P. (2003). Images as Evidence in Seventeenth-Century Europe. *Journal of the History of Ideas*, *64*(2), 273–96.

Cambi, F. (2012). *Il ruolo degli oppida e la difesa del territorio in Etruria: casi di studio e prospettive di ricerca*. Trento: Tangram.

Cambi, F., and Acconcia, V. (2011). Hidden urban landscape: Populonia between survey and excavations. In M. van Leusen, G. Pizziolo, and L. Sarti (Eds.), *Hidden landscapes of Mediterranean Europe: cultural and methodological biases in pre- and protohistoric landscape studies* (pp. 1–9). Oxford: BAR.

Cambi, F., and Di Paola, G. M. F. (2013). Etruscan strategies of defense: late classical and early hellenistic hilltop fortresses in the territory of Populonia. *Etruscan Studies*, *16*(2), 190–209.

Camilli, A. (2004). Le strutture 'portuali' dello scavo di Pisa-San Rossore. In A. G. Zevi and R. Turchetti (Eds.), *Le strutture dei Porti e degli approdi antichi* (pp. 67–86). Soveria Mannelli: Rubbettino.

Camporeale, G. (1967). *Vetulonia*. Florence: Leo S. Olschki.

Cappuccini, L. (2007). I kyathoi etruschi di Santa Teresa di Gavorrano e il ceramista dei Paiθina. *Römische Mitteilungen*, *113*, 217–40.

Cappuccini, L. (2012). Il castellum di Poggio Civitella (Montalcino, Siena). In F. Cambi (Ed.), *Il ruolo degli oppida e la difesa del territorio in Etruria. Casi di studio e prospettive di ricerca* (pp. 299–322). Trento: Tangram.

Carancini, G. L. (2018). La lezione di metodo di Renato Peroni e la sua visione della protostoria come evoluzione della dialettica dei gruppi sociali: dalla comunità di villaggio alla vigilia delle società di classi. *Ostraka*, *XXVII*, 23–34.

Cavani, V. (2009). La paletnologia in Romagna tra XIX e XX secolo. *IpoTESI di Preistoria*, *2*, 166–91.

Cecconi, G. A. (2006). Romanizzazione, diversità culturale, politicamente corretto. *Mélanges de l'École française de Rome. Antiquité*, *118*(1), 81–94.

Cella, E., Gori, M., and Pintucci, A. (2016). The trowel and the sickle: Italian archaeology and its Marxist legacy. *EX NOVO. Journal of Archaeology*, *1*(1), 71–83.

Cerasuolo, O., Pulcinelli, L., and Rubat Borel, F. (2008). Rofalco (Farnese, VT). Una fortezza vulcente tra la metà del IV e i primi decenni del III sec. a.C. In O. Paoletti (Ed.), *La città murata in Etruria* (pp. 533–8). Pisa: Fabrizio Serra.

Cerchiai, L. (2001). The ideology of the Etruscan city. In M. Torelli (Ed.), *The Etruscans* (pp. 243–53). London : Thames and Hudson.

Cerchiai, L. (2008). Riflessioni sull'immaginario dionisiaco nella pittura tombale etrusca di età arcaica. In S. Estienne, D. Jaillard, N. Lubtchansky, and C. Pouzadoux (Eds.), *Image et religion dans l'Antiquité gréco-romaine* (pp. 439–47). Naples: Publications du Centre Jean Bérard.

Cerchiai, L. (2011). Culti dionisiaci e rituali funerari tra poleis magnogreche e comunità anelleniche. In M. Lombardo, A. Siciliano & A. Alessio (Eds.),

La vigna di Dioniso. Vite, vino e culti in Magna Grecia (pp. 483–514). Taranto: Istituto per la storia e l'archeologia della Magna Grecia.

Cerchiai, L. (2012). Questioni di metodo. *Mélanges de l'École française de Rome*, 124–2 online.

Chastel, A. (1961). *Art et Humanisme à Florence au Temps de Laurent le Magnifique: Études sur la Renaissance et l'Humanisme Platonicien* (2nd edn). Paris: P.U.F.

Chiaramonte Treré, C., and Bagnasco Gianni, G. (1999). *Tarquinia: scavi sistematici nell'abitato: campagne 1982–1988: i materiali 1*. Rome: L'Erma di Bretschneider.

Chiesa, F. (2005). *Tarquinia: archeologia e prosopografia tra ellenismo e romanizzazione*. Rome: L'Erma di Bretschneider.

Cianferoni, G. C. (1999). La tomba della Mula. In F. Martini, G. Poggesi, and L. Sarti (Eds.), *Lunga memoria della piana. L'area fiorentina dalla preistoria alla romanizzazione* (pp. 81–4). Florence: Centro Stampa 2P.

Cianferoni, G. C., and Celuzza, M. (2010). *Signori di Maremma: elites etrusche fra Populonia e Vulci*. Florence: Polistampa.

Cifani, G. (2003). *Storia di una frontiera: dinamiche territoriali e gruppi etnici nella media Valle Tiberina dalla prima età del ferro alla conquista romana*. Rome: Istituto poligrafico e Zecca dello Stato, Libreria dello Stato.

Cifani, G. (2008). *Architettura romana arcaica: edilizia e società tra monarchia e repubblica*. Rome: L'Erma di Bretschneider.

Cifani, G. (2015a). Il sepolcro dei Cacni a Perugia. Ideologia e cultura di una famiglia aristocratica tra ellenismo e romanizzazione. *Römische Mitteilungen* (121), 125–76.

Cifani, G. (2015b). Osservazioni sui paesaggi agrari, espropri e colonizzazione nella prima età repubblicana *Mélanges de l'École française de Rome - Antiquité* [*En ligne*], 127–2. https://doi.org/10.4000/mefra.2938.

Cinquantaquattro, T., and Pellegrino, C. (2017). Southern Campania. In A. Naso (Ed.), *Etruscology* (pp. 1359–94). Berlin; Boston: De Gruyter.

Cipriani, G. (1980). *Il mito Etrusco nella Firenze repubblicana e medicea nei secoli XV e XVI*. Florence: Leo S. Olschki.

Ciuccarelli, M. R. (2015). Etruscan tombs in a 'Roman' city: the necropolis of Caere between the late fourth and the first century B.C.E. *Etruscan Studies*, *18*(2), 200–10.

Coarelli, F. (1983). Le pitture della Tomba François a Vulci: una proposta di lettura. *Dialoghi di Archeologia, III serie, 1*(2), 43–69.

Cocchi Genick, D. (2014). L'analisi tipologica delle ceramiche preistoriche e protostoriche dal 1959 a oggi. In A. Guidi (Ed.), *150 anni di preistoria e protostoria in Italia* (pp. 529–34). Florence: Osanna Edizioni.

Colini, G. A. (1909). Le antichità di Tolfa e Allumiere e il principio dell'età del ferro in Italia. *Bullettino di Paletnologia Italiana 35*, 104–49.

Colivicchi, F. (2015). After the fall: *Caere* after 273 B.C.E. *Etruscan Studies, 18*(2), 178–99.

Colombi, C. (2018). *La necropoli di Vetulonia nel periodo orientalizzante.* Wiesbaden: Reichert Verlag.

Colonna, G. (1985). *Santuari d'Etruria.* Florence; Milan: Regione toscana Electa.

Colonna, G. (1988). Il lessico istituzionale etrusco e la formazione della città, specialmente in Emilia Romagna. In G. A. Mansuelli (Ed.), *La Formazione della città preromana in Emilia Romagna* (pp. 15–36). Bologna: Centro Studi sulla città antica, Università di Bologna.

Colonna, G. (1991). Riflessioni sul dionisismo in Etruria. In F. Berti (Ed.), *Dionysos. Mito e mistero* (pp. 117–55). Ferrara: Liberty House.

Colonna, G. (1996). Il dokanon, il culto dei Dioscuri e gli aspetti ellenizzanti della religione dei morti nell'Etruria arcaica. In L. Bacchielli and M. Bonanno Aravantinos (Eds.), *Scritti di antichità in memoria di Sandro Stucchi* (pp. 165–84). Rome: L'Erma di Bretschneider.

Colonna, G. (2000). Il santuario di Pyrgi dalle origini mitistoriche agli altorilievi frontonali dei Sette e di Leucotea. *Scienze dell'antichità*, 10, 251–336.

Colonna, G. (2001). Porsenna, la lega etrusca e il Lazio. In M. Iozzo (Ed.), *La lega etrusca dalla Dodecapoli ai Quindecim populi* (pp. 29–35). Pisa: Istituti editoriali e poligrafici internazionali.

Colonna, G. (2002). *Il Santuario di Portonaccio a Veio*. Rome: Accademia nazionale dei Lincei.

Colonna, G. (2003). Ossevazioni sulla Tomba tarquiniese della nave. In A. Minetti (Ed.), *Pitture Etrusca. Problemi e prospettive* (pp. 63–77). Siena: Protagon Editori Toscani.

Colonna, G. (2019). The sanctuary of Portonaccio. In J. Tabolli and O. Cerasuolo (Eds.), *Veii* (pp. 117–26). Austin: University of Texas Press.

Cornelio Cassai, C., Giannini, S., and Malnati, L. (2013). *Spina: scavi nell'abitato della città etrusca, 2007–2009*. Florence: Cooperativa Archeologica.

Cosentino, R., and Maggiani, A. (2010). Caere: necropoli della Banditaccia - complesso monumentale di Campo della Fiera. *Studi Etruschi, LXXVI*, 267–71.

Cox-Rearick, J. (1982). Themes of time and rule at Poggio a Caiano: the Portico Frieze of Lorenzo il Magnifico. *Mitteilungen des Kunsthistorischen Institutes in Florenz*, 26(2), 167–210.

Cremaschi, M. (2017). Il contesto geoarcheologico dell'abitato etrusco di Spina: la stratigrafia lungo il raccordo secondario canale Anita (Ostellato - Ferrara). In C. Reusser (Ed.), *Spina. Neue Perspektiven der archäologischen Erforschung* (pp. 35–40). Rahden/Westf: VML Verlag Marie Leidorf GmbH.

Cristofani, M. (1969). *Le tombe da Monte Michele nel Museo Archeologico di Firenze*. Florence: Leo S. Olschki.

Cristofani, M. (1976a). Storia dell'arte e acculturazione. Le pitture tombali arcaiche di Tarquinia. *Prospettiva*, 7, 2–10.

Cristofani, M. (1976b). Winckelmann, Heyne, Lanzi e l'arte etrusca. *Prospettiva* 4, 16–21.

Cristofani, M. (1978). *L'arte degli etruschi: produzione e consumo*. Turin: G. Einaudi.

Cristofani, M. (1978). *Le urne volterrane*. Rome: CNR.

Cristofani, M. (1979). Per una storia del collezionismo archeologico nella Toscana granducale. I. I grandi bronzi. *Prospettiva* 17, 4–15.

Cristofani, M. (1981). Linee di una storia del 'revival' etrusco in Toscana nel XVI secolo. In *'Mito' etrusco e ideologia medicea* (Vol. Annali della Facoltà di lettere e filosofia di Siena, pp. 195–8). Florence: Leo S. Olschki.

Cristofani, M. (1983). *La scoperta degli etruschi: archeologia e antiquaria nel '700*. Rome: Consiglio nazionale delle ricerche.

Cristofani, M. (1985). *Il commercio etrusco arcaico: atti dell'incontro di studio, 5–7 dicembre, 1983*. Rome: Consiglio nazionale delle ricerche.

Cristofani, M. (1992). *Caere 3. Lo scarico arcaico della Vigna Parrocchiale*. Rome: Consiglio nazionale delle ricerche.

Cristofani, M. (1993a). Il 'von Kunst der Hetrurien' nelle due edizioni della 'Geschichte'. In M. Fancelli (Ed.), *J. J. Winckelmann tra letteratura e archeologia* (pp. 133–43). Venice: Marsilio.

Cristofani, M. (1993b). Un etrusco a Egina. *Studi Etruschi*, 59, 159–62.

Cristofani, M. (2003). *Caere 4. Vigna Parrocchiale. Scavi 1983–1989. Il santuario, la 'residenza' e l'edificio ellittico*. Rome: Consiglio nazionale delle ricerche.

Cristofani, M., and Martelli, M. (1994). Lo stile del potere e i beni di prestigio. In S. Settis and J. Guilaine (Eds.), *Storia di Europa II, Preistoria e antichità* (pp. 1147–66). Turin: Einaudi.

Cruciani Fabrozzi, G. (1976). Le 'Antichità figurate etrusche' e l'opera di Anton Francesco Gori. In Kunsthistorisches Institut in Florenz (Ed.), *Kunst des Barock in der Toskana. Studien zur Kunst unter den letzten Medici* (pp. 275–88). Munich: Bruckmann.

Crum, R. J. (1989). 'Cosmos, the World of Cosimo': the iconography of the Uffizi Façade. *The Art Bulletin*, *71*(2), 237–53. doi:10.1080/00043079.1989.10788497

Cultrera, G. (1932). Tarquinia. Il primo tumulo della Doganaccia. *Notizie degli Scavi*, *14*, 100–16.

Cuozzo, M. A. (2007). Ancient Campania: cultural interaction, political borders and geographical boundaries. In G. Bradley, E. Isayev, and C. Riva (Eds.), *Ancient Italy: regions without boundaries* (pp. 224–67). Exeter: Exeter University Press.

Cunliffe, B. W., and Osborne, R. (2005). *Mediterranean urbanization, 800–600 BC*. Oxford: Oxford University Press.

Cygielman, M., and Rafanelli, S. (2004). *Io sono di Rachu Kakanas: la tomba etrusca del Duce di Vetulonia*. Vetulonia: Museo Civico Archeologico 'Isidoro Falchi'.

d'Agostino, B., and Cerchiai, L. (1999). *Il mare, la morte, l'amore: gli etruschi, i greci e l'immagine*. Rome: Donzelli.

D'Oriano, R., and Sanciu, A. (2013). Phoenician and Punic Sardinia and the Etruscans. In J. MacIntosh Turfa (Ed.), *The Etruscan World* (pp. 231–43). Abingdon: Routledge.

De Angelis, F. (1999). Tragedie familiari. Miti Greci nell'arte sepolcrale etrusca. In T. Hölscher et al. (Eds.), *Im Spiegel des Mythos. Bilderwelt und Lebenswelt. Lo specchio del mito. Immaginario e realtà* (pp. 53–66). Wiesbaden: Dr. Ludwig Reichert Verlag.

De Angelis, F. (2015). *Miti Greci in tombe Etrusche: le urne cinerarie di Chiusi*. Rome: Giorgio Bretschneider Editore.

De Francesco, A. (2013). *The antiquity of the Italian nation: the cultural origins of a political myth in modern Italy, 1796–1943* (1st edn). Oxford: Oxford University Press.

De Grummond, N. T., Edlund-Berry, I. E. M., and Bagnasco Gianni, G. (2011). *The archaeology of sanctuaries and ritual in Etruria*. Portsmouth, R.I: Journal of Roman Archaeology.

Décultot, E. (2010). *Musées de papier: l'antiquité en livres, 1600–1800 [published on the occasion of the exhibition held at the Musée du Louvre, Paris, 25 September 2010 –3 January 2011]*. Paris: Musée du Louvre.

Décultot, E. (2000). *Johann Joachim Winckelmann: enquête sur la genèse de l'histoire de l'art* (1re édn). Paris: Presses Universitaires de France.

Della Fina, G. M. (2002). *Perugia etrusca: atti dell'IX convegno internazionale di studi sulla storia e l'archeologia dell'Etruria*. Rome: Quasar.

Della Fina, G. M. (2004). *Citazioni archeologiche: Luciano Bonaparte archeologo: catalogo della Mostra, Orvieto, Museo Claudio Faina, 10 settembre 2004–9 gennaio 2005*. Rome: Quasar.

Delpino, F. (1991). Documenti sui primi scavi nel sepolcreto arcaico della Arcatelle a Tarquinia. *Archeologia Classica*, *XLIII*(1), 123–51.

Delpino, F. (1999). La 'scoperta' di Veio etrusca. In A. Mandolesi and A. Naso (Eds.), *Ricerche archeologiche in Etruria meridionale nel XIX secolo* (pp. 73–86). Florence: All'Insegna del Giglio.

Demetriou, D. (2012). *Negotiating identity in ancient Mediterranean. The archaic and classical Greek multiethnic emporia*. Cambridge: Cambridge University Press.

Dennis, G. (1907). *The cities and cemeteries of Etruria*. London: Dent.

Dezzi Bardeschi, M. (1976). Archeologismo e neoumanesimo nella cultura architettonica fiorentina sotto gli ultimi Medici. In Kunsthistorisches Institut in Florenz (Ed.), *Kunst des Barock in der Toskana. Studien zur Kunst unter den letzten Medici* (pp. 245–67). Munich: Bruckmann.

di Fazio, M. (2007). Porsenna e la società di Chiusi. *Athenaeum*, *88*, 393–412.

di Fazio, M. (2018). Figures of memory. Aulus Vibenna, Valerius Publicola and Mezentius between history and legend. In K. Sandberg and C. Smith (Eds.), *Omnium annalium monumenta: historical writing and historical evidence in Republican Rome* (pp. 322–48). Leiden; Boston: Brill.

Di Giuseppe, H. (2008). Assetti territoriali nella media valle del Tevere dall'epoca orientalizzante a quella repubblicana. In H. L. Patterson and F. Coarelli (Eds.), *Mercator placidissimus. The Tiber Valley in antiquity. New research in the upper and middle river valley* (pp. 431–65). Rome: Quasar.

Di Giuseppe, H. (2012). Veii in the Republican period. In R. Cascino, H. Di Giuseppe, and H. L. Patterson (Eds.), *Veii. The historical topography of the ancient city: a restudy of John Ward-Perkins's survey* (pp. 359–66). London: British School at Rome.

Diaz, F. (1976). *Il Granducato di Toscana: i Medici*. Turin: UTET.

Dietler, M. (2005). *Consumption and colonial encounters in the Rhône Basin of France: a study of Early Iron Age political economy*. Lattes: Association pour le Développement de l'Archéologie en Languedoc-Roussillon.

Dolfini, A. (2013). The gendered house: exploring domestic space in later Italian prehistory. *Journal of Mediterranean Archaeology*, *26*(2), 131–57.

Donati, L. (1994). *La Casa dell'Impluvium: architettura etrusca a Roselle*. Rome: Giorgio Bretschneider.

Donati, L. (2000). Civil, religious and domestic architecture. In M. Torelli (Ed.), *The Etruscans* (pp. 313–33). London: Thames and Hudson.

Dore, A., and Morigi Govi, C. (2014). La protostoria a Bologna dalla scoperta di Villanova all'inaugurazione del Museo Civico. In A. Guidi (Ed.), *150 anni di preistoria e protostoria in Italia* (pp. 93–8). Firenze: Osanna Edizioni.

Drago Troccoli, L. (1997). Le tombe 419 e 426 del sepolcreto di Grotta Gramiccia a Veio. Contributo alla conoscenza di strutture tombali e ideologia funeraria a Veio tra il VI e il V secolo a. C. In G. Nardi and M. Pandolfini (Eds.), *Etrusca et Italica. Scritti in ricordo di Massimo Pallottino* (pp. 239–80). Pisa: Istituti Editoriali e Poligrafici Internazionali.

Drago Troccoli, L. (2003). Rapporti tra Fermo e le comunità tirreniche nella prima età del ferro. In Istituto nazionale di studi etruschi e italici (Ed.), *I Piceni e l'Italia medio-adriatica* (pp. 35–84). Pisa: Istituti Editoriali e Poligrafici Internazionali.

Dyson, S. L. (2013). Cosa. In J. DeRose Evans (Ed.), *A companion to the archaeology of the roman republic* (pp. 472–84). Chichester: Wiley.

Edlund-Berry, I. (2019). Cult evidence from the urban sanctuaries at Veii. In J. Tabolli and O. Cerasuolo (Eds.), *Veii* (pp. 127–38). Austin: University of Texas Press.

Eisenbichler, K. (2001). *The cultural politics of Duke Cosimo I de'Medici*. Aldershot: Ashgate.

Eles, P. von (2002). *Guerriero e sacerdote: autorità e comunità nell'età del ferro a Verucchio: la tomba del Trono*. Florence: All'Insegna del Giglio.

Eles, P. von (2013). Research in Villanovan necropoleis of Verucchio, 9th to 7th century BC. In A. J. Nijboer, S. M. Willemsen, P. A. J. Attema, and J. F. Seubers (Eds.), *Research into pre-Roman burial grounds in Italy* (pp. 83–102). Leuven: Peeters.

Emiliozzi, A. (1999). *Carri da guerra e principi etruschi: Catalogo della Mostra*. Rome: L'Erma di Bretschneider.

Emiliozzi, A. (2011). The Etruscan Chariot from Monteleone di Spoleto. *Metropolitan Museum Journal*, 46, 9–132. doi: 10.1086/668454

Esposito, A. M. (1999). *Principi guerrieri: la necropoli etrusca di Casale Marittimo (guida alla mostra)*. Milan: Electa.

Esposito, A. M., and Burchianti, F. (2009). L'insediamento orientalizzante e arcaico di Casalvecchio. In G. Camporeale and A. Maggiani (Eds.), *Volterra alle origini di una città etrusca* (pp. 191–224). Rome: Fabrizio Serra.

Falchi, I. (1965). *Vetulonia e al sua necropoli antichissima*. Rome: L'Erma di Bretschneider.

Fedeli, L. (2012). Gli scavi della Soprintendenza dal 1992 al 2012. In P. Bruschetti, F. Cecchi, P. Giulierini, and P. Pallecchi (Eds.), *Restaurando la storia: l'alba dei principi etruschi* (pp. 45–64). Cortona (AR): Tiphys edizioni.

Feruglio, A. E. (1995). *Porano: gli Etruschi.* Perugia: Quattroemme.

Feruglio, A. E. (2003). Le necropoli etrusche. In G. M. Della Fina (Ed.), *Storia di Orvieto I. Antichità* (pp. 275–328). Foligno (PG): Editoriale Umbra SAS.

Ferrari, S. (2003). Le transfert italien de Johann J. Winckelmann pendant la seconde moitié du XVIIIe siècle. *Recherches Germaniques, 33*, 1–19.

Findlen, P. (2012). Uffizi Gallery, Forence: the rebirth of a museum in the eighteenth century. In C. Paul (Ed.), *The first modern museums of art: the birth of an institution in 18th- and early-19th-century Europe* (pp. 73–111). Los Angeles: J. Paul Getty Museum.

Findlen, P. (2013). The 2012 Josephine Waters Bennett Lecture: the eighteenth-century invention of the renaissance: lessons from the Uffizi. *Renaissance Quarterly, 66*(1), 1–34. doi:10.1086/670403.

Fiore, C. S. (2012). Parmi d'andare peregrinando dolcissimamente per quell'Etruria. Scoperte antiquarie e natura nell'Etruria di Curzio Inghirami e Athansius Kircher. *Storia dell'Arte, 133*, 53–81.

Fiorini, L. (2005). *Topografia generale e storia del santuario: analisi dei contesti e delle stratigrafie*. Bari: Edipuglia.

Fiorini, L. (2015). Le ancore di Gravisca. *Aristonothos, 10*, 65–90.

Fiorini, L., and Materazzi, F. (2017). Un Iseion a Gravisca? Fotogrammetria, telerilevamento multispettrale da APR e dati archeologici per una possibile identificazione. *FastiOnLine Documents & Research, 396*, 1–23.

Fiorini, L., and Torelli, M. (2010). Quarant'anni di ricerche a Gravisca. In L. B. van der Meer (Ed.), *Material aspects of Etruscan religion* (pp. 29–49). Leiden: Peeters.

Fiorini, L., and Winter, N. A. (2013). La Vigna Marini-Vitalini. In F. Gaultier, L. Haumesser, and P. Santoro (Eds.), *Gli etruschi e il Mediterraneo: la città di Cerveteri* (pp. 162–9). Paris: Somogy.

Firpo, G. (2008). Roma, etruschi e italici nel 'secolo senza Roma'. In G. Urso (Ed.), *Patria diversis gentibus una? Unità, politica e identità etniche nell'Italia antica* (pp. 267–304). Pisa: ETS.

Fontaine, P. (2010). *L'Étrurie et l'Ombrie avant Rome: cité et territoire.* Bruxelles: Insititut Historique Belge de Rome.

Fortunelli, S. (2007). *Il deposito votivo del santuario settentrionale.* Bari: Edipuglia.

Fugazzola Delpino, M. A. (1979). The Proto-Villanovan: a survey. In D. Ridgway and F. Ridgway (Eds.), *Italy before the Romans: the Iron Age, orientalizing and Etruscan periods* (pp. 31–47). London; New York, San Francisco: Academic Press.

Fulminante, F. (2014). *The urbanization of Rome and Latium Vetus: from the Bronze Age to the Archaic Era*. Cambridge: Cambridge University Press.

Fusco, L., and Corti, G. (2006). *Lorenzo de'Medici, collector of antiques*. Cambridge: Cambridge University Press.

Gaertner, J. F. (2008). Livy's Camillus and the political discourse of the late republic. *Journal of Roman Studies*, *98*, 27–52. doi:10.3815/007543508786239283

Gailledrat, E. (2015). New perspectives on emporia in the western Mediterranean: Greeks, Etruscans and native populations at the mouth of the Lez (Hérault, Grance) during the sixth-fifth centuries BC. *Journal of Mediterranean Archaeology*, *28*, 23–50.

Gailledrat, E., Dietler, M., and Plana Mallart, R. (2018). *The emporion in the Ancient Western Mediterranean: trade and colonial encounters from the Archaic to the Hellenistic period*. Montpellier: Presses Univeritaires de la Méditerranée.

Galdy, A. M. (2009). *Cosimo I de'medici as collector: antiquities and archaeology in Sixteenth-century Florence*. Newcastle upon Tyne: Cambridge Scholars Publishing.

Gallo, D. (1999). Per una storia degli antiquari romani nel Settecento *Mélanges de l'École française de Rome. Italie et Méditerranée*, 111(2), 827–45.

Garagnani, S., Gaucci, A., and Gruška, B. (2016). From the archaeological record to ArchaeoBIM: the case study of the Etruscan temple of Uni in Marzabotto. *Virtual Archaeology Review* 7(15), 77–86.

Gaucci, A. (2010). Adria. Iscrizioni etrusche tardo-arcaiche. *Ocnus*, *18*, 35–51.

Gaucci, A. (2012). Le iscrizioni etrusche tardo-arcaiche di Adria. Nuove iscrizioni e analisi epigrafica e dei contesti. *Padusa*, *48*, 143–79.

Gaultier, F. (2013). La scultura funeraria in età arcaica. In F. Gaultier, L. Haumesser, P. Santoro, V. Bellelli, A. Russo Tagliente, and R. Cosentino (Eds.), *Gli etruschi e il Mediterraneo: La città di Cerveteri* (pp. 185–9). Paris: Somogy éditions d'art.

Gaultier, F., Haumesser, L., and Santoro, P. (2013). *Gli etruschi e il Mediterraneo: la città di Cerveteri*. Paris: Somogy éditions d'art.

Gauna, C. (2003). *La Storia pittorica di Luigi Lanzi: arti, storia e musei nel Settecento*. Florence: Leo S. Olschki.

Ghirardini, G. (1882). Corneto-Tarquinia. *Notizie degli Scavi*, *1882*, 136–215.

Giardino, C. (2013). Villanovan and Etruscan mining and metallurgy. In J. MacIntosh Turfa (Ed.), *The Etruscan World* (pp. 721–37). Abingdon: Routledge.

Gleba, M. (2008). *Textile production in pre-Roman Italy*. Oxford Oakville, CT: Oxbow Books.

Gleba, M. (2009). Textile tools and specialisation in the early Iron Age female burials. In E. Herring and K. Lomas (Eds.), *Gender identities in Italy in the first millennium BC* (pp. 69–78). Oxford: Archaeopress.

Gleba, M. (2016). Etruscan textiles in context. In S. Bell and A. A. Carpino (Eds.), *A Companion to the Etruscans* (pp. 237–46). Chichester: Wiley Blackwell.

Gleba, M., and Laurito, R. (2017). *Contextualising textile production in Italy in the1st millennium BC*. Rome: Gangemi Editore.

Gleba, M., Mandolesi, A., and Lucidi, M. R. (2017). New textile finds from Tomba dell'Aryballos Sospeso, Tarquinia: context, analysis and preliminary interpretation. *Origini*, *XL*, 29–44.

Gori, S., and Bettini, M. C. (2006). *Gli Etruschi da Genova ad Ampurias: atti del XXIV Convegno di studi etruschi ed italici, Marseille, Lattes, 26 settembre - 1 ottobre 2002*. Pisa: Istituti editoriali e poligrafici internazionali.

Govi, E. (2009). L'archeologia della morte a Bologna: spunti di riflessione e prospettive di ricerca. In R. Bonaudo, L. Cerchiai, and C. Pellegrino (Eds.), *Tra Etruria, Lazio e Magna Grecia: indagini sulle necropoli* (pp. 21–35). Paestum (SA): Pandemos.

Govi, E. (2015a). Il linguaggio figurativo delle stele felsinee. In E. Govi (Ed.), *Studi sulle stele etrusche di Bologna tra V e IV sec. a. C.* (pp. 7–42). Rome: Edizioni Quasar.

Govi, E. (2015b). *Studi sulle stele etrusche di Bologna tra V e IV sec. A.C.* Rome: Edizioni Quasar.

Govi, E. (2017). Kainua-Marzabotto: the archaeological framework. *Archeologia e Calcolatori*, *28*(2), 87–97.

Govi, E., and Sassatelli, G. (2010a). Considerazioni conclusive. In E. Govi and G. Sassatelli (Eds.), *Marzabotto. La Casa 1 della Regio IV, insula 2. Lo scavo* (pp. 291–310). Bologna: Ante Quem.

Govi, E., and Sassatelli, G. (2010b). *Marzabotto: la casa 1 della Regio IV, insula 2*. Bologna: Ante Quem.

Gregori, M. (1983). Luigi Lanzi e il riordinamento della galleria. In P. Barocchi and G. Ragionieri (Eds.), *Gli Uffizi. Quattro secoli di una galleria* (pp. 367–93). Florence: Leo S. Olschki.

Gunter, A. C. (2013). Orientalism and orientalization in the Iron Age Mediterranean. In B. A. Brown and M. H. Feldman (Eds.), *Critical approaches to ancient near eastern art* (pp. 79–108). Boston; Berlin: De Gruyter.

Haack, M.-L. (2008). Il concetto di 'transferts culturels': un'alternativa soddisfacente a quello di 'romanizzazione'? Il caso etrusco. In G. Urso (Ed.), *Patria diversis gentibus una? Unità politica e identità etniche nell'Italia antica* (pp. 135–46). Pisa: ETS.

Hankins, J. (1990). *Plato in the Italian renaissance, Volume I*. Leiden: E.J. Brill.

Hankins, J. (1991). Forging links with the past. *Journal of the History of Ideas*, *52*(3), 509–18.

Harari, M. (1993). Cultura moderna e arte etrusco-italica. *Rivista Storica Italiana 105*(3), 730–43.

Harari, M. (2007). Lo scudo 'spezzato' di Vel Saties. *Ostraka*, *16*(1), 45–54.

Harari, M. (2011). Perché all'inferno cresce la barba ai draghi. In G. F. La Torre and M. Torelli (Eds.), *Pittura ellenistica in Italia e in Sicilia. Linguaggi e tradizioni* (pp. 387–97). Rome: Giorgio Bretschneider.

Harari, M. (2012). Etruscologia e fascismo. *Athenaeum 100*, 405–18.

Harloe, K. (2013). *Winckelmann and the invention of antiquity: aesthetics and history in the age of altertumswissenschaft*. Oxford: Oxford University Press.

Harvey, F. D. (1976). Sostratos of Aegina. *Parola del Passato*, *31*, 206–14.

Hemelrijk, J. M. (2009). *More about Caeretan Hydriae: addenda et clarificanda*. Amsterdam: Allard Pierson Museum.

Holberton, P. (1985). Of antique and other figures: metaphor in early renaissance art. *Word & Image*, *1*(1), 31–58. doi:10.1080/02666286.1985.10435666

Iaia, C. (1999). *Simbolismo funerario e ideologia alle origini di una civiltà urbana: forme rituali nelle sepolture villanoviane a Tarquinia e Vulci, e nel loro entroterra*. Florence: All'Insegna del Giglio.

Iaia, C. (2005). *Produzioni toreutiche della prima età del ferro in Italia centro-settentrionale: stili decorativi, circolazioni, significato*. Pisa: Istituti editoriali e poligrafici internazionali.

Iaia, C. (2006). Servizi cerimoniali da 'simposio' in bronzo del primo ferro in Italia centrosettentrionale. In P. von Eles (Ed.), *La ritualità funeraria tra età del ferro e orientalizzante in Italia* (pp. 103–10). Pisa: Istituti Editoriali e Poligrafici Internazionali.

Iaia, C. (2009–2012). Warrior identity and the materialisation of power in Early Iron Age Etruria. *Accordia Research Papers*, *12*, 71–95.

Iaia, C. (2010). Fra Europa Centrale e Mediterraneo: modelli di recipienti e arredi in bronzo nell'Italia centrale della prima età del Ferro. *Bollettino di Archeologia On Line, Volume Speciale Congresso di Archeologia AIAC, 2008*, 31–44.

Iaia, C. (2013). Metalwork, rituals and the making of elite identity in central Italy at the Bronze age-Iron Age transition. In M. E. Alberti and S. Sabatini (Eds.), *Exchange networks and local transformations: interaction and local change in Europe and the Mediterranean from the Bronze Age to the Iron Age* (pp. 102–16). Oxford: Oxbow Books.

Iaia, C., and Pacciarelli, M. (2012). La cremazione in area mediotirrenica tra Bronzo Finale e Primo Ferro. In M. C. Rovira Hortalà, F. J. López Cachero, and F. Mazière (Eds.), *Les necròpolis d'incineració entre l'Ebre i el Tíber (segles IX–VI aC): metodologia, pràctiques funeràries i societat* (pp. 341–55). Barcelona: Museu d'Arqueologia de Catalunya.

Isler-Kerényi, C. (1998). K. O. Müllers Etrusker. In W. M. Calder III, and R. Schlesier (Eds.), *Zwischen Rationalismus und Romantik. Karl Otfried Müller und die antike Kultur* (pp. 239–81). Hildesheim: Weidmann.

Izzet, V. (2007). *The archaeology of Etruscan society*. Cambridge: Cambridge University Press.

Jannot, J.-R. (2005). *Religion in ancient Etruria*. Madison: University of Wisconsin Press.

Johnston, A. W. (1979). *Trade marks on Greek vases*. Warminster: Aris & Philips.

Johnston, A. W. (2001). Sailors and sanctuaries of the ancient Greek world. *Archaeology International*, *5*, 25–8.

Johnston, A. W. (2006). *Trademarks on Greek vases: addenda*. Oxford: Aris & Phillips (an imprint of Oxbow).

Johnston, A. W. (2019). Votive inscriptions from Naukratis. *British Museum Studies in Ancient Egypt and Sudan*, *24*, 105–17.

Johnston, A. W., and Pandolfini Angeletti, M. (2000). *Le iscrizioni*. Bari: Edipuglia.

Jolivet, V. (2013). A long twilight (396–90 BC): romanization of Etruria. In J. MacIntosh Turfa (Ed.), *The Etruscan World* (pp. 151–79). Abingdon: Routledge.

Jones, R. E., Levi, S. T., Bettelli, M., and Vagnetti, L. (2014). *Italo-Mycenaean pottery: the archaeological and archaeometric dimensions*. Rome: CNR.

Keay, S., Millett, M., Poppy, S., Robinson, J., Taylor, J., and Terrenato, N. (2000). Falerii Novi: A new survey of the walled area. *Papers of the British School at Rome*, *68*, 1–93.

Kent, F. W. (2004). *Lorenzo de' Medici and the art of magnificence*. Baltimore; London: Johns Hopkins University Press.

Kistler, E., Öhlinger, B., Mohr, M., and Hoernes, M. (2015). *Sanctuaries and the power of consumption: Networking and the formation of elites in the archaic Western Mediterranean world: proceedings of the international conference in Innsbruck, 20th–23rd March 2012*. Wiesbaden: Harrassowitz verlag.

Knoop, R. R. (1987). *Antefixa Satricana: sixth-century architectural terracottas from the sanctuary of Mater Matuta at Satricum (Le Ferriere)*. Assen, The Netherlands; Wolfeboro, N.H: Van Gorcum.

Krauskopf, I. (2016). Myth in Etruria. In S. Bell and A. A. Carpino (Eds.), *A companion to the Etruscans* (pp. 388–409). Chichester: Wiley Blackwell.

Lanzi, L. (1824–5). *Saggio di lingua etrusca e di altre antiche d'Italia: per servire alla storia de' popoli, delle lingue e delle belle arti*. Florence: tipografia di Attilio Tofani.

Lanzi, L. (1982). *La Real Galleria di Firenze accresciuta e riordinata per comando di S. A. R. l'Arciduca Granduca di Toscana*. Florence: Amministrazione comunale di Firenze, Assessorati alla Cultura e allo Sviluppo Economico.

Leighton, R. (2002). *Tarquinia*. London: Duckworth.

Leighton, R., and Castelino, C. (1990). Thomas Dempster and Ancient Etruria: a review of the autobiography and de Etruria Regali. *Papers of the British School at Rome*, *58*, 337–52.

Lejars, T. (2006). Les Celtes d'Italie. In M. Szabó (Ed.), *Celtes et Gaulois, l'Archéologie face à l'Histoire. Les Civilisés et les Barbares (du Ve au IIe siècle avant J.-C.)*. (pp. 1–20). Glux-en-Glenne: Centre archéologique européen.

Ligota, C. (1987). Annius of Viterbo and historical method. *Journal of the Warburg and Courtauld Institutes*, *50*, 44–56.

Lippolis, E. (2005). Nuovi dati sull'acropoli e sulla forma urbana di Marzabotto. In G. Sassatelli and E. Govi (Eds.), *Culti, forma urbana e artigianato a Marzabotto. Nuove prospettive di ricerca* (pp. 139–66). Bologna: Ante Quem.

Liverani, P. (1989). Il rilievo con i popoli etruschi: proposta di ricostruzione e interpretazione. In M. Fuchs, P. Liverani, and P. Santoro (Eds.), *Il teatro e il ciclo statuario giulio-claudio* (pp. 145–57). Rome: CNR.

Lo Schiavo, F. (2008). La navicella nuragica in bronzo dalla tomba del Duce di Vetulonia. In F. Lo Schiavo, P. Falchi, and M. Milletti (Eds.), *Gli Etruschi e la Sardegna tra la fine dell'età del Bronzo e gli inizi dell'età del Ferro* (pp. 31–9). Florence: Contemporanea Progetti.

Locatelli, D. (2005). La 'fonderia' della Regio V, insula 5. In G. Sassatelli and E. Govi (Eds.), *Culti, forma urbana e artigianato a Marzabotto. Nuove prospettive di ricerca* (pp. 213–38). Bologna: Ante Quem.

Long, L., Gantès, L.-F., and Rival, M. (2006). L'épave grand Ribaud F. In S. Gori and M. C. Bettini (Eds.), *Gli Etruschi da Genova ad Ampurias* (pp. 455–95). Pisa: Istituti editoriali e poligrafici internazionali.

Long, L., Pomey, P., and Sourisseau, J.-C. (2002). *Les Etrusques en mer: épaves d'Antibes à Marseille*. Aix-en-Provence; Marseille: Edisud Musées de Marseille.

Lugli, F. (2014). La preistoria e la protostoria italiana e l'etnoarcheologia. In A. Guidi (Ed.), *150 anni di preistoria e protostoria in Italia* (pp. 501–6). Florence: Osanna Edizioni.

Lulof, P. (2000). Archaic terracotta acroteria representing Athena and Heracles: manifestations of power in central Italy. *Journal of Roman Archaeology*, *13*, 207–19.

Lulof, P. (2006). 'Roofs from the south': campanian architectural terracottas in Satricum. In I. Edlund-Berry, G. Greco, and J. Kenfield (Eds.), *Deliciae Fictiles III. Architectural terracottas in ancient Italy: new discoveries and interpretations* (pp. 235–42). Oxford: Oxbow Books.

Lulof, P. (2008). Le Amazzoni e i Guerrieri di Vigna Marini-Vitalini. *Mediterranea*, *5*, 197–214.

Lulof, P. (2016). New perspectives on the Acroteria of Caeretan temples. In N. Thomson de Grummond and L. Pieraccini (Eds.), *Caere* (pp. 131–40). Austin: University of Texas Press.

Lulof, P., and Smith, C. (2017). The age of Tarquinius Superbus: history and archaeology. In P. Lulof and C. Smith (Eds.), *The age of Tarquinius Superbus: Central Italy in the late 6th century BC* (pp. 3–13). Leuven: Peeters.

Maggiani, A. (1996). Appunti sulle magistrature etrusche. *Studi Etruschi*, *62*, 95–138.

Maggiani, A. (2001). Magistrature cittadine, magistrature federali. In M. Iozzo (Ed.), *La lega etrusca dalla Dodecapoli ai Quindecim populi* (pp. 37–48). Pisa: Istituti editoriali e poligrafici internazionali.

Maggiani, A. (2002). La libbra etrusca. Sistemi ponderali e monetazione. *Studi Etruschi*, *LXXII*, 135–47.

Maggiani, A. (2005). Simmetrie architettoniche, dissimetrie rappresentative. Osservando le pitture della Tomba degli Scudi a Tarquinia. In F. Gilotta (Ed.), *Pittura Parietale, pittura Vascolare. Ricerche in corso tra Etruria e Campania* (pp. 115–32). Naples: Arte Tipografica.

Maggiani, A. (2006). Dinamiche del commercio arcaico: le tesserae hospitales. *Annali della Fondazione per il Museo «Claudio Faina»*, *13*, 317–50.

Maggiani, A. (2012). Ancora sui sistemi ponderali in Etruria. Pesi di pietra dal territorio fiesolano. *Mélanges de l'École française de Rome - Antiquité [En ligne]*, 124–2. doi: 10.4000/mefra.795

Maggiani, A. (2013). Il santuario in località Sant'Antonio: la fase arcaica. In F. Gaultier, L. Haumesser, and P. Santoro (Eds.), *Gli etruschi e il Mediterraneo: la città di Cerveteri* (pp. 176–8). Paris: Somogy.

Maggiani, A. (2016). The Vicchio Stele: the inscription. *Etruscan Studies, 19*(2), 220–4.

Mandolesi, A. (1999). *La 'prima' Tarquinia: l'insediamento protostorico sulla Civita e nel territorio circostante.* Florence: All'Insegna del Giglio.

Mandolesi, A., and de Angelis, D. (2011). Il tumulo della Regina di Tarquinia fra tradizioni levantine e innovazioni etrusche. *Archeologia Classica, 62*, 7–40.

Mandolesi, A., Lucidi, M. R., and Altilia, E. (2015). La Doganaccia di Tarquinia: organizzazione di un sepolcreto principesco. *Annali della Fondazione per il Museo «Claudio Faina»*, 22, 369–86.

Maras, D. (2002). Le iscrizioni. In G. Colonna (Ed.), *Il santuario di Portonaccio a Veio. 1, Gli scavi di Massimo Pallottino nella zona dell'altare (1939–1940)* (pp. 261–73). Rome: Giorgio Bretschneider.

Maras, D. F. (2009). *Il dono votivo: gli dei e il sacro nelle iscrizioni etrusche di culto.* Pisa: Fabrizio Serra.

Maras, D. (2013). Interferenza e concorrenza di modelli alfabetici e sistemi scrittori nell'Etruria arcaica. *Mélanges de l'École française de Rome - Antiquité* [*En ligne*], 124–2. https://doi.org/10.4000/mefra.742.

Maras, D., and Sciacca, F. (2011). Ai confini dell'oralità. Le forme e i documenti del dono nelle aristocrazie orientalizzanti etrusche. In V. Nizzo (Ed.), *Dalla nascita alla morte. Antropologia e archeologia a confronto* (pp. 703–13). Rome: Editorial Service System.

Marchand, S. L. (1996). *Down from Olympus: archaeology and philhellenism in Germany, 1750–1970.* Princeton: Princeton University Press.

Marchesini, M., and Marvelli, S. (2017). Indagini botaniche nell'abitato di Spina: paesaggio vegetale, ambiente e dieta alimentare. In C. Reusser (Ed.), *Spina. Neue Perspektiven der archäologischen Erforschun* (pp. 41–50). Rahden/Westf: VML Verlag Marie Leidorf GmbH.

Marcone, A. (2017). Romanization. In A. Naso (Ed.), *Etruscology* (pp. 665–83). Berlin; Boston: De Gruyter.

Martelli, M. (1987). *La Ceramica degli Etruschi: la pittura vascolare.* Novara: Istituto Geografico de Agostini.

Marzullo, M. (2017). *Spazi sepolti e dimensioni dipinte nelle tombe etrusche di Tarquinia.* Milan: Ledizioni.

Masseria, C. (2009). Ceramiche attiche dalla necropoli di Tarquinia e dall'emporion di Gravisca. Un confronto. In S. Fortunelli and C. Masseria (Eds.), *Ceramica attica da santuari della Grecia, della Ionia e dell'Italia* (pp. 329–68). Venosa (PZ): Osanna Edizioni.

Mazzoli, M., and Pozzi, A. (2015). I troni di Verucchio tra archeologia e iconografia. In P. von Eles, L. Bentini, P. Poli, and E. Rodriguez (Eds.),

Immagini di uomini e di donne dalle necropoli villanoviane di Verucchio (pp. 89–98). Florence: All'Insegna del Giglio.

Meer, L. B. van der (1987). *The bronze liver of Piacenza: analysis of a polytheistic structure*. Amsterdam: J.C. Gieben.

Meer, L. B. van der (2007). *Liber linteus zagrabiensis. The linen book of Zagreb: a comment on the longest Etruscan text*. Louvain; Dudley, MA: Peeters.

Meer, L. B. van der (2011). *Etrusco ritu: case studies in Etruscan ritual behaviour*. Louvain; Walpole, MA: Peeters.

Meer, L. B. van der (2013). Campo della Fiera at Orvieto and *Fanum Voltumnae*: identical places? *BABESCH*, *88*, 99–108.

Menichetti, M. (1994). *Archeologia del potere: re, immagini e miti a Roma e in Etruria in età arcaica*. Milan: Longanesi.

Mercuri, L., and Fiorini, L. (2014). *Il mare che univa: Gravisca santuario mediterraneo*. Rome: Gangemi.

Meyers, G. E. (2013). Approaching monumental architecture: mechanics and movement in Archaic Etruscan palaces. *Papers of the British School at Rome*, *81*, 39–66. doi:10.1017/S0068246213000044

Michetti, L. (2002). Considerazioni sui materiali. In G. Colonna (Ed.), *Il santuario di Portonaccio a Veio. 1, Gli scavi di Massimo Pallottino nella zona dell'altare (1939–1940)* (pp. 229–45). Rome: Giorgio Bretschneider.

Michetti, L. (2016). Ports: trade, cultural connections, sanctuaries, and Emporia. In N. Thomson de Grummond and L. Pieraccini (Eds.), *Caere* (pp. 73–86). Austin: University of Texas Press.

Miller, M. (2015). Archeologi e linguisti tedeschi e l'Istituto di Studi Etruschi prima della Seconda Guerra Mondiale. In M.-L. Haack (Ed.), *La construction de l' étruscologie au début du XXe siècle* (pp. 107–19). Bordeaux: Ausonius.

Minetti, A. (2004). *L'orientalizzante a Chiusi e nel suo territorio*. Rome: L'Erma di Bretschneider.

Minetti, A. (2006). *La tomba della quadriga infernale nella necropoli delle Pianacce di Sarteano*. Rome: L'Erma di Bretschneider.

Minto, A. (1921). *Marsiliana d'Albegna. Le scoperte archeologiche del Principe Don Tommaso Corsini*. Florence: Istituto di Edizioni Artistiche.

Minto, A. (1930). Le scoperte archeologiche nell'Agro Volterrano dal 1897 al 1899 (da appunti manoscritti di Gherardo Gherardini). *Studi Etruschi*, *IV*, 9-ff.

Momigliano, A. (1950). Ancient history and the antiquarian. *Journal of the Warburg and Courtauld Institutes*, *13*(3/4), 285–315. doi:10.2307/750215

Momigliano, A. (1966). *Terzo contributo alla storia degli studi classici e del mondo antico*. Rome: Edizioni di Storia e Letteratura.

Momigliano, A. (1975). *Quinto contributo alla storia degli studi classici e del mondo antico*. Rome: Edizioni di storia e letteratura.

Morandi, L. (2013). La necropoli orientalizzante della Banditella a Marsiliana d'Albegna. *BABESCH*, *88*, 13–38.

Moretti Sgubini, A. M. (2000). Il museo nazionale etrusco di Villa Giulia. In M. Torelli (Ed.), *Gli Etruschi* (pp. 523–9). Milan: Bompiani.

Morigi Govi, C., and Dore, A. (2005). Le necropoli: topografia, strutture tombali, rituale funerario, corredi e ideologia della morte. In R. Zangheri (Ed.), *Storia di Bologna* (pp. 164–80). Bologna: Bononia University Press.

Müller, C. O. (1847). *Ancient art and its remains, or, A manual of the archaeology of art*. London: Fullarton.

Müller, K. O., and Deecke, W. (1877). *Die Etrusker* (Neu bearbeitet von Wilhelm Deecke. edn). Stuttgart: Heitz.

Munzi, M., and Terrenato, N. (2000). *Volterra: il teatro e le terme. Gli edifici, lo scavo, la topografia*. Florence: All'Insegna del Giglio.

Musti, D. (2005). Temi etici e politici nella decorazione pittorica della Tomba François. In A. M. Sgubini Moretti (Ed.), *Dinamiche di sviluppo delle città nell'Etruria meridionale. Veio, Caere, Tarquinia Vulci* (pp. 485–508). Pisa: Istituti editoriali e poligrafici internazionali.

Najemy, J. M. (2000). *Civic humanism and Florentine politics*. Cambridge: Cambridge University Press.

Naso, A. (1996). *Architetture dipinte: decorazioni parietali non figurate nelle tombe a camera dell'Etruria meridionale : VII–V sec. a. C.* Rome: L'Erma di Bretschneider.

Naso, A. (1998). Tumuli monumentali in Etruria meridionale: caratteri propri e possibili ascendenze orientali. In P. Schauer (Ed.), *Archäologische Untersuchungen zu den Beziehungen zwischen Altitalien und der Zone nordwärts der Alpen während der frühen Eisenzeit Alteuropas* (pp. 117–57). Regensburg: Universitätsverlag Regensburg.

Naso, A. (2001). La Tomba del Convegno. In A. Barbet (Ed.), *La peinture funéraire antique. IVe siècle av. J.-C.-IVe siècle ap. J.-C.* (pp. 21–7). Paris: Editions Errance.

Naso, A. (2004). *Appunti sul bucchero: atti delle giornate di studio*. Florence: All'Insegna del Giglio.

Naso, A. (2007). Etruscan style of dying: funerary architecture, Tomb groups, and social range at Caere and its Hinterland during the Seventh-Sixth centuries B.C. In N. Lanieri (Ed.), *Performing death: social analyses of funerary traditions in the ancient Near East and Mediterranean* (pp. 141–62). Chicago: Oriental Institute of the University of Chicago.

Naso, A. (2012). Gli influssi del vicino Oriente sull'Etruria nell'VIII–VII sec. a.C.: un bilancio. In V. Bellelli (Ed.), *Le origini degli Etruschi. Storia Archeologia Antropologia* (pp. 433–54). Rome: L'Erma di Bretschneider.

Naso, A., and Botto, M. (2018). *Caere orientalizzante: nuove ricerche su città e necropoli.* Rome; Paris: CNR, Istituto di studi sul Mediterraneo antico Musée du Louvre, Département des antiquités grecques, étrusques et romaines.

Negrini, C., Mazzoli, M., and Di Lorenzo, G. (2018). The helmets of Verucchio: production and significance. *Etruscan Studies*, *21*(1–2), 78–97.

Nielsen, M. (2013). The last Etruscans: family tombs in northern Etruria. In J. MacIntosh Turfa (Ed.), *The Etruscan World* (pp. 180–93). Abingdon: Routledge.

Nijboer, A. J. (1998). *From household production to workshops: archaeological evidence for economic transformation, pre-monetary exchange and urbanisation in central Italy from 800 to 400 BC.* Groningen: Groningen Institute of Archaeology.

Nizzo, V. (2014). Il dibattito sull'origine degli italici nell'età di L. Pigorini: dall'antiquaria all'archeologia. In A. Guidi (Ed.), *150 Anni di Preistoria e Protostoria in Italia* (pp. 161–8). Florence: Osanna Edizioni.

North, J. A. (2006). The Constitution of the Roman Republic. In N. Rosenstein and R. Morstein-Marx (Eds.), *A companion to the Roman Republic* (pp. 256–77). Oxford: Blackwell.

Nowlin, J. (2016). *Reorienting orientalization: intrasite networks of value and consumption in central Italy* (Unpublished PhD thesis). Brown University.

Orestano, F. (2016). Gli Etruschi nella memoria culturale britannica, tra Otto e Novecento: ovvero il sublime fascino di un braccialetto. *Aristonothos 11*, 145–76.

Orlin, E. M. (2010). *Foreign cults in Rome: creating a Roman Empire.* New York; Oxford: Oxford University Press.

Osanna, M., and Pellegrino, C. (2017). Nuove ricerche nel santuario extra-urbano di Fondo Iozzino a Pompei. In E. Govi (Ed.), *La città etrusca e il sacro. Santuari e istituzioni politche* (pp. 373–93). Bologna: Bononia University Press.

Östenberg, C. E. (1961). Luni sul Mignone: Prima campagna di scavi. *Notizie degli Scavi*, *1960*, 103–24.

Östenberg, C. E. (1967). *Luni sul Mignone e problemi della preistoria d'Italia.* Lund: Gleerup.

Pacciarelli, M. (2000). *Dal villaggio alla città: la svolta protourbana del 1000 a.C. nell'Italia tirrenica.* Florence: All'Insegna del Giglio.

Pacciarelli, M. (2010). Verso i centri protourbani. Situazioni a confronto da Etruria meridionale, Campania e Calabria. *Scienze dell'antichità*, *15*, 371–416.

Pacciarelli, M., Cupitò, M., Grifoni Cremonesi, R., Cremaschi, M., and Tagliaferri, T. (2014). Progressi, polemiche e accentramento: La preistoria e la protostoria italiane al tempo di Luigi Pigorini (1871–1925). In A. Guidi (Ed.), *150 anni di Preistoria e Protostoria in Italia* (pp. 149–62). Florence: Osanna Edizioni.

Pairault Massa, F.-H. (1992). *Iconologia e politica nell'Italia antica. Roma, Lazio, Etruria dal VII al I secolo a.C.* Milan: Longanesi.

Paleothodoros, D. (2002). Purquoi les Étrusques achetaient-ils des vases Attiques? *Les Etudes Classiques*, *70*, 139–60.

Paleothodoros, D. (2007). Dionysiac imagery in Archaic Etruria. *Etruscan Studies*, *10*, 187–201.

Paleothodoros, D. (2010). Etruscan black-figure in context. *Bollettino di Archeologia On Line I 2010, Volume Speciale C/C4/2. Congresso di Archeologia AIAC 2008*. https://bollettinodiarcheologiaonline.beniculturali.it/wp-content/uploads/2019/01/2_PALEOTHODOROS.pdf.

Pallottino, M. (1939). Sulle facies culturali arcaiche dell'Etruria. *Studi Etruschi*, *13*, 85–129.

Pallottino, M. (1942). *Etruscologia*. Milan: U. Hoepli.

Pallottino, M. (1947). *L'origine degli Etruschi*. Rome: Tumminelli.

Pallottino, M. (1965). Orientalizing style. In *Encyclopedia of World Art* (Vol. X, pp. 782–96). New York: McGraw-Hill.

Pallottino, M. (1990). Per una immagine di Roma arcaica. In M. Cristofani (Ed.), *La Grande Roma dei Tarquini* (pp. 3–6). Rome: L'Erma di Bretschneider.

Pallottino, M., and Wikander, Ö. (1986). *Architettura etrusca nel viterbese: ricerche svedesi a San Giovenale e Acquarossa, 1956–1986*. Rome: De Luca.

Paltineri, S. (2012). I segni della discordia. Annotazioni sui sodales della Tomba François. In M. Harari and S. Paltineri (Eds.), *Segni e colore. Dialoghi sulla pittura tardoclassica ed ellenistica* (pp. 115–22). Rome: L'Erma di Bretschneider.

Paltineri, S., and Robino, M. T. A. (2016). Le ultime fasi del sito di San Cassiano di Crespino e le trasformazioni nell'entroterra di Adria. In E. Govi (Ed.), *Il mondo etrusco e il mondo italico di ambito settentrionale prima dell'impatto con Roma (IV–II sec. a.C.)* (pp. 275–301). Rome: Giorgio Bretschneider.

Paoletti, O. (2014). *Gli umbri in età preromana: atti del XXVII Convegno di studi etruschi ed Italici: Perugia · Gubbio · Urbino, 27–31 Ottobre 2009*. Pisa: Fabrizio Serra editore.

Paolucci, G. (2007). *Immagini etrusche: tombe con ceramiche a figure nere dalla necropoli di Tolle a Chianciano Terme*. Cinisello Balsamo (Milan): Silvana.

Paolucci, G. (2010). I canopi di Tolle tra restituzione del corpo e memoria del defunto. *Scienze dell'Antichitá*, *16*, 109–18.

Paolucci, G. (2015). *Canopi etruschi: Tombe con ossuari antropomorfi dalla necropoli di Tolle (Chianciano Terme)*. Rome: Giorgio Bretschneider.

Pareti, L. (1947). *La Tomba Regolini-Galassi del Museo Gregoriano Etrusco e la civiltà dell'Italia centrale nel sec VII a. C.* Città del Vaticano: Tipografia Poliglotta Vaticana.

Pasquinucci, M. (2003). Pisa e i suoi porti in età etrusca e romana. In M. Tangheroni (Ed.), *Pisa e il Mediterraneo. Uomini, merci, idee dagli etruschi ai Medici* (pp. 93–7). Milan: Skira.

Pasquinucci, M., and Menchelli, S. (2010). Il sistema portuale di Pisa: dinamiche costiere, import-export, interazioni economiche e culturali (VII sec. a.C.-I sec. d.C.). *Bollettino di Archeologia on line I 2010/ Volume speciale B / B6 / 1. Congresso di Archeologia AIAC 2008*. https://bollettinodiarcheologiaonline.beniculturali.it/wp-content/uploads/2019/01/1_PASQUINUCCI_MENCHELLI.pdf.

Pearce, M., and Gabba, E. (1995). Wolfgang Helbig e la teoria delle origini degli Italici. *Rivista Storica Italiana*, *CVII*(1), 119–32.

Pébarthe, C., and Delrieux, F. (1999). La transaction du plomb de Pech-Maho. *Zeitschrift für Papyrologie und Epigraphik*, *126*, 155–61.

Pellegrini, G. (1899). Fregi arcaici etruschi in terracotta a piccole figure. In L. Milani (Ed.), *Studi e materiali di archeologia e numismatica* (pp. 87–118). Florence: Leo S. Olschki.

Perazzi, P., and Poggesi, G. (2011). *Carta archeologica della provincia di Prato: dalla preistoria all'età romana*. Florence: All'Insegna del Giglio.

Perini, G. (1982). Luigi Lanzi: questioni di stile, questioni di metodo. In P. Barocchi (Ed.), *Gli Uffizi. Quattro secoli di una galleria. Fonti e Documenti* (pp. 215–65). Florence: Leo S. Olschki.

Peroni, R. (1959). Per una definizione dell' aspetto culturale 'subappenninico' come fase cronologica a sé stante. *Atti Accademia Nazionale dei Lincei, Serie 8*(9), 3–253.

Peroni, R. (1960). Allumiere: scavo di tombe in località 'La Pozza'. *Notizie degli Scavi*, *14*, 341–62.

Peroni, R. (1971). *L'età del bronzo nella penisola italiana*. Florence: Leo S. Olschki.

Peroni, R. (1992). Preistoria e protostoria. La vicenda degli studi in Italia. In M. Angle, A. Bietti, A. M. Bietti Sestieri, G. Canova, R. Ceserani, R. Dottarelli, A. Guidi, A. Iacono, R. Peroni, K. Randsborg, and M. Tosi (Eds.), *Le vie della preistoria* (pp. 9–70). Rome: Il Manifesto Libri.

Peroni, R. (2004). *L'Italia alle soglie della storia*. Rome: Laterza.

Perkins, P. (1999). *Etruscan settlement, society and material culture in Central coastal Etruria*.Oxford: BAR International Series.

Perkins, P., and Walker, L. (1990). Survey of an Etruscan City at Doganella, in the Albegna valley. *Papers of the British School at Rome*, *58*, 1–143. doi:10.1017/S0068246200011624

Pitts, M., and Versluys, M. J. (2015). *Globalisation and the Roman world: world history, connectivity and material culture*. Cambridge: Cambridge University Press.

Pizzirani, C. (2009). Iconografia dionisiaca e contesti tombali tra Felsina e Spina. In R. Bonaudo, L. Cerchiai, and C. Pellegrino (Eds.), *Tra Etruria, Lazio e Magna Grecia: indagini sulle necropoli* (pp. 37–49). Paestum (SA): Pandemos.

Pizzirani, C. (2010). Ceramica attica e ideologia funeraria. Dioniso in Etruria padana. *Bollettino di Archeologia on line I 2010/ Volume speciale D / D2 / 4. Congresso di Archeologia AIAC 2008*. https://bollettinodiarcheologiaonline.beniculturali.it/wp-content/uploads/2019/05/4_Pizzirani_paper.pdf.

Pieraccini, L. C. (2009). The English, Etruscans and 'Etouria': the grand tour. *Etruscan Studies*, *12*(1), 3–20. doi:10.1515/etst.2009.12.1.3

Poggesi, G. (2011). Il popolamento del territorio in epoca etrusca e romana. In P. Perazzi and G. Poggesi (Eds.), *Carta archeologica della provincia di Prato. Dalla preistoria all'età romana* (pp. 31–54). Florence: All'Insegna del Giglio.

Pohl, I. (1972). *The iron age necropolis of Sorbo at Cerveteri*. Stockholm; Lund: Paul Åström (Sölveg. 2).

Pommier, E. (2001). La nascita della storia dell'arte da Winckelmann a Séroux d'Agincourt. In F. C. a. M. G. D'Arcano (Ed.), *Fabio di Maniago e la storiografia in Italia e in Europa tra Sette e Ottocento* (pp. 275–88). Udine: Forum Edizioni.

Potter, T. W. (1979). *The changing landscape of South Etruria*. New York: St. Martin's Press.

Potter, T. W. (1998). *Dennis of Etruria: a celebration*. Cambridge: Antiquity.

Potts, A. (2000). *Flesh and the ideal: Winckelmann and the origins of art history*. New Haven; London: Yale University Press.

Potts, C. R. (2018). *Religious architecture in Latium and Etruria, c. 900–500 BC*. Oxford: Oxford University Press.

Prag, J. (2010). Tyrannizing Sicily: the despots who cried 'Carthage!'. In A. J. Turner, J. H. Kim On Chong-Gossard, and F. J. Vervaet (Eds.), *Private and public lies: the discourse of despotism and deceit in the Graeco-Roman world* (pp. 51–71). Leiden; Boston: Brill.

Pratt, C. E. (2015). The 'SOS' amphora: an update. *The Annual of the British School at Athens*, *110*, 213–45. doi:10.1017/S0068245414000240

Prayon, F. (1974). Zum ursprünglichen Aussehen und zur Deutung des Kulturraumes in der Tomba delle Cinque Sedie bei Cerveteri. *Marburger Winckelmann-Programm*, *1974*, 1–15.

Prayon, F. (1975). *Frühetruskische Grab- und Hausarchitektur*. Heidelberg: F. H. Kerle.

Prayon, F. (2016). *Castellina del Marangone: un abitato etrusco tra i monti della Tolfa e il mare Tirreno*. Civitavecchia: Associazione Archeologica Centumcellae.

Puglisi, S. M. (1959). *La civiltà appenninica: origine delle comunità pastorali in Italia*. Florence: Sansoni.

Quint, D. (1985). Humanism and modernity: a reconsideration of Bruni's dialogues. *Renaissance Quarterly*, *38*(3), 423–45. doi:10.2307/2861078

Quirino, T. (2012). Forcello di Bagnolo San Vito (Mn): dalle strutture abitative alla forma urbana. Alcune riflessioni sull'architettura etrusca della pianura padana. *Padusa*, *48*, 89–107.

Raaflaub, K. A. (2006). Between myth and history: Rome's rise from village to empire (the Eighth Century to 264). In N. Rosenstein and R. Morstein-Marx (Eds.), *A companion to the Roman Republic* (pp. 126–45). Oxford: Blackwell.

Rasmussen, T. B. (1979). *Bucchero pottery from southern Etruria*. Cambridge: Cambridge University Press.

Rathje, A. (2014). Self-representation and identity-creation by an Etruscan family. The use of the past in the François Tomb at Vulci. In B. Alroth and C. Scheffer (Eds.), *Attitudes towards the past in antiquity. Creating identities* (pp. 55–65). Stockholm: Stockholm University.

Rebenich, S. (2011). The making of a bourgeois antiquity: Wilhelm von Humboldt and Greek history. In A. Lanieri (Ed.), *The western time of ancient history: historiographical encounters with the Greek and Roman past* (pp. 119–38). Cambridge: Cambridge University Press.

Regoli, C. (2017). Un nuovo contributo da Regisvilla. *Scienze dell'antichità*, 23(2), 305–10.

Reusser, C. (2017). *Spina. Neue Perspektiven der archäologischen Erforschung*. Rahden/Westf: VML Verlag Marie Leidorf GmbH.

Rich, J. W. (2017). Warlords and the Roman Republic. In T. Ñaco del Hoyo and S. López-Sánchez (Eds.), *War, warlords and interstate relations in the ancient mediterranean* (pp. 266–94). Leiden; Boston: Brill.

Riedweg, C. (2005). *Pythagoras: his life, teaching, and influence*. Ithaca, NY; Bristol: Cornell University Press.

Riva, C. (2006). The orientalizing period in Etruria: sophisticated communities. In C. Riva and N. Vella (Eds.), *Debating orientalization: multidisciplinary approaches to change in the ancient Mediterranean* (pp. 11–135). London: Equinox Publishing.

Riva, C. (2010a). Ingenious inventions: welding ethnicities east and west. In T. Hodos and S. Hales (Eds.), *Material culture and social identities in the ancient world* (pp. 79–113). Cambridge: Cambridge University Press.

Riva, C. (2010b). *The urbanisation of Etruria: funerary practices and social change, 700–600 BC*. Cambridge: Cambridge University Press.

Riva, C. (2017). Wine production and exchange and the value of wine consumption in sixth-century BC Etruria. *Journal of Mediterranean Archaeology*, *30*(2), 237–61.

Riva, C. (2018). The freedom of the Etruscans: Etruria between Hellenization and Orientalization. *International Journal of the Classical Tradition*, *25*(2), 101–26.

Riva, C., and Vella, N. (2006). Introduction. In C. Riva and N. Vella (Eds.), *Debating orientalization: multidisciplinary approaches to processes of change in the ancient Mediterranean* (pp. 1–20). London: Equinox Publishing.

Rizzo, M. A. (1989). Veio. Tomba delle Anatre. In M. A. Rizzo (Ed.), *Pittura etrusca al Museo di Villa Giulia* (pp. 103–7). Rome: De Luca.

Rizzo, M. A. (1990). *Le Anfore da trasporto e il commercio etrusco arcaico*. Rome: De Luca.

Rizzo, M. A. (2015). *Principi etruschi: le tombe orientalizzanti di San Paolo a Cerveteri*. Rome: Ministero dei beni e della attività culturale e del turismo, Direzione generale belle arti e paesaggio.

Robino, M. T. A., Paltineri, S., and Smoquina, E. (2009). Scavi dell'Università di Pavia a San Cassiano di Crespino (RO). Un complesso abitativo etrusco nella chora di Adria, in *Atti del Congresso internazionale di Archeologia Classica*, Roma, 22–26 settembre 2008, *Fastionline Documents & Research*, http://www.fastionline.org/docs/FOLDER-it-2009-157.pdf.

Romagnoli, S., Calastri, C., Cremonini, S., and Desantis, P. (2014). *Il santuario etrusco di Villa Cassarini a Bologna*. Bologna: Bononia University Press.

Roncalli, F. (2001). Spazio reale e luogo simbolico: alcune soluzioni nell'arte funeraria etrusca. *Acta Hyperborea*, *8*, 242–72.
Roppa, A. (2012). L'età del Ferro nella Sardegna centro-occidentale. Il villaggio di Su Padrigheddu, San Vero Milis. *FastiOnLine documents & research* www.fastionline.org/docs/FOLDER it-2012-2252.pdf.
Rossi, M. (2006). *Le fila del tempo: il sistema storico di Luigi Lanzi*. Florence: Leo S. Olschki.
Roth, R. (2004). Ritual abbreviations in the Etruscan funeral: an Etruscan red-figured skyphos in the Fitzwilliam Museum. *Accordia Research Papers*, *9*, 93–103.
Rowland, I. D. (2005). *The scarith of Scornello: a tale of Renaissance forgery*. Chicago, IL; Bristol: University of Chicago Press.
Rubinstein, N. (2004). *Studies in Italian history in the Middle Ages and the Renaissance. 1, Political thought and the language of politics: art and politics*. edited by Giovanni Ciappelli. Rome: Storia e letteratura.
Russo Tagliente, A., and Guarneri, F. (2016). *Santuari mediterranei tra Oriente e Occidente: interazioni e contatti culturali: atti del Convegno internazionale, Civitavecchia - Roma 2014*. Rome: Scienze e lettere.
Sacchetti, F. (2012). *Les amphores grecques dans le nord de l'Italie: échanges commerciaux entre les Apennins et les Alps aux époques archaïque et classique*. Paris; Aix-en-Provence: Editions Errance: Centre Camille Jullian.
Sacchetti, F. (2016). Transport Amphorae in the West Hallstatt Zone: reassessing socio-economic dynamics and long-distance Mediterranean exchange in western Central Europe in the early Iron Age. *Oxford Journal of Archaeology*, *35*(3), 247–65. doi:10.1111/ojoa.12088
Said, E. W. (1995). *Orientalism*. London: Penguin.
Salvestrini, G. (2002). Giovanni Villani and the aetiological myth of Tuscan cities. In E. Kooper (Ed.), *The Medieval Chronicle II: proceedings of the second international conference on the Medieval Chronicle* (pp. 199–211). Amsterdam: Rodopi.
Sannibale, M. (2013). Orientalizing Etruria. In J. MacIntosh Turfa (Ed.), *The Etruscan World* (pp. 99–133). Abingdon: Routledge.
Sassatelli, G., and Govi, E. (2005). Il tempio di Tina in area urbana. In G. Sassatelli and E. Govi (Eds.), *Culti, forma urbana e artigianato a Marzabotto: nuove prospettive di ricerca* (pp. 9–62). Bologna: Ante Quem.
Sassatelli, G., and Govi, E. (2010). Cults and foundation rites in the Etruscan City of Marzabotto. In L. B. van der Meer (Ed.), *Material aspects of Etruscan religion* (pp. 27–37). Leuven: Peeters.

Sassi, M. M. (1984). Ermeneutica del mito in Karl Otfried Müller. *Annali della Scuola Normale Superiore di Pisa. Classe di Lettere e Filosofia*, *14*(3), 911–35.

Sciacca, F. (2005). *Patere baccellate in bronzo: Oriente, Grecia, Italia in età orientalizzante*. Rome: L'Erma di Bretschneider.

Schnapp, A. (2009). Naissance des savoirs antiquaires. In I. Aghion, M. Avisseau-Broustet and A. Schnapp (Eds.), *Histoires d'archéologie. De l'objet à l'étude* (pp. 2–8). Paris: Publications de l'Institut national d'histoire de l'art.

Schoonhoven, E. (2010). A literary invention: the Etruscan myth in early Renaissance Florence. *Renaissance Studies*, *24*(4), 459–71. doi:10.1111/j.1477-4658.2010.00662.x

Serra Ridgway, F. R., and Pieraccini, L. (2010). *Pithoi stampigliati ceretani: una classe originale di ceramica etrusca*. Rome: L'Erma di Bretschneider.

Settis, S. (1984). Dal sistema all'autopsia: l'archeologia di C. O. Müller. *Annali della Scuola Normale Superiore di Pisa. Classe di Lettere e Filosofia*, *14*(3), 1069–96.

Sewell, J. (2016). Higher-order settlements in early Hellenistic Italy: a quantitative analysis of a new archaeological database. *American Journal of Archaeology*, *120*(4), 603–30. doi:10.3764/aja.120.4.0603

Sgubini Moretti, A. M. (1998). La Tomba del Carro, 680–670 a. In C. A. Emiliozzi (Ed.), *Carri da guerra e principi etruschi* (pp. 139–45). Rome: L'Erma di Bretschneider.

Sisani, S. (2009). *Umbrorum gens antiquissima Italiae: studi sulla società e le istituzioni dell'Umbria preromana*. Perugia: Deputazione di storia patria per l'Umbria.

Smith, C. (1998). Traders and Artisans in Archaic central Italy. In H. Parkins and C. Smith (Eds.), *Trade, Traders and the Ancient City* (pp. 31–51). London and New York: Routledge.

Smith, C. J. (2014). *The Etruscans. A very short introduction*. Oxford: Oxford University Press.

Smith, C. (2018). J.B. Ward-Perkins, the BSR and the landscape tradition in post-war Italian archaeology. *Papers of the British School at Rome*, *86*, 271–92.

Smith, C. (2019). Furius Camillus and Veii. In J. Tabolli and O. Cerasuolo (Eds.), *Veii* (pp. 219–24). Austin: University of Texas Press.

Spalletti, E. (2010). *La Galleria di Pietro Leopoldo: gli Uffizi al tempo di Giuseppe Pelli Bencivenni*. Florence: Centro Di.

Spivey, N. J. (1987). *The Micali Painter and his followers*. Oxford: Clarendon.

Spivey, N. J. (1997). *Etruscan art*. London: Thames & Hudson.
Steingräber, S. (1986). *Etruscan painting: catalogue raisonné of Etruscan wall paintings*. New York: Johnson Reprint Corp; Harcourt Brace Jovanovich.
Stefani, E. (1944). Scavi archeologici a Veio in contrada Piazza d'Armi. *Monumenti Antichi dei Lincei*, *40*, 122–290.
Steingräber, S. (2006). *Abundance of life: Etruscan wall painting*. Los Angeles: J. Paul Getty Museum.
Stek, T. (2015). Cult, conquest, and 'religious Romanization'. In T. Steck and J.-G. Burgers (Eds.), *The impact of Rome on cult places and religious practices in ancient Italy* (pp. 1–28). London: Bulletin of the Institute of Classical Studies.
Stephens, W. (2004). When Pope Noah ruled the Etruscans: Annius of Viterbo and his forged 'Antiquities'. *MLN*, *119*(1), S201–23. doi:10.1353/mln.2004.0038
Stoddart, S. (2012). Between text, body and context: expressing 'Umbrian' identity in the landscape. In G. Cifani and S. Stoddart (Eds.), *Landscape, ethnicity and identity in the Archaic Mediterranean area* (pp. 173–86). Oxford: Oxbow.
Stopponi, S. (2003). I templi e l'architettura templare. In G. M. Della Fina (Ed.), *Storia di Orvieto 1. Antichità* (pp. 235–73). Foligno (PG): Editoriale Umbra SAS.
Stopponi, S. (2011). Campo della Fiera at Orvieto: new discoveries. In N. T. De Grummond and I. Edlund-Berry (Eds.), *The archaeology of sanctuaries and ritual in Etruria* (pp. 17–44). Porstmouth, RI: Journal of Roman Archaeology
Stopponi, S. (2012). Il Fanum Voltumnae: dalle divinità Tluschva a San Pietro. *Annali della Fondazione per il Museo «Claudio Faina»*, *19*, 7–75.
Stopponi, S. (2013). Orvieto, Campo della Fiera. In J. MacIntosh Turfa (Ed.), *The Etruscan World* (pp. 632–54). Abingdon: Routledge.
Strandberg Olofsson, M. (1989). On the reconstruction of the monumental area at Acquarossa. *Opuscola Romana*, *17*, 163–83.
Swaddling, J. (2002). *Seianti Hanunia Tlesnasa: the story of an Etruscan noblewoman*. London: British Museum.
Szilágyi, J. G. (1992). *Ceramica etrusco-corinzia figurata*. Florence: Leo S. Olschki.
Talocchini, A. (1980). Castelnuovo Berardenga. *Studi Etruschi*, *48*, 550.
Tassi Scandone, E. (2001). *Verghe, scuri e fasci littori in Etruria: contributi allo studio degli insignia imperii*. Pisa: Istituti editoriali e poligrafici internazionali.

Tavernor, R. (1998). *On Alberti and the art of building*. New Haven, CT; London: Yale University Press.

Ten Kortenaar, S., Neri, S., and Nizzo, V. (2006). La necropoli di Piano e Poggio delle Granate. In M. Aprosio and C. Mascione (Eds.), *Materiali per Populonia 5* (pp. 325–57). Pisa: Edizioni ETS.

Terrenato, N. (2019). *The early Roman expansion into Italy: elite negotiation and family agendas*. Cambridge: Cambridge University Press.

Thomas, M. L., and Meyers, G. E. (2013). *Monumentality in Etruscan and early Roman architecture: ideology and innovation*. Austin: University of Texas Press.

Thomson de Grummond, N. (2016). Ritual and religion: life at the sanctuaries. In N. Thomson de Grummond and L. Pieraccini (Eds.), *Caere* (pp. 149–65). Austin: University of Texas Press.

Torelli, M. (1975). *Elogia tarquiniensia*. Florence: Sansoni.

Torelli, M. (1985). *L'arte degli Etruschi*. Rome: Laterza.

Torelli, M. (2014). Conclusioni. In M. Aberson, M. C. Biella, M. di Fazio, and M. Wullschleger (Eds.), *Entre archéologie et histoire. Dialogues sur divers peuples de l'Italie préromaine* (pp. 349–62). Berne: Peter Lang.

Torelli, M. (2016). The Roman period. In N. Thomson de Grummond and L. Pieraccini (Eds.), *Caere* (pp. 263–70). Austin: University of Texas Press.

Torelli, M. (2017). The Etruscan legacy. In A. Naso (Ed.), *Etruscology* (pp. 685–720). Berlin; Boston: De Gruyter.

Torelli, M. (2019). *Gli Spurinas. Una famiglia di principes nella Tarquinia della 'rinascita'*. Rome: L'Erma di Bretschneider.

Tortarolo, E. (2003). *La ragione interpretata: la mediazione culturale tra Italia e Germania nell'età dell'illuminismo*. Rome: Carocci.

Tronchetti, C. (2015). Cultural interactions in Iron Age Sardinia. In A. B. Knapp and P. van Dommelen (Eds.), *The Cambridge prehistory of the Bronze and Iron Age mediterranean* (pp. 266–84). Cambridge: Cambridge University Press.

Tsingarida, A. (2009). Vases for heroes and gods: early Red-Figure parade cups and large-scaled phialai. In A. Tsingarida (Ed.), *Shapes and uses of Greek vases (7th–4th centuries B.C.)* (pp. 185–202). Bruxelles: CReA-patrimoine.

Tuck, A. S. (2009). *The necropolis of Poggio Civitate (Murlo): burials from Poggio Aguzzo*. Rome: Giorgio Bretschneider.

Tuck, A. (2017). The evolution and political use of élite domestic architecture at Poggio Civitate (Murlo). *Journal of Roman Archaeology*, *30*, 227–43. doi:10.1017/S1047759400074092

Tuck, A., and Wallace, R. (2013). Letters and non-alphabetic characters on roof tiles from Poggio Civitate (Murlo). *Etruscan Studies*, *16*(2), 210–62.

Urso, G. (2008). *Patria diversis gentibus una? unità, politica e identità etniche nell'Italia antica: atti del convegno internazionale, Cividale del Friuli, 20–22 settembre 2007*. Pisa: ETS.

Vacano, O. W. von (1985). *Gli Etruschi a Talamone: la baia di Talamone dalla preistoria ai giorni nostri*. Bologna: Cappelli.

Vacano, O. W. von (1988). *Der Talamonaccio: alte und neue Probleme*. Florence: Leo S. Olschki.

Vagnetti, L. (1999). Mycenaean pottery in the central Mediterranean: imports and local production in their context. In J. P. Crielaard, V. Stiss, and J. van Wijngaarden (Eds.), *The complex past of pottery: production, circulation and consumption of Mycenaean and Greek pottery (sixteenth to early fifth centuries BC)* (pp. 137–55). Amsterdam: J. C. Gieben.

van Dommelen, P. (2012). Colonialism and migration in the Ancient Mediterranean. *Annual Review of Anthropology*, *41*, 393–409.

van Veen, H. T. (1992). Republicanism in the visual propaganda of Cosimo I de' Medici. *Journal of the Warburg and Courtauld Institutes*, *55*, 200–9.

Vanzetti, A. (2002). Some current approaches to protohistoric centralization and urbanization in Central Italy. In P. Attema, J.-G. Burgers, E. van Joolen, v. L. M., and B. Mater (Eds.), *New developments in Italian landscape archaeology* (pp. 36–51). Oxford: Archaeopress.

Versluys, M. J. (2014). Understanding objects in motion: an archaeological dialogue on Romanization. *Archaeological Dialogues*, *21*(1), 1–20. doi:10.1017/S1380203814000038

Vianello, A. (2005). *Late bronze age Mycenaean and Italic products in the West Mediterranean: a social and economic analysis*. Oxford: Archaeopress.

Vitali, D., Brizzolara, A. M., and Lippolis, E. (2001). *L'acropoli della città etrusca di Marzabotto*. Imola: University Press Bologna.

Vitali, D., Guidi, F., and Minarini, L. (1997). La stipe di Monte Bibele (Monterenzio, Bologna). In M. Pacciarelli (Ed.), *Acque, grotte e dei. 3000 anni di culti preromani in Romagna, Marche e Abruzzo* (pp. 127–53). Imola: Musei civici di Imola.

Wallace, R. (2016). Literacy and epigraphy of an Etruscan town. In N. Thomson de Grummond and L. Pieraccini (Eds.), *Caere* (pp. 41–8). Austin: University of Texas Press.

Wallace-Hadrill, A. (2008). *Rome's cultural revolution*. Cambridge: Cambridge University Press.

Warden, P. G. (2016). The Vicchio Stele and its context. *Etruscan Studies*, *19*(2), 208–19.

Warden, P. G., Thomas, M. L., Steiner, A., and Meyers, G. (2005). Poggio Colla: a N Etruscan settlement of the 7th–2nd c. B.C. (1998-2004 excavations). *Journal of Roman Archaeology, 18*, 252–66. doi:10.1017/S1047759400007340

Wallace, R. E. (2008). *Muluvanice* Inscriptions at Poggio Civitate (Murlo). *American Journal of Archaeology, 112*(3), 449–58.

Watt, M. A. (2001). The reception of Dante in the time of Cosimo I. In K. Eisenbichler (Ed.), *The cultural politics of Duke Cosimo I de' Medici* (pp. 121–34). Aldershot: Ashgate.

Werner, I. (2005). *Dionysos in Etruria: the ivy leaf group*. Stockholm: Svenska institutet i Rom.

Wikander, Ö. a., and Tobin, F. a. (2017). *Roof-tiles and tile-roofs at Poggio Civitate (Murlo): the emergence of central Italic tile industry*. Stockholm: Svenska Institutet i Rom.

Willemsen, S. M. (2013). A changing funerary ritual at Crustumerium (ca. 625 BC). In A. J. Nijboer, S. M. Willemsen, P. Attema, and J. F. Seubers (Eds.), *Research into pre-Roman burial grounds in Italy* (pp. 35–50). Leuven: Peeters.

Wikander, Ö. (1993). *Acquarossa: results of excavations conducted by the Swedish Institute of Classical Studies at Rome and the Soprintendenza alle antichità dell'Etruria meridionale*. Stockholm: Svenska Institutet i; Rome: Paul Åströms Förlag.

Wilson, J.-P. (1997–98). The 'illiterate trader'? *Bulletin of the Institute of Classical Studies, 42*, 29–56.

Winckelmann, J. J. (1760). *Description des pierres gravées du feu Baron de Stosch*. Florence: André Bonducci.

Winckelmann, J. J., and Borbein, A. H. (2002). *Geschichte der Kunst des Alterthums*. Mainz am Rhein: Verlag Phillip von Zabern.

Winckelmann, J. J., and Potts, A. (2006). *History of the art of antiquity*. Los Angeles, CA; Garsington: Getty Research Institute.

Winter, N. A. (2009). *Symbols of wealth and power: architectural terracotta decoration in Etruria and Central Italy, 640–510 B.C.* Ann Arbor, MI: Published for the American Academy in Rome by the University of Michigan Press.

Winter, N. A. (2017). Traders and refugees: contributions to Etruscan architecture. *Etruscan Studies, 20*(2), 123–51.

Winter, N. A., and Lulof, P. (2016). Temple decor and civic pride. Caere's place in the evolution of Etruscan architectural terracotta decoration, 550–510 BC. In N. Thomson de Grummond and L. Pieraccini (Eds.), *Caere* (pp. 125–40). Austin: University of Texas Press.

Witt, R. G. (2000). *'In the footsteps of the ancients': the origins of humanism from Lovato to Bruni*. Leiden: Brill.

Woolf, G. (2000). *Becoming Roman: the origins of provincial civilization in Gaul*. Cambridge: Cambridge University Press.

Wrede, H. (2000). L'antico nel Seicento. In E. Borea and C. Gasparri (Eds.), *L'idea del Bello. Viaggio per Roma nel Seicento con Giovan Pietro Bellori* (pp. 7–15). Rome: De Luca.

Zamarchi Grassi, P. (2006). *Il tumulo II del Sodo di Cortona: la tomba di età tardo arcaica*. Cortona: Arti Tipografiche Toscane.

Zamboni, L. (2016). *Spina città liquida: gli scavi 1977–1981 nell'abitato e i materiali tardo-arcaici e classici*. Rahden/Westf: VML, Verlag Marie Leidorf GmbH.

Zamboni, L. (2017a). Case di legno e d'argilla. Urbanistica, tecniche edilizie e vita quotidiana a Spina tra VI e IV sec. a. C. In C. Reusser (Ed.), *Spina. Neue Perspektiven der archäologischen Erforschung* (pp. 51–60). Rahden/Westf: VML Verlag Marie Leidorf GmbH.

Zamboni, L. (2017b). L'abitato di Verucchio nella prima Età del Ferro. *Studi Romagnoli*, LXVIII, 381–94.

Zannoni, A. (1876). *Gli scavi della Certosa di Bologna*. Bologna: Regia Tipografia.

Zifferero, A. (1991). Forme di possesso della terra e tumuli orientalizzanti nell'Italia centrale tirrenica. In E. Herring, R. Whitehouse, and J. Wilkins (Eds.), *Papers of the fourth conference of Italian archaeology I. The archaeology of power. Part I* (pp. 107–34). London: Accordia Research Institute.

Zifferero, A. (2017). Le attività artigianali nel territorio vulcente: la valle dell'Albegna e Marsiliana. In M. C. Biella (Ed.), *Gli artigiani e la città: officine e aree produttive tra VIII e III sec. a. C. nell'Italia centrale tirrenica* (pp. 311–29). Rome: Edizioni Quasar.

Index

Note: Page numbers followed by "n" refer to notes.

Accademia degli Umidi 12
Accademia dei Lincei
Monumenti Antichi 124
Accademia del Cimento 13
Accademia della Crusca 13
Accademia Etrusca 16
Accademia Fiorentina 9, 11–12
Achilles (Etruscan *Achle*) 166
Acquarossa 94–5
acroterion/acroteria 88, 96, 119, 120
Adria 102, 132, 133
San Cassiano di Crespino 131
Adriani, Giovan Battista 11
Adriatic Italy, sheet-bronze helmets 52
Aegean 103
Aeneid 169
aes rude 129
aes signatum 130
Ahal Trutitis 139
Ainsley, Samuel James 27
Aita (Greek Hades) 156, 157, 161
alabaster urns 23
Albani, Alessandro 17
Alberti, Leon Battista
church of Sant'Andrea, design of 5–6
Alsium 81, 174
Altertumswissenschaft 24–5, 26
Amazonomachy 143
Amoretti, Carlo 20
amphorae 82, 103–7, 134, 157, 159, 195
Annius of Viterbo 12
Anti, Carlo 31
antiquarianism 16, 20
Aphaia, temple of (Aegina) 101
Apollo (Etruscan *Aplu*) 119
Appennines 38, 135, 137, 153, 173, 174, 185
Apulia 174
Apulian vessels 166
Ara della Regina, Tarquinia 117, 124, 144
Arcatelle cemetery, Tarquinia 51
sheet-bronze helmet 52–4
archaic period, urban growth in 91–121
building revolution 94–6
buoyant trade and productive economy 97–110
religion 111–21
Archinto, Cardinal 17

Arezzo 12
Aria, Giuseppe 123
Ariminum (modern Rimini) 174
Arretium (modern Arezzo) 175, 176
Arringatore 23
aryballos/aryballoi 159
Assyrian museum, Louvre 26
Athena (Etruscan *Menrva*) 98, 119
Ati family 183
atrium house 129, 166
Attica 101
auguraculum 127
Augustus 165, 185, 192, 193
Aventine 164
Avile Vipiiennas 119, 166, 168

bacula 173
Bagnasco Gianni, G. 100
Banditaccia *necropolis*, *Caere* 78
Banditella *necropolis*, Marsiliana d'Albegna 76
Barnabei, Felice
  Notizie degli Scavi 49
Battle of *Aricia* 168
Battle of *Cumae* 154
Battle of *Sentinum* 173, 174
Battle of the Sardinian Sea 96, 111, 154
Bellelli, V. 202 n.5
Belvedere temple, *Volsinii* (Orvieto) 141
Beneventum 174
Berlin 26
Bianchi Bandinelli, Ranuccio 31, 201 n.5
Bianchini, Francesco 16
biconical urns 49
Bisenzio 43, 46
  Olmo Bello *necropolis* 72
Black Death 187
Blera 146
Bollettino d'Arte 31
Bologna 128, 133
  archaeological record of the settlement 130
  ceremonial warrior accoutrements 56
  chariots in burials 52
  First International Congress of Etruscology 33
  funerary *stelai* 153, 156
  Iron Age cemeteries 33, 49
  Misala (*Sala*) 170
  Museo Civico 31
  tumulus burial 73–4
  Villa Cassarini 130
Bonaparte, Lucien 27
Botto, M. 202 n.3
Bourdin, S. P. 204 n.6, 204 n.6
Brizio, Edoardo 48–9, 50, 124, 125, 130
Bronze Age xiv, 33, 80, 202 n.5
  continuity and change 41–7
  settlement 37–41
Bryn Mawr College 35
bucchero 63, 66, 77, 81, 83, 89, 93, 98, 104, 107, 119, 146, 168, 189
  bucchero kantharoi 106
  bucchero kyathos 85
  bucchero oinochoe 67
  bucchero olla/ollae 128
  bucchero sottile 82, 84, 85
building revolution 94–6
Bullettino dell'Instituto di Corrispondenza Archeologica 28, 123
Bünau, Heinrich von 17
Buonarroti, Filippo
  De Etruria Regali 14, 15, 18–19
buoyant trade 97–110

burial xv, 82, 85, 116, 117, 142, 145, 146, 150, 151, 155, 169, 175, 185, 189
  Bronze Age 43
  chariots in 52, 75–6
  Copper Age 39
  grounds, establishment of 141
  Iron Age 47, 49
  lavishness and monumentality of 65–6
  ritual 49, 54, 69, 72–80, 137, 149, 159
  tumulus 61–4, 68, 72–4, 81, 113, 143, 147–8
  see also cremation

Caere 26, 27, 34, 114, 117, 119, 146, 169, 170, 178
  amphorae 104–5
  Banditaccia *necropolis* 78
  Bronze Age cemeteries 42, 43
  Bucchero oinochoe 67
  building revolution 95
  burial ritual 72, 146
  Calabresi Tomb, Sorbo cemetery 85
  coastal hinterland 181
  dado tombs 151
  Iron Age cemeteries 48, 49
  Petrographic analysis 98
  pithoi 80
  Pyrgi 34, 99, 101, 105, 111–16, 119, 121, 162, 174, 178
  Regolini Galassi Tomb 26, 64, 68, 81–2
  religious buildings, roof's decoration of 99
  Roman conquest 176–7
  San Giuliano 146
  San Paolo Olpe 81–5
  Sant'Antonio 177
  symbolism of warriorhood 54–5
  Thefarie Velianas 113, 115, 121
  Tomb of the Five Chairs 78, 79
  Tomb of the Sarcophagi 160
  Tomb of the Triclinium 160
  tumulus burials 68, 146
  Vigna Marini Vitalini 115, 177
  Vigna Parrocchiale 99, 144, 177
Caesar 183
Caile Vipinas 119, 166, 167, 168
Calabresi Tomb, Sorbo cemetery, *Caere* 85
Calindri, Abbot Serafino 123
Calvario, Tarquinia 176
Camillus 164
Campana, Giovanni Pietro 27
Campanari, Vincenzo 27
Campana Tomb, *Veii* 74
Campania 107
  Battle of *Cumae* 154
Campiglia Marittima 129
Campo della Fiera, *Volsinii* (Orvieto) 83, 187–91, 203 n.2
Canina, Luigi 48, 61, 91
Cannicella *necropolis*, *Volsinii* (Orvieto) 140
canopic urns 73
Capena 165
Capitoline Jupiter 181
Caprifico 99
Capua 138
Carthage
  S. Monica *necropolis* 110
Casa dell'Impluvium, Roselle 145
Casal del Fosso *necropolis*, *Veii* 48
casa-officina (house-workshop) 129

cassetta (box tomb) 140, 146
Castel d'Asso 175
Castel Di Decima 34
Castellina del Marangone
Iron Age settlement 45–6
Castellina Tumulus, Chianti hills 5
Castel San Mariano 142, 143, 202 n.2
Castelsecco, Arezzo 128
Castrum Novum 174
cataloguing 15, 17, 25, 28
Cavatha 100, 112, 189
Caylus, Comte
Recueil d'antiquités égyptiennes, étrusques, grecques, romaines 19, 23
Cecina Valley Survey 183
Ceicna/Caecina family 183–4
cella, temple 114
cepen 170
Cerchiai, L. 201 n.4, 201 n.5
Cerveteri *see Caere*
chariots in burials 52, 75–6
Charun 157, 158, 166
Chierici, Gaetano 124
Chimera of Arezzo 12, 23
Chiusi 12, 23, 26, 43, 46, 119, 155, 203 n.2
burial ritual 72–4, 146
Hellenistic alabaster *sarcophagi* 156
magistracies 171
chronology 21, 25, 33, 50, 51, 64, 191, 202 n.1
Church of San Pietro, Orvieto 187
Church of Santa Maria della Neve, Velletri 92
church of Sant'Andrea, Mantova 5–6
Cicero 184
CIE (*Corpus Inscriptionum Etruscarum*) 29
Cilnia family 175
Cilnius 176
cinerary urn 53–5, 76, 146, 163, 172, 177, 183, 184
cippus/cippi 126, 131, 140, 155, 170, 171
Cipriani, G. 201 n.1
Circolo degli Avori, Marsiliana d'Albegna 84
Circolo dei Lebeti, Vetulonia 68
Circolo della Fibula, Vetulonia 76
Civiltà del Lazio Primitivo 34
civitas 37, 171, 172
civitas foederata 181
Civitella di Montalcino 179
classicism 30, 31
Claudius 167–8, 193
Clepsina, C. Genucius 177
Cneve Tarchunies Rumach 166
coarseware 104, 105
Coke, Thomas 13
De Hetruria Regali 14
Colonia Augusta, Volterra 183
colonization 137–43
condottieri 168
Conze, Alexander 26, 64
Copper Age 38
Corciano 142
Corinth 95–6
Corneto-Tarquinia, *see* Tarquinia
corridors, funerary 22, 23, 75, 78, 79, 82, 155, 156, 166, 176
Cortona 143
Sodo Tumulus II 151
cortonesi 16
Cosa (modern Ansedonia) 181, 182
Cosimo I, Medici 5, 9–14
Accademia degli Umidi 12
Accademia Fiorentina 11–12

Chimera of Arezzo 12
as *Etruriae Dux* 11
as Grand Duke of Tuscany 9
Minerva of Arezzo 12
political–cultural ideology 9
Salone dei Cinquecento, Palazzo della Signoria (or Palazzo Vecchio), Florence 9–11
Cosimo II, Medici 13
Cosimo III, Medici 14
cremation 47, 49, 50, 52, 55, 56, 72–5, 77, 80, 85, 145, 146, 148–50, 153, 183
see also burial
Cristina di Borbone, Teresa 48
Cristofani, Mauro 75
Crocifisso del Tufo, *Volsinii* (Orvieto) 140–2, 146
Crustumerium 145
cubism 31
Cultrera, Giovanni 61–4
cultural bricolage 191–6, 204 n.5
cultural change 66
cultural *facies* 51, 137
cursus honorum 170
Cyprus 103

d'Agostino, Bruno 201 n.5
Danubian-Carpathian basin
sheet-bronze helmets 52
Dasti, Luigi 49
De Angelis, F. 203 n.5
decolonization 194
Deecke, Wilhelm 25, 29
De Francesco, A. 30, 201 n.3
del Pozzo, Cassiano 15
Demaratus 86
Dempster, Thomas 13–14, 24
De Hetruria Regali 13
Dennis, George 61, 91, 123
Cities and Cemeteris of Etruria, The 27, 28, 74
Deputazione per la conservazione e l'ordinamento dei musei e delle antichità etrusche 30
Dialoghi di Archeologia 201 n.5
Dietler, M. 202 n.2
diffusionism 68
Dionysiac rites 148, 149, 189
Dionysius of Halicarnassus 50, 64, 163
Roman Antiquities 2
Dionysos (Etruscan *Fufluns*) 112, 150–4
disciplina etrusca 124, 125, 193
Doganaccia *necropolis*, Tarquinia 85
Doganella 106
domus 191
Dresden 17
dromos 155, 159
Ducal Regency 16
Ducati, Pericle 65

ekklesiasterion of *Metapontum* 145
Elogia Tarquiniensia 176, 193
Emilia Romagna 48, 50
Emporion 109
epigraphy 28
eschatological beliefs 153, 158–64
eschatological dimension of mystery cults 152
Este, Veneto 131
Eteokles 114, 178, 203 n.5
Etruria Padana 102, 105, 130–7, 149, 153, 174
Etruscan civilization 5
Etruscan Museum, Florence 31
Etruscan myth 3–9
Etruscan *oppida* 178, 179
Etruscan revival 192

Etruscans, The, Palazzo Grassi, Venice 35
etruscheria/etruscherie 12, 24
Etruscology xiii, xv, 3, 16, 20, 24, 25, 30–5, 194–196, 202 n.1, 204 n.5
Etruscorum more 5
evocatio 164, 203 n.6
excavation 14, 24, 26–8, 31, 33, 35, 37, 38
  campaigns 34
  illegal, xv
  intensification of 16
  Iron Age cemeteries 48, 49, 51
  Luni sul Mignone 39–41, 43
expressionism 31

Falchi, Isidoro 48, 76
Falerii 173
Falerii Novi 173
Faliscan vessels 166
Fanum Voltumnae 173, 187–92
fasces 162, 163, 173
Fea, Carlo 20
Ferdinando, son of Cosimo I 13
Fermo 137
fibulae 55
Fifth Congress of Prehistoric Archaeology 48
Fiorelli, Giuseppe 49, 125
Fiorini, L. 99, 100
First International Congress of Etruscology 33
First National Congress of Etruscology 31
flabellum 76
Flaccus, M. Fulvius 174
Florence 7–12, 14, 16, 17, 46, 134, 135
  artistic and cultural world 5
  civic identity 4
  Etruscan Museum 31
  First National Congress of Etruscology 31
  Museo Archeologico 74–5
  republican ideology 4
  Salone dei Cinquecento, Palazzo della Signoria (or Palazzo Vecchio) 9–11
  tholos tombs 72
Florentine humanism 3–9
Fondo Iozzino, *Pompeii* 138
Fondo Scataglini *necropolis*, Tarquinia 176
Forcello di Bagnolo San Vito 130, 132, 133, 153
Forma Italiae, Rome 35
Forum Boarium, Rome 98
Fosso della Mola, *Veii* 91
Francesco, son of Cosimo I 13
François, Alessandro 166
François Tomb, Vulci 119, 166, 167, 169, 172, 178
Fregenae 174
funerary architecture 146–8, 151
funerary rites 149, 161, 183
funerary *stelai* 150, 153, 156
funerary symbolism 72–80

gabinetti, Real Galleria, Uffizi 22
Gabrici, Ettore 91
Gailledrat, E. 202 n.2
Galileo 13, 14
Gallery of the Statues (*corridoio/Galleria delle Statue*), Real Galleria, Uffizi 23
Gallic Celts 124
Gallic Sack 164
Gaultier, F. 202 n.5
Gauls 164, 173, 178
gens/gentilicial 86, 109, 110, 119, 129, 138, 140, 161, 163, 189
Genucii 177

Gerhard, Edward
Etruskische Spiegel 28
Rapporto intorno i vasi volcenti 28
Germanism 30
Ghirardini, Gherardo 48–9, 51, 61
gift exchange 85
Gigantomachy 143
Giglio Island 105
Giglioli, Giulio Quirino 31
Gli Etruschi e l'Europa 34
globalization 187–96
Gori, Anton Francesco 14–15
Herculaneum 15
Museum Etruscum 15, 18, 24
Museum Florentinum 15
Govi, E. 202 n.1
Gozzadini, Count Giovanni 49, 123, 124, 137
Gravisca 34, 99–101, 103, 105, 114, 144
Le Saline 99
Gray, Lady Hamilton 27
Tour to the Sepulchres of Etruria in 1839, 61
Greek fineware 63, 82, 85, 93, 104–6, 134, 143, 150, 159
Greek settlements 38, 46, 51, 65, 69, 105
Grosseto 145
Grotta Gramiccia *necropolis*, *Veii* 48
Gsell, Stéphane
Fouilles dans la Nécropole de Vulci 27
Guarnacci, Mario 16
Origini Italiche (*Italic Origins*) 24
Guarneri, F. 202 n.4
guilloches 76, 80
Gustav VI Adolph, king of Sweden 37

Hades (Etruscan *Aita*) 112
Hadria (modern Atri) 174
Hankins, James 7
Hardcastle, A. 61
haruspices 193
Haumesser, L. 202 n.5
Heba 178
Helbig, Wolfgang 49
Hellenistic political institutions 169–73
Herakles (Etruscan *Herkle*) 98, 112, 113, 114, 119, 143, 144
Herodotus 20, 64, 96
Heyne, Christian Gottlob 20
hipukrates 86
Hoernes, M. 202 n.4
Homer 17
Odyssey 83
human mobility 123–54
hypogeum
of the *Cacni* 184
of the Palazzone *necropolis*, Perugia 184

impasto 62, 63, 72, 76, 77, 82, 84, 146
Inghirami Tomb, Volterra 183
inhumation 69, 72–5, 146, 149, 155, 159
inscriptions 10, 12, 14, 23, 29, 34, 82–5, 101, 109, 112, 113, 119, 131, 137, 138, 139, 150, 152, 157, 159, 161–3, 166, 168–72, 175, 177, 195
Fufluns 153
Greek 21, 103
hipukrates of 86
Kanuta 189, 190

Latin 13, 21, 167, 176, 183, 193
muluvanice 85, 89
Institute for Italic and Etruscan Studies 48
Instituto di Corrispondenza Archeologica 28
Ionian Asia Minor 97
Ionian Greeks 97
Iron Age 38, 41, 68, 81, 91
burial ritual 49, 54, 72
cemeteries 33, 47–51
continuity and change 41–7
Etruscan civilization of 33
growing communities 47–51
Istituto di Studi Etruschi e Italici 34
Italian unification 25, 29
Izzet, V. 203 n.3

Jolivet, V. 204 n.5
Juno (Etruscan *Uni*) 164, 165

Kainua 126
kantharos/kantharoi 106, 153
Kanuta 189, 190
Kircher, Athanasius 14
Kistler, E. 202 n.4
kline 155, 156, 159, 162
kunstwollen 31
kyathos/kyathoi 85, 87
kylikeion 158

La Castellina, Tarquinia 43
Lake Bolsena 43, 44, 46
Lake Trasimeno 143
Lanciani, Rodolfo 48, 91
Languedoc 106
Lanzi, Luigi 16–17, 20–3, 25, 28
Galleria delle Statue 22
Museo Etrusco 22, 23
Real Galleria 20, 22
Saggio di lingua etrusca e di altre antiche d'Italia: per servire alla storia de' popoli, delle lingue e delle belle arti 20–1
Storia Pittorica della Italia 21
Laris Velchaina 98
Larth Velcha 161, 162, 164
La Téne 154
latifundia 183
Latium (Lazio) 34, 44, 94, 95, 99, 107, 176
Lattes 109
lautni 175
lauχume 170
Lavinium
Sanctuary of the Thirteen Altars 34
Layard, Henry 26
League of the *Duodecim Populi* 173, 192
'Le Arcatelle,' Tarquinia 49
Le Colonne, *Cosa* 181
Leinies 161, 203 n.2
lekythoi 159
lekythos 159
Leonardo Bruni of Arezzo (1370–1444)
Historiae Florentini Populi Libri XII (1416–42) 4
Leopold, Peter 20
Le Saline, Gravisca 99
Levantine craftsmanship 68
L'Italia Avanti il dominio de' romani (*Italy before the dominion of Rome*) 30
lituus 116, 172
Livy 66, 124, 137, 164, 175, 176
Ab Urbe Condita 2, 4
London 26
Louvre 27, 146
Assyrian museum 26
Lucania 174

Lucanian sanctuary, Rossano di Vaglio 192
Lucius Tarquinius 170
lucumones 4, 16, 169, 170
Luni sul Mignone 35
  Bronze Age cemeteries 37–42, 44
  Iron Age cemeteries 48
  Mycenaean fragments at 51
  Tre Erici 38
Lunum 37
Lyon 167

Macstrna 166, 167, 168
Maecenas 176
magistracies 169–73
Magliano 170
Magna Graecia: Tarentum (modern Taranto) 174
Mandolesi, Alessandro 38
Mansuelli, Guido Achille 126
Mantova
  church of Sant'Andrea 5–6
Marcone, A., 204 n.5
Margrethe, Princess 37
Marius 183
Marsiliana d'Albegna
  amphorae 106, 107
  Banditella *necropolis* 76
  burial ritual 73, 76
  Charun 159
  Circolo degli Avori 84
  House of Amphorae 107, 108
Mars of Todi 138–40
Martha, Jules
  L'art Etrusque 31
marunuχ 170
Marzabotto 26, 98, 121, 123–31, 133, 134, 137, 145, 154
  Pian di Misano 123
  Poggio Misanello 123
  Villa Aria 124
Massalia 97, 106
Mater Matuta 98
Medici, Lorenzo 12, 13, 22, 23
  dynasty 12, 13
    rise to power 7–8
  Uffizi Gallery 16
Medici villa, Poggio a Caiano 7, 8
Mengarelli, Raniero 48
Micali, Giuseppe 123
  L'Italia Avanti il dominio de' romani (*Italy before the dominion of Rome*) 30
migration theories 50
Minerva of Arezzo 12, 23
Minto, Antonio 48
Misala (*Sala*), Bologna 170
mobility 137–43
Mohr, M. 202 n.4
Momigliano, Arnaldo 1–2, 3
Montagnola
  tholos tombs 72
Montefortini
  tholos tombs 72
Monteleone di Spoleto 143
Montepulciano 82
Monte Santo
  high-altitude settlement 43
Montesanto of Todi 138
Montfaucon, Bernard de 15
Müller, K. O.
  Die Etrusker 25–6
Müller-Karpe, Hermann 50
muluvanice inscriptions 85, 89
Murlo (Poggio Civitate)
  amphorae 105
  Archaic complex, reconstruction 80
  Corinthian vase painting 96
  Orientalizing complex, reconstruction 87–9, 95
Musarna 175
Musei Vaticani
  Mars of Todi 138–9

Museo Archeologico, Florence 74–5
museo cartaceo (paper museum) 15
Museo Civico, Bologna 31
Museo Gregoriano Etrusco, Vatican Museum 27

Nanni, Giovanni
  Commentaria super opera diversorum auctorum de antiquitatibus loquentium 12
Napoleon III 27
Narce, Treia valley 40
National Museum of Naples 92
National Museum of Tarquinia 52, 144
nation state 24–30
Naukratis 101
nenfro 148, 151
Nepi 165
Norchia 175
North-West Palace, Nimrud 26

Öhlinger, B. 202 n.4
oinochoe/oinochoai 63, 67
olla/ollae 62, 75, 80, 85, 128
Olmo Bello *necropolis*, Bisenzio 72
olpe 82–4, 86
  bucchero olpe 83
Oltos 160
Orientalism 26, 65
Orientalizing culture 66, 68, 69, 113
Orientalizing period 26, 33, 56, 62–5
orthogonal 91, 94, 126, 131, 146, 147
Östenberg, C. E. 37, 38, 40, 41
ostentation 72–80
Osteria dell'Osa 34
Osteria *necropolis*, Vulci 79

Pairault Massa, F.-H., 201 n.4
Palazzo Grassi, Venice
  Etruscans, The 35
Palidoro, Lazio 39
Pall Mall exhibition 27
Pallottino, Massimo 33, 34, 50, 51, 65, 66
Pania *pyxides* 82
pan-Mediterranean Orientalizing culture 66
Paris 26
Pasqui, Angelo 49
Passeri, Giambattista
  Picturae Etruscorum in vasculis 24
paterae 68
Patroclus (Etruscan *Patrucle*) 166
Patroni, Giovanni 49, 50
Pauli, Carl
  CIE (*Corpus Inscriptionum Etruscarum*) 29
Pech Maho lead letter 109, 110
peripteral 121, 128
Peroni, Renato 32, 39, 50–1
Persephone (Etruscan *Phersiphnai*, *Kore*) 112, 157, 161
Perugia 15, 26, 138, 141, 143, 153, 184
petrographic analysis 98
Phersiphnai (Greek *Persephone*) 156
philhellenism 24, 25, 31, 64, 65
Phoenician craftsmanship 68
Phoenician palmettes 78
Phoenician settlements 46, 65, 69, 105, 106
Piacenza liver 29, 127–8
Pian della Regina, Tarquinia 43
Pian di Civita, Tarquinia 43
Pian di Luni 37

Pian di Misano, Marzabotto 123
Piano di Comunità, *Veii* 165
Piazza d'Armi, *Veii* 91–5, 120
Picentine region 138
Picentine settlement 138
Pigorini, Luigi 48, 50
Pindar 154
Pinza, Giovanni 26
Piranesi, Giambattista 16
Pisa 73, 134, 153
pit (*tomba a buca/pozzetto*) 146
pithoi 80, 195
Pithekoussai, Ischia 46
Pius V, Pope 9
Plana Mallart, R. 202 n.2
Pliny the Elder 5, 6, 97, 138
Plutarch 97
podium 114, 115, 124
Poggio a Caiano
  Medici villa 7, 8
Poggio Buco 92
Poggio Colla 135
Poggio Misanello, Marzabotto 123
Polyneikes/Polineikes 114, 178, 203 n.5
Pompeii 99, 124, 125, 129, 138
  Fondo Iozzino 138
Pontecagnano 138
Ponte Rotto *necropolis*, Vulci 166
Populonia 178
  Bronze Age cemeteries 43, 46
  inhumation burials 72
  Iron Age cemeteries 48
  Poggio al Castello 46
  Poggio del Telegrafo 46, 87
  sheet-bronze helmet 54
  technological innovation 87
populus 171
Porsenna of Chiusi 168, 170
Po Valley 26, 101, 103, 125, 129, 131, 173
Prato Gonfienti 134–6
productive economy 97–110
prothesis 83
proto-Corinthian pottery 82
proto-urban settlements 44, 47
proto-Villanovan
  period 41, 49
  relationship with Sub-Appennine 50–1
  relationship with Villanovan 51
Puglisi, Salvatore 39, 40
Punic Wars 181
Pyrgi 34, 99, 101, 105, 111–16, 119, 121, 162, 168, 169, 174, 178
Pythagoreanism 152
pyxides 82

Rachu Kakanas 86
rasna 171
Rath 119
Rathje, A. 203 n.4
Regae-Regisvilla, Vulci 100, 105
Regolini Galassi Tomb, *Caere* 26, 27, 64, 68, 81–2
  Regolini, Alessandro 26
  Vincenzo Galassi 26
religion, and the city 111–21
religious buildings, roof's decoration of 98–9
republican heritage 4
republicanism 4
resources, controlling 80–90
Rhodes 103
rhyton 152
Riegl, Aloïs
  kunstwollen 31
Risorgimento 29, 201 n.3
Riva, C. 201 n.2, 202 n.3
Rofalco, Selva del Lamone nature reserve 180
Roman citizenship 183

Roman colonization and colonies 164–9
Romanization 173, 185, 193, 194, 203 n.7, 204 n.5
Rome xiii, xv, xvi, 2, 13, 14, 16, 17, 35, 37, 43, 44, 94–9
  Basilica of Maxentius 5
  Etruscan National Museum, Villa Giulia 31, 76
  in Etruria 155–86
  Forum Boarium 98
  imperial expansion 154
  Instituto di Corrispondenza Archeologica 28
  La Grande Roma dei Tarquini 34
  multi-city alliance against 164
  Regia 93
  republican legacy 4
  role in the assimilation of Italy 30
  Sant' Omobono 110, 119
  University of 113
  urbanization 34
  urban landscape 5
Rosa, Salvator 14
Roselle 88, 178
  Casa dell'Impluvium 145
Russo Tagliente, A. 202 n.4
rutile hipucrates 63

Sacred Way (*Via Sacra*), *Volsinii* (Orvieto) 187
Saint Blaise 109
Salamis 154
Salerno Gulf 138
Salone dei Cinquecento, Palazzo della Signoria (or Palazzo Vecchio), Florence 9–11
Salutati, Coluccio 4
Samnites 173
Samos 101
San Cassiano di Crespino, Adria 131
Sanctuary of the Thirteen Altars, *Lavinium* 34
San Giovenale 37, 88
San Giuliano, *Caere* 146
San Paolo Olpe, *Caere* 81–5
San Rocchino 134
Sant'Antonio, *Caere* 177
Sant'Imbenia 105
Sant' Omobono 98, 110, 119
Santoro, P. 202 n.5
San Valentino di Marsciano 143
sarcophagus/sarcophagi 27, 146, 155, 162, 163, 166, 177, 178
Sardinia 105, 107
Sarteano
  Museum of Sarteano 155
  Tomb of the Infernal Chariot (*Quadriga Infernale*) 155–8
Satricum 98, 119
Sassatelli, G. 202 n.1
Scipio Africanus' campaign 181
Second Punic War 181
Seianti Hanunia Tlesnasa 156
Selinus 114
sella curulis 162
Selva del Lamone, Vulci 44
Sena Gallica (modern Senigallia) 174
Serlio, Sebastiano 8–9
Servius 169
Servius Tullius 168
Seta, Alessandro Della 65
Settefinestre 181
Seven Against Thebes, Villa Giulia Museum 114, 115, 177
sheet-bronze helmets 52–4
Sicily 103, 105, 107
Siena 16
silen 153
skyphoi 63
S. Monica *necropolis*, Carthage 110

social power 72–80
sodales 168, 178
sodalis fidelissimus 168
Sodo Tumulus II, Cortona 151
Sorgenti della Nova 44, 45
Sostratos 101, 102
South Etruria Survey 35
Sovana 44
Spina 103, 131–4, 153
  house unit 133
  town plan 132
spura 172
Spurianas 110
Spurinna family, Tarquinia 176
Stefani, Enrico 91–3, 120
Stesichorus
  Geryoneis 83
Stopponi, Simonetta 187, 203 n.1
Strabo 138
Sulki 110
Sulla 183
Śuri 100, 112
Sutri 165
Swedish Institute of Classical Studies 35
symposia/*symposium* 148, 158

tablinum 166
Tabula Cortonensis 171, 175
Tacitus 167
Talamone 178, 179
Tarchon 193
Tarquinia 26, 42, 59, 110, 178
  amphora 105
  Ara della Regina 117, 124, 144
  Arcatelle cemetery at 52
  Bronze Age 43
  burial ritual 146
  Calvario 176
  continuity of cult 116
  Doganaccia *necropolis* 85
  Fondo Scataglini *necropolis* 176
  Iron Age cemeteries 33, 49
  La Castellina 43
  La Civita di Tarquinia 116
  'Le Arcatelle' 49
  magistracies 170, 172
  Monterozzi hill 61, 62, 148, 149, 159
  multi-city alliance against Rome 164
  National Museum of Tarquinia 52, 144
  nenfro slab 151
  Pian della Regina 43
  Pian di Civita 43
  sheet-bronze helmet 54
  Spurinna family 193
  standardization of tomb architecture 147
  symbols of political rule 163
  technological innovation 81
  Tomb of Hunting and Fishing 160
  Tomb of Orco II 156
  Tomb of the Blue Demons 158, 203 n.1
  Tomb of the Bulls 160
  Tomb of the Lionesses 149
  Tomb of the Meeting (*Tomba del Convegno*) 163, 164
  Tomb of the Pygmies 160
  Tomb of the Shields (*Tomba degli Scudi*) 161–4
  Tomb of the Ships 159
  Tomb of the Warrior 56
  Tumulo della Regina (Tumulus of the Queen) 62, 63, 68–71, 73
  Tumulo del Re (Tumulus of the King) 62–4, 66, 85
  tumulus burials 61–3
Tarquinius Priscus 97
Tarquinius Superbus 97
technological innovation 80–90
Telamon 178

templum 127, 128
tenute 27
terracotta 23, 31, 40, 43, 51, 54, 72, 80, 81, 86, 88, 89, 91–8, 111, 112, 114, 115, 117, 119, 120, 141, 144, 146, 151, 156, 178, 187, 189, 202 n.1
  helmets, warrior graves in 55
  roofs and related decoration 76
Terrenato, N. 203 n.3, 204 n.5
tesserae hospitales 110, 119
textile production 56–8
Thefarie Velianas, Villa Giulia Museum 113, 115, 169
thyrsus 152
Tiber Valley 138, 139, 145, 165, 173
Titian 12
Todi 138–9, 143
  Montesanto of Todi 138
togae 161
toga picta 172
Tolfa Hills 49, 146
Tolle (Chianciano)
  burial ritual 73, 146
tomba a dado 146, 147
Tomba dei Leoni Ruggenti, Veii 73
Tomba del Carro, Vulci 73, 79–80
Tomba del Duce, Vetulonia 76, 77, 85, 86
Tomba delle Anatre, Veii 73
Tomb 5 at Monte Michele, *Veii* 74, 75, 81
tombe a pozzo (pit cremation tombs) 49
Tomb Golini I, *Volsinii* (Orvieto) 156, 157, 161, 171
Tomb of Hunting and Fishing, Tarquinia 160
Tomb of Orco II, Tarquinia 156
Tomb of the Blue Demons, Tarquinia 158, 203 n.1
Tomb of the Bulls, Tarquinia 160
Tomb of the Five Chairs, *Caere* 78, 79
Tomb of the Infernal Chariot (*Quadriga Infernale*), Sarteano 155–8
Tomb of the Lictor (*Tomba del Littore*), Vetulonia 172
Tomb of the Lionesses, Tarquinia 149
Tomb 89 of the Lippi cemetery, Verucchio 56
Tomb of the Meeting (*Tomba del Convegno*), Tarquinia 163, 164
Tomb of the Pygmies, Tarquinia 160
Tomb of the Sarcophagi, *Caere* 160
Tomb of the Shields (*Tomba degli Scudi*), Tarquinia 161–4
Tomb of the Ships, Tarquinia 159
Tomb of the Silver Hands, Vulci 73, 74
Tomb of the Triclinium, *Caere* 160
Tomb of the Warrior, Ripagretta cemetery, Tarquinia 56
Torelli, Mario 192
Torlonia, Giulio 27
Tour to the Sepulchres of Etruria in 1839, 27
trachite euganea 131
Tragliatella 170
Tre Erici, Luni sul Mignone 38
Tuck, A. 202 n.4
tufa 37, 42–4, 46, 72, 73, 78, 91, 116, 140, 146, 147, 163, 187
tular rasnal 171

Tumulo della Regina (Tumulus of the Queen), Tarquinia 62, 63, 68–71, 73
Tumulo del Re (Tumulus of the King), Tarquinia 62–4, 66, 85
tumulus burials 61–4, 68, 72–4, 81, 113, 143, 147–8
Tuscania 146, 175
Tuscanic temple 114
Twelve Tables 145
Tyrrhenian Etruria 123–54, 174

Uffizi 11, 13
  Uffizi Gallery/*Real Galleria* 16, 20, 22
Umbria 138, 140, 142
Umbrians 173
Uni 112, 113, 117, 119, 128, 137, 164, 165
University of Pisa 9, 13
urban growth, in archaic period 91–121
  building revolution 94–6
  buoyant trade and productive economy 97–110
  religion 111–21
urbanization 34, 61–90
  burial ritual 72–80
  funerary symbolism 72–80
  resources, controlling 80–90
  technological innovation 80–90
urban planning 94, 124–6, 130, 133, 140
  Attic foot 126, 131
urban societies, public and private 143–50
Urnfield Culture 47
Urso, G. 204 n.6

Valdichiana 43, 46, 143, 155
Valli di Comacchio 131
Vanth 159, 166
Varro 97
Vasari, Giorgio 11, 12
vase painting 26
Vatican Museum 64
  Museo Gregoriano Etrusco 27
Vei 189
Veian Juno 174
Veii 42, 97, 117, 153, 154, 164, 165, 203 n.3
  amphorae 106
  Bronze Age settlement 43
  burial ritual 72, 145, 146
  Campana Tomb 74
  Casal del Fosso *necropolis* 48
  chariots in burials 52
  Fosso della Mola 91
  Grotta Gramiccia *necropolis* 48
  Iron Age cemeteries 48
  Piano di Comunità 165
  Piazza d'Armi 91–5, 120
  Portonaccio sanctuary 31, 32, 118, 120
  Quattro Fontanili *necropolis* 55
  religious buildings, roof's decoration of 98
  symbolism of warriorhood 55
  Tomb AA1, Quattro Fontanili 55, 57
  Tomba dei Leoni Ruggenti 73
  Tomba delle Anatre 73
  Tomb 5 at Monte Michele 74, 75, 81
  tumulus burials 68
  The Walking Apollo, Portonaccio sanctuary 31, 32, 118, 120
Vel Leinies 161
Velletri 92, 99
Vel Saties 168, 172
Velthur Velcha 161

Veneto 131
Venice
Etruscans, The, Palazzo Grassi 35
Versluys, M. J. 203 n.4
Verucchio
occupation 137–8
textile production 58
Tomb 89 of the Lippi cemetery 56
warrior graves 56
vestibulum 161
Vettori, Piero 11
Vetulonia
Bronze Age cemeteries 43, 46
burial ritual 77
Circolo dei Lebeti at 68
Circolo della Fibula 76, 77
Iron Age cemeteries 48
Tomba del Duce 76, 85, 86
Tomb of the Lictor (*Tomba del Littore*) 172
warrior graves 56
Vibenna brothers 167–8
Vicchio *stele* 136, 137
Vigna Marini Vitalini, *Caere* 115, 177
Vigna Parrocchiale, *Caere* 99, 144, 177
Villa Aria, Marzabotto 124
Villa Cassarini, Bologna 130
Villa Giulia Museum 31, 91, 120, 146
Bucchero oinochoe, *Caere* 67
Seven against Thebes 115
Thefarie Velianas 113
Villani, Giovanni
Nuova Cronica 4
Villanova di Forlì 26, 49
Villanovan
burial ritual 137
civilization 33, 50
material culture 51
period 49, 50, 64
Viterbo
Luni sul Mignone 35, 37–41
technological innovation 87
Vitruvius 5, 114
Vives-Ferrándiz, J. 202 n.3
Volsinii (Orvieto) 28, 46, 138–43, 169, 174, 175, 203 n.2
amphorae 157
Belvedere temple 141
burial ritual 146
Campo della Fiera 83, 187–91, 203 n.2
Cannicella cemetery 140, 151
Church of San Pietro 187
Crocifisso del Tufo 140–2, 146
magistracies 171
Sacred Way (*Via Sacra*) 187
Settecamini *necropolis* 156
Tomb Golini I 156, 157, 161, 171
Volterra 16, 24, 46, 181
alabaster urns 23
cinerary urns 172
citizenship rights 183
Colonia Augusta 183
Inghirami Tomb 183
Poggio alle Croci 56
Roman *municipium* 173
Roman theatre 184
symbols of political rule 163
technological innovation 86
von Merhart, Gero 52
von Stosch, Philipp 17
Vortumnus-Voltumna 173, 174, 192
Vulca 97
Vulci 110, 119, 168, 170, 174, 178, 179
amphorae 106
Bronze Age settlements 42–4
burial ritual 146
François Tomb 119, 166, 167, 169, 172, 178

Fufluns Pachie 152
Osteria *necropolis* 79
painted fineware 104
pillaging of 27
Ponte Rotto *necropolis* 166
Regae-Regisvilla 100, 105
Selva del Lamone 44
Tomba del Carro 73, 79–80
Tomb of the Silver Hands 73, 74
Vulcian vessels 152

Ward-Perkins, John 35
warriors
graves 52, 54–7
in tombs 51–9
Wickhoff, Franz 31
Winckelmann, Joan Joachim 16–18, 21, 23
Altertumswissenschaft 24–5, 26
Description des pierres gravées du feu baron de Stosch 17
evolutionistic view of classical art 31
Geschichte der Kunst des Alterthums (*A History of the Art of Antiquity*) 17–20
Winter, N. 202 n.1
Woolf, G. 203 n.7

'Year of the Etruscans, the' 34

Zagreb mummy 29, 170–1
Zannoni, Antonio 124
Zeus (Etruscan *Tinia*) 119, 121, 126, 128, 137, 143, 192
zilac selaita 113
zilath 171
zilχ ceχaneri 162–4